Creation and the Flood

An Alternative to Flood Geology
and Theistic Evolution

Creation and the Flood

An Alternative to Flood Geology and Theistic Evolution

DAVIS A. YOUNG

Associate Professor of Geology

University of North Carolina at Wilmington

BAKER BOOK HOUSE

Grand Rapids, Michigan

Copyright © 1977 by Baker Book House Company

ISBN: 0-8010-9912-9

Printed in the United States of America

Quotations from the following books have been used with the permission of the publishers: Alexander Heidel, *Babylonian Genesis* (The University of Chicago Press); E. J. Young, *Genesis 3* (The Banner of Truth Trust Publishers); P. Teilhard de Chardin, *The Phenomenon of Man* (Harper and Row, Publishers, Inc.); J. C. Whitcomb and H. M. Morris, *The Genesis Flood,* H. M. Morris, *Studies in the Bible and Science,* R. J. Rushdoony, *The Mythology of Science,* E. J. Young, *Studies in Genesis One,* and B. Davidheiser, *Evolution and Christian Faith* (The Presbyterian and Reformed Publishing Co.); and J. Lever, *Where Are We Headed?,* R. H. Bube, *The Encounter Between Christianity and Science,* F. F. Bruce, *The Epistle to the Hebrews,* E. J. Young, *The Book of Isaiah,* C. Hodge, *Systematic Theology,* and C. F. Keil and F. Delitzsch, *Biblical Commentary on the Old Testament, I, The Pentateuch* (Wm. B. Eerdmans Publishing Co.).

This book is dedicated

to the memory of my father

EDWARD J. YOUNG

"For to me to live is Christ, and to die is gain."

Preface

Since the last century evangelical Christianity has been engaged in intense controversy over the relationship of geology and the Bible. This controversy received fresh impetus with the publication a decade ago of *The Genesis Flood* by John C. Whitcomb and Henry M. Morris. Their work has brought about a stunning renaissance of flood geology in Christian circles. Their influence has led to the formation of such organizations as the Creation Research Society, the Creation Science Research Center, and the Institute for Creation Research. Journals, radio programs, lecture tours, and curriculum materials devoted to the propagation of flood geology and special creationism have proliferated and met with astounding success among ministers, educators, scientists, and laymen from a wide spectrum of denominations. The impact of this movement has been felt in the recent California education controversy.

As an evangelical Christian who is a professional geologist, I am greatly concerned about this movement. On the one hand I am in agreement with many of the theological emphases of the movement. I am particularly in agreement with the high view of the Bible held by most members of the flood geology school (though they tend to rely on selected Scriptural texts which seem to support flood geology at the expense of other texts which do not). On the other hand I believe that the flood geology is based on misunderstanding, misinterpretation, and misapplication of fundamental geologic facts and principles. In short this movement is guilty of bad geological science. A basically healthy theology is no excuse for poor science.

Many other evangelicals are also appalled by the flood geology movement and the impact it is having on the American ecclesiastical and educational scene. In contrast to the flood geology movement these evangelicals are strong supporters of good science but often at the expense of sound Biblical principles. In particular I have observed a pronounced tendency for many evangelicals in scientific professions to hold to a very weak view of the Bible, a view which ultimately undermines the very foundations of Christianity. A basically healthy science is no excuse for poor theology.

I believe that it is possible to combine good theology and good geology by having a truly *Biblical* view of geology. To do this one needs to reject both the flood geology and theistic evolutionism. It is imperative that theologians, pastors, evangelical scientists, educators, and students, and Christian lay people have this Biblical perspective on science if they are to avoid undermining Christianity itself and if they are to avoid detracting from the gospel of Jesus Christ by adding to it the human foolishness of pseudo-science. This book seeks to develop such a Biblical perspective of geology through a fresh re-examination of both Biblical and geological data.

It is, of course, impossible to write such a book without the help of many people. My father, Edward J. Young, and I had originally intended to collaborate on such a book as this. His untimely death in 1968 after 33 years as Professor of Old Testament at Westminster Theological Seminary in Philadelphia eliminated that possibility. Nonetheless I have been aided greatly by his voluminous writings. Even more decisive an influence on me was the fact that the theological perspective so plain in his writings was lived out so consistently in our home. My father loved his Lord, he loved his Lord's Word, he loved his family, and he lived in obedience to the commands of his Lord as revealed in Holy Scripture. Hence the truly Biblical theology which he loved and gave his life to has rubbed off on me and, I trust, is evident in this book.

The entire text has been read by Richard B. Gaffin, Associate Professor of New Testament at Westminster Theological Seminary, by Edwin Karp, Associate Professor of Geology at New York University, and by Meredith G. Kline, Professor of Old Testament at Gordon-Conwell Theological Seminary. Their many constructive criticisms have been deeply appreciated, if not in every case acted upon. Both my wife and my mother have made numerous helpful suggestions for improving the clarity and force of the text. Miss Mercedes Duran graciously spent long hours typing the manuscript, John Hostettler labored diligently on the line drawings, and Mrs. Audrey Baris contributed the sketches of the hominid skulls.

Davis A. Young
Wilmington, North Carolina
August, 1974

Contents

1

Fanning the Flames
of an Old Debate

The last two centuries have seen intensive debate between Biblical
religion and the natural sciences. A great deal of this debate has
centered specifically around the interaction between the science of
geology, that is, the science of the earth and its history, and Biblical
interpretation. In this work I am continuing the debate by attempting to present a consistently Biblical approach to the science of
geology.

The Modern Bias Against the Bible and Its Development

At this point the question may legitimately be raised as to the
sense of adding still another book about science and Scripture to the
already voluminous literature. Does it really matter that a different
way of viewing these issues is here developed? Specifically, does it
matter that a truly Biblical approach to these issues is developed?
Furthermore haven't others in recent times tried to develop Biblical
approaches to geology and ended up with rather bizarre results?
Besides, am I not here dealing with *dead* issues? Am I not guilty of
trying to resurrect matters that were settled in the nineteenth
century? Isn't genuine Biblical Christianity already dead, and with
good reason? Modern society is now basically humanistic and secu-
larized. Even "Christianity" has become a secular, humanistic

13

religion that is no longer Christianity. Modern man is not especially concerned about a Biblical perspective on science. For that matter modern man is not especially interested in a Biblical perspective on anything. This is presumably the post-Christian era in which the Bible is regarded as a book that is basically irrelevant to the massive issues of the present. Of course, there are and, no doubt, always will be a few individuals who think that the Bible is not only relevant but the very Word of God. Christianity means something to these individuals. It is, of course, their privilege to believe unusual things in the modern democratic world. Society will not bother such individuals as long as these Christians do not try to change society. Hence, despite the presence of isolated pockets of Biblical belief, it appears that as a molding, shaping, driving, and permeating force in modern culture Biblical thinking has seen its day. In the light of the realities of our day is not a serious attempt to demonstrate that the Bible has something to say about scientific matters a quaint, trivial, and irrelevant exercise?

The historical development of this modern bias against Scripture is without question extremely complex. I believe that a large measure of the antibiblical bias of the present is traceable to the previous battles between the sciences and the Christian church. During the eighteenth and particularly the nineteenth centuries many discoveries in the growing and developing science of geology were at variance with interpretations of the opening chapters of the Biblical Book of Genesis that were widely held by Christian people at that time.[1] The supporters of the Bible, it seems, continually lost ground in the intensifying warfare between geology and the church. One Biblical interpretation after another was gradually abandoned in the face of the avalanche of new data dug from the earth. The steady advance of scientific discovery was accompanied by a gradual erosion in the widespread acceptance of the infallibility of the Bible. This slowly but inexorably increasing distrust in the complete reliability of Scripture perhaps came to a climax with the appearance of Darwin's theory of organic evolution. The tiny rift between scientific facts and theories and the established religious dogmas had developed into a Grand Canyon of irreconcilability. The established interpretation of

---

1. For excellent discussions of the historical development of geological science and its interaction with Christian thought see C. C. Gillispie, *Genesis and Geology* (New York: Harper and Brothers, 1951), and S. Toulmin and J. Goodfield, *The Discovery of Time* (New York: Harper and Row, 1965).

Genesis suggested that the earth had been created in six days; geology now indicated that it had developed over a period of millions of years. The established interpretation of Genesis said that the earth was very young; geology said it was very old. Scripture recorded the occurrence of a gigantic flood; geology could find no evidence for such a flood. The current interpretation of Scripture suggested that life had been created directly by God; geology said that life had evolved from more primitive life and ultimately from non-life. Scripture said that man was created by God in His own image; geology said that man was an advanced animal and was related to the apes. The accumulating facts seemed always to tip the balance of argument in favor of geology. The increasingly obvious conclusion of the whole debate was that, *inasmuch as the traditional or current interpretations of Genesis were virtually identified with the teachings of Genesis itself,* Genesis must be in error about the origins of the universe, the earth, life, and man himself.

The logical consequences of this conclusion, whether recognized consciously or not, worked themselves out in subsequent thinking. The Bible makes the claim that a God who cannot lie or make mistakes is its author. The Bible, however, was believed by many to contain a large number of mistakes. Therefore part, or perhaps all, of the Bible could not have been given by such a God as it claimed. For that reason the Bible no longer had to be regarded as an absolutely authoritative book. There was not much reason for giving any more heed to its message than to that of any other religious book or to the wisdom of the world's great philosophers or to the collective moral conscience of society. The nineteenth century conflict between science and religion served to undermine the authority of the Bible. Hence the current general disinterest in and low regard for the Bible have been inherited from earlier generations.

The Need for a New Look at Scripture and Geology

It is my belief that modern society is absolutely wrong in its attitude toward the Scriptures. There is no compelling reason why belief in the authority and infallibility of the Bible should ever have been undermined as a result of this debate. The debate has *not* demonstrated the existence of any mistakes in the Bible. I am convinced that many (not all) of the interpretations of the Biblical teaching of origins that were widely held in the eighteenth and nineteenth centuries were either incorrect or else merely possible alterna-

tives among equally plausible alternatives. Men did well to learn from
the new discoveries of geology, but they were wrong in rejecting the
Bible because certain dogmas presumably based on the Bible were
wrong. Many of the ideas that were held by Christians in those years
are not taught in the Bible. Moreover, the church should have evidenced more willingness to exegete the Scriptures very carefully to
see whether those ideas were tenable. Regrettably many Christians in
our day still adhere doggedly to interpretations of origins that are
either incorrect or merely possible. Many of these Christians have
developed unorthodox theories of geology that are out of accord
with observable data. Of course, the only conclusion for the informed individual, and especially the scientist with no commitment
to Biblical faith, must be, as it was a century ago, that if these bizarre
kinds of earth history are the kinds of earth history really taught by
the Bible, then the Bible is a very unreliable book indeed. It is
therefore imperative that some of the damage done and still being
done to the Christian cause be undone by developing a truly Biblical
approach to geology. Perhaps men will be more willing and ready to
listen earnestly to the message of the Scriptures if the existing cultural milieu already manifests within itself general respect and high
regard for the Bible. And such respect and regard can be manifested
only where Christians develop intellectual honesty, carefulness, and
humility in such complex matters as that of origins.

Other Christian Approaches to Scripture and Geology

Of course, other Christians in our day have discussed the problems
of science and Scripture. A wide spectrum of views has been
advanced.[2] However, in recent years, two major Christian approaches
have tended to develop. On the one hand is the approach which
entails the unusual theories of geology already referred to. In this
approach the words of both the Old and New Testaments are regarded as directly identifiable with the Word of God. Men who adopt
this approach believe that the Bible speaks with absolute and infallible authority upon whatever matter it happens to speak. They
further hold that Scripture speaks on matters of science as well as
religion. The Bible, not geology, is therefore viewed as the ultimate

---

2. A great many of these views have been ably summarized by B. Ramm, *The
Christian View of Science and Scripture* (Grand Rapids: Wm. B. Eerdmans,
1954).

authority in matters of earth history. Many members of this school are convinced that the Bible teaches that the universe was created miraculously by God in the span of six successive 24-hour days, that man is a special creation of God rather than a product of evolution, and that the earth experienced profound geological disturbances on a global scale during the flood of Noah only a few thousand years ago. In the eyes of these men the Biblical view of earth history is at odds with modern scientific views on many major points. There is therefore great concern on the part of what I term *Biblical neo-catastrophists*[3] to defend Christianity against the presumed attacks of what is believed to be a hostile, humanistic science. In addition, other Christian approaches to science are viewed with great suspicion by Biblical neo-catastrophism. These approaches are typically regarded as compromise positions that weaken Christianity.

I am sympathetic with certain views of Biblical neo-catastrophists. I am in agreement with them that Scripture is the Word of God. I also agree that man is a special creation of God. Basically, however, the neo-catastrophist position is very unsatisfactory in that its interpretation of Scripture is at many points incorrect or too narrow. Many relevant passages in Scripture are ignored. Moreover, many of the scientific theories of Biblical neo-catastrophism are untenable in the light of the facts of nature.

A second approach prevails among those I would term *theistic evolutionists*. These men are scientists who believe that the Bible is an authoritative book of religion and a reliable guide to faith and morals. As *Christians*, these men are concerned to defend their faith and to win adherents to it. As *scientists*, they are comfortable with the methods and results of modern science. They accept the major ideas of current science including the general theory of evolution and the uniformitarian approach to geological history. Because of their belief that the Scriptures are concerned with matters of religion and not of science, they do not feel that science conflicts with Biblical faith in any significant way. In terms of this belief the conflicts in the past between theology and science can be seen as having arisen from misinterpretations of the nature of the Bible and of its message as well as misunderstanding of the nature of scientific thought.

---

3. I have referred to these men as Biblical neo-catastrophists in order to distinguish them from other catastrophists (such as Immanuel Velikovsky) who apparently do not regard Scripture as an error-free book from God.

I am also sympathetic to large blocks of thinking within theistic evolutionism. I agree with the theistic evolutionists as regards the antiquity of the universe and as regards a generally uniformitarian approach to geology. I am strongly in disagreement with them regarding the origin of man and regarding the nature of the Bible and the methods of Biblical interpretation.

I am therefore sympathetic to elements of thought from both Biblical neo-catastrophism and theistic evolutionism, but each has very serious pitfalls and fallacies that must be avoided. As a practicing geologist who is a Christian I am convinced that there must be a workable solution to the problem of the relationship between Christian thought and experience and geological science. The solution, however, has not been provided by the theistic evolutionists, nor has it been provided by the neo-catastrophists. The position of theistic evolutionism leads logically and ultimately to the death of *genuinely Biblical* religion. The position of neo-catastrophism weakens Biblical religion and leads to the death of science. My concern is to develop a new approach, *not* a synthesis of theistic evolutionism and neo-catastrophism, but a *third way* which can preserve both genuine Christianity and genuine science.

The Nature of the Bible and the Methods of Biblical Interpretation

The fact that we have several approaches to the debate on science and Scripture that claim to be Christian and to do justice to the Bible raises the question as to how to decide what is Christian. What is Biblical? What does justice to the Bible? What is the proper way to understand and interpret the Bible? Numerous opinions have been given as to how one is to understand and interpret the Bible, but it seems to me quite evident that if we wish to arrive at a truly *Biblical* way of understanding and interpreting the Bible, we should read the Bible to see what it says about itself. One should avoid insofar as it is humanly possible pouring the apparent content of the Bible into some kind of preformed philosophical mold. We should let the Bible speak for itself. For example, it is a rather odd procedure to say that the Bible is concerned to speak in one area, such as religion, but that it is not the least bit interested in speaking about some other matter, such as science, without deriving such opinions from the Bible. It will not do to make the assumption that the Bible cannot be concerned with science because it is fundamentally a religious book unless it can be demonstrated *from the Bible* that the Bible is not concerned with science. If we want to learn what the Bible says about its nature and purpose, we do not go to history, art, science, philosophy, or common sense. Logic tells us to go to the Bible. Only then can a *Biblical* approach to a certain subject be developed. Having ascertained what the Bible *does* and *does not* say about itself or about some topic, we may *then* go on to argue about whether or not what the Bible says is true. Many well-meaning adherents of the Bible miss this point entirely in an attempt to water down the teaching of the Bible so that its message will be more palatable to modern man. For example, some Christians say that the Bible does not really intend to teach that the entire human race descended from a first pair of individuals, Adam and Eve. Instead the story of Adam and Eve is said to be an allegory. I believe that this allegorizing is a very misleading practice, for the Bible *does,* as will be seen, teach that Adam and Eve were historical individuals. Therefore it would be a far more honest procedure for such Christians to say that the Bible teaches that the human race descended from two first parents, Adam and Eve, but that they do not believe that teaching. They believe that the Bible is mistaken on this point. Such a procedure is preferable to distorting the actual teaching of the Bible for the sake of gaining a few supporters.

There ought to be very little difficulty in arriving at some understanding of the Bible's opinion of itself. II Timothy 3:16 serves as an excellent starting point. In this text the Apostle Paul not only notes the practical qualities of Scripture, but he also observes that every Scripture is God-breathed. God is the ultimate source, the ultimate author of the Scripture even though several human authors may have written down the actual words. Paul's view of Scripture had to be colored by his view of God. There is no doubt that, for Paul, God is the very Truth itself. God cannot lie or make mistakes. Paul, as a Scriptural writer himself, regarded Scripture as being totally reliable, true, and authoritative inasmuch as Scripture ultimately was breathed out by the altogether reliable, true, and authoritative God.

Paul's view of Scripture was corroborated by the Apostle Peter. II Peter 1:21 indicates that prophecy came about because holy men of God were borne and superintended by the Spirit of God in their prophetic activity. Peter, too, sees Scripture as having its source in God and hence we have a surer word of prophecy. It is worthy of note that Peter clearly regarded the writings of Paul as falling into the category of Scripture (II Peter 3:16).

Jesus, too, subscribed to the indefectible authority of Scripture. He maintained that the Scripture cannot be broken (John 10:35), and stated that not one jot or one tittle would pass from the law. Every stroke of every letter of Scripture was of extreme importance to Jesus. Jesus' life was characterized by continuous appeal to the Old Testament Scriptures. He was *always* concerned to say, "It is written."

Admittedly this is a very brief presentation of the Bible's view of itself. Many outstanding theologians have dealt with the doctrine of Scripture at great length.[4] Then, too, the reader ought to study the Bible carefully for himself to see just what claims the Bible does make. Let it suffice for now to say that the Bible views itself as a book whose author is *God*. It is absolutely authoritative because it is from the God who created the total universe and upon whom all men are completely dependent, *not* because it expresses the collective wisdom of the greatest religious experts—for it does not. Scripture is infallible in its doctrine for it is the God of *truth* who speaks. Scripture is free of mistakes whether in doctrine, ethics, historical details, geographic matters, or scientific facts because Scripture is the *Word* of God. The words, jots, and tittles of Scripture are *directly identical* to the speech of God.

In this book Scripture's view of itself is adopted. I regard Scripture as directly identical to God's Word and therefore absolutely authoritative, infallible, and inerrant. Naturally there are many "problems" and "intellectual difficulties" with regard to this view of Scripture. Many theologians have dealt with these difficulties, but a particularly excellent defense of this view of Scripture has been presented in the writings of Cornelius Van Til.[5]

---

4. The Biblical view of Scripture has been thoroughly developed in such works as B. B. Warfield, *The Inspiration and Authority of the Bible* (Philadelphia: Presbyterian and Reformed, 1948); E. J. Young, *Thy Word Is Truth* (Grand Rapids: Wm. B. Eerdmans, 1957); N. B. Stonehouse and P. Wooley, eds., *The Infallible Word* (Philadelphia: Presbyterian and Reformed, 1946); M. J. Arntzen, "Inspiration and Trustworthiness of Scripture," in *Interpreting God's Word Today* (Philadelphia: Presbyterian and Reformed, 1970), pp. 179-212; R. B. Gaffin, Jr., "Contemporary Hermeneutics and the Study of the New Testament," in *Westminster Theological Journal* 31 (1969), pp. 129-44; and J. I. Packer, "Biblical Authority, Hermeneutics and Inerrancy," in *Jerusalem and Athens* (Philadelphia: Presbyterian and Reformed, 1971), pp. 141-53.

5. The ablest, most consistent and thorough *Biblical* defense of the historic Christian faith may be found in the writings of Cornelius Van Til of Westminster Theological Seminary. Van Til's apologetics have been set forth in numerous

In terms of the view adopted here, if one finds an apparent contradiction between Scripture and some group of facts from any realm of human thought, there are three possibilities: (1) the exact human interpretation of Scripture on that point is incorrect or not clear; (2) the interpretation of the group of facts is incorrect; or (3) the "facts" are not really facts. But the words of Scripture are *never* incorrect. *The words and real teachings of Scripture are never in ultimate conflict with the real facts of science or history.*

It is therefore a very serious matter to charge that there are mistakes in the Bible as has been done so often in the long struggle between geology and Christianity. Consequently in this book let us look very carefully at as many Scripture passages as possible in order to ascertain exactly what the Bible does and does not teach regarding the origin and history of the earth. The reader will find that the charge that there are geological errors in the Bible cannot be substantiated.

Let me reiterate that the message of Scripture must not be twisted to make it appear that there are no geological errors in the Bible. The message of Scripture must never be twisted to fit historically-conditioned prevailing philosophical winds simply to win friends. Rather as situations of conflict arise and as new attacks on Scripture or teachings of Scripture develop in time, Christians must continue to exegete Scripture, to ask new questions of the Biblical text that may be spawned in the context of new cultural and intellectual settings, and to examine old prejudices, traditions, and interpretations in the light of Scripture. Christians have often failed to increase their understanding of the teaching of Scriptural texts because they have not asked enough questions of the text. Many questions may not even have suggested themselves in the past. Even though we might ask new questions, the exegesis of Scripture still means that *Scripture*, not the scientific and philosophical strands of the cultural fabric which provides the interrogative material, is its own interpreter. Scripture says what it says, not what we want it to say.

---

books, classroom syllabi, and pamphlets. The most extensive expositions of his views are to be found in *The Defense of the Faith* (Philadelphia: Presbyterian and Reformed, 1963), and *A Christian Theory of Knowledge* (Philadelphia: Presbyterian and Reformed, 1969). Van Til's defense of the historic doctrine of Scripture may be found in *The Doctrine of Scripture*, a classroom syllabus available from the Presbyterian and Reformed Publishing Company.

We will see that Scripture contains no geological errors. This is not to say that all the problems regarding geology and Scripture are solved herein. It is to say that Scripture's claim to be the Word of God has not been disproved by the science of geology as has so often been asserted in the past. And it is to say that men ought therefore to give more heed to the Bible than they have been doing in recent years.

2

Theistic Evolutionism—
A House Built on Sand

Before developing the positive aspects of the *third way*, I wish to indicate at some length why theistic evolutionism and Biblical neo-catastrophism are unsatisfactory as Christian approaches to the debate between geology and Biblical religion.

In this chapter we will take a look at theistic evolutionism. Theistic evolutionists are found among both Roman Catholic and Protestant circles. There is considerable variation, theologically, philosophically, and scientifically, among theistic evolutionists. Quite naturally then there is some danger in grouping many different individuals into one broad category. I will, however, sketch a generalized picture of the beliefs of a theistic evolutionist which without doubt does not apply completely to any individual thinker falling into this group. Characteristic of the thought of these men, however, is what I believe to be an unbiblical view of Scripture and hence of science. science.

The proponent of theistic evolutionism is first of all a *theist* for the simple reason that he claims to believe and trust in the God of the Bible. He accepts the Bible as a revelation from God, he confesses his own sinfulness and need for deliverance from sin, and he believes that Jesus Christ is his personal Lord and Savior. He is a theist in that he believes that the God of the Bible has created and providentially controls and upholds the totality of existence.

The proponent of theistic evolutionism is also an *evolutionist* in that he maintains that *all* of life has evolved through time from more primitive to more complex forms. He claims that the first living organisms were developed through the complex interplay of natural chemical and physical processes without the miraculous intervention of God. He sees no necessity for the special creation of any groups of animals or plants. Rather these are seen as having evolved gradually from simpler types of animals or plants. The theistic evolutionist also maintains that mankind has evolved from lower animals, most immediately from apelike ancestors. In all these matters the formal scientific beliefs of the theistic evolutionist are much the same as those of the non-Christian, orthodox evolutionist. The theistic evolutionist also generally accepts the current interpretations of scientific data, such as fossils, provided by the scientific community. He has great faith in the entire scientific enterprise. He more or less accepts the total picture of the physical world that is being developed by modern science. Hence he sees no need for divine interventions in the course of earth history apart from the initial act of creation. The major difference between the theistic evolutionist and the non-Christian evolutionist is that the former believes and is concerned to point out that it is *God,* and specifically the God of the Bible, who has providentially and wonderfully directed and controlled the entire evolutionary process in such a way that the culmination of that process is *man.* He believes, too, that man is responsible to God. The theistic evolutionist is totally opposed to any philosophy of materialistic, naturalistic, or atheistic evolutionism. He wants to be a *Christian* evolutionist.

The theistic evolutionist is far removed from the Biblical neo-catastrophists, who invoke many direct, miraculous acts of God in earth history. The theistic evolutionist is not inclined to invoke the miraculous in earth history apart from the *initial* creation. Yet theistic evolutionist and neo-catastrophist are generally agreed that miracles have occurred during *human* history. Most proponents of both positions would readily agree that Jesus of Nazareth was born of a virgin, that He rose from the dead, and ascended to heaven. Most agree, too, that Christ will return bodily at the end of this age. There is, then, on the part of theistic evolutionists, general acceptance of the Biblical narrative.

In many respects the position of theistic evolutionism is acceptable. Nonetheless theistic evolutionism offers an inadequate inter-

pretation of the *theism*, that is, of the *Christian faith* that the theistic
evolutionist is concerned to defend. True theism can flourish only
where God reveals Himself and man responds correctly and be-
lievingly to that revelation. True theism can thus develop only where
Scripture, the revelation of God, is taken seriously. Scripture must be
permitted to tell us what we ought to believe about God, ourselves,
the world, and Scripture itself. Theistic evolutionists, however, tend
to have views of Scripture that are not themselves derived from
Scripture. Where such faulty views of Scripture have arisen, typically
faulty views of other Christian doctrines have developed. For
example, distortion of the Biblical doctrine of Scripture will lead
ultimately to a distortion of the heart of the Christian message. This
has already happened to varying degrees in the thinking of a number
of theistic evolutionists. These assertions are, of course, serious, and
are substantiated below in a consideration of the writings of representative theistic evolutionists.

Jan Lever

Jan Lever is a professor of zoology at the Free University of
Amsterdam and a member of the Reformed Churches in the Netherlands. An unusually concise and meaty exposition of Lever's views
has been given in a recent booklet, *Where Are We Headed?* The
booklet consists of a series of brief radio talks delivered in the
Netherlands.

As a thoughtful, informed scientist Lever is aware of many conflicts between Scriptural interpretation and science. Many discoveries
have been made which Christian scientists cannot in good conscience
deny. Lever suggests that there is only one conclusion to which such
men can come, "namely, that certain views regarding the origin of
the world that have long been held in the Christian community must
be wrong."[1] But this does not question the credibility of their Christian faith. "These Christians surely do not reject biblical revelation
and the gospel of Christ."[2] It becomes evident that another interpretation of the Bible's first chapters is "not only necessary, but also
possible and even enriching."[3] This is the opinion held by Lever
himself.[4]

------

1. J. Lever, *Where Are We Headed?* (Grand Rapids: Wm. B. Eerdmans, 1970),
p. 8.

2. Ibid.   3. Ibid.   4. Ibid., p. 9.

How then shall we interpret the early chapters of Scripture so that they enrich the Christian experience? At this point Lever introduces the concept of "pictures of reality." "Our picture of reality always concerns what we know or think we know about this earthly reality. An obvious but important characteristic of it is that it changes. As science progresses our insight is enlarged and we must correct our notions about the world."[5] Of course, any writer is influenced by the picture of reality of his day and age.

> The Bible was written in times when people had far less factual knowledge about the world than we have. They had no telescopes, no microscopes, no laboratories. . . . As far as factual knowledge of the world is concerned, they had little more to go by than daily experience. It constituted the picture of reality of that time. . . . And it need not at all surprise us that the writers of the Bible also shared this picture of reality, for their notions were completely embedded in it.[6]

To clarify his point Lever asks us

> to imagine that science and technology had made great progress by the time the Bible was being written, that there were universities, radio and television, refrigerators and automobiles, airplanes and tanks, space flights and nuclear power stations. Don't you suppose that if that had been the case many expressions and pictures in the Bible would have been different from what they now are. . . ?[7]

We must recognize that this cultural clothing does not alter the religious perspective of Scripture. "The Bible definitely is not concerned with scientific knowledge. The entire Bible was written within the framework of existing notions about nature."[8] And, again, Lever argues that

> it would be extremely helpful if everyone would only realize that the religious perspective of the Bible holds for all time, even when it is conveyed in stories, concepts, and pictures that are quite obviously characteristic of the time in which the Bible was written.[9]

Now, of course, says Lever, time and again the old picture of reality found in the Bible is wrong. Modern scientific knowledge has demonstrated that this is the case.

> The earth is not flat, the sun does not revolve around the earth. The earth, the organisms, and man are not just a few thousand years old.

---

5. Ibid., p. 16.   7. Ibid., p. 17.   9. Ibid.
6. Ibid., pp. 16-17.   8. Ibid.

Death in plants and animals did not originate after man's appearance on earth. The present species of organisms have not existed ever since the beginning of the earth, and they cannot be regarded as being constant.[10]

These were aspects, according to Lever, of the common-sense picture of reality found in the Bible. Clearly "we must give up the picture of reality held by the writers of the Bible."[11] But if we give up the picture of reality held by the Biblical writers, is the Biblical message left? Emphatically yes and "the fact is that we can now understand its message all the better."[12]

How then can we better understand Genesis 1, clothed as it is in the erroneous picture of reality of the ancients? The concern of the writer of Genesis 1 was to set the one true God, the Creator, over against the pagan gods of the surrounding nations. Genesis 1 is thus a *confession*.

Genesis 1, we conclude, does not give us any scientific, historical, astronomical, or biological information. It is rather a grandiose confession of God who brought forth this reality and all that is in it. . . .

Although Genesis does not give us a picture of reality or scientific information about the world, it does provide us with the fundamentals for a *life and world view*, a religious perspective on the nature of this reality, its finitude and its dependence upon God in becoming and in being.[13]

Of paramount importance in the mind of any thinking Christian is the account of the origin and the fall of man. How shall we interpret the paradise story? We cannot, says Lever, take the story literally. If, for example, we read Genesis 1 and 2 literally, we have obvious internal contradictions inasmuch as these two accounts of creation are given in different chronological order. If we do not take these creation accounts literally, then "the only conclusion to which we can come is that quite obviously these chapters do not aim to give a report of events that took place then and there."[14] And if we do not consider the paradise account to be concerned with history, then it "is concerned with whether man makes or misses contact with God and the destiny God has for him. . . ."[15] "By referring the paradise story back in time and reducing it to the account of a single event that took place in one small spot on the globe and involved just two

---

10. Ibid., p. 21.   12. Ibid.   14. Ibid., p. 28.

11. Ibid., p. 22.   13. Ibid., p. 23.   15. Ibid., p. 29.

people, particular trees, and one speaking snake, one greatly impover-
ishes the significance of the story."[16] Because of staring ourselves
blind at these details "we have often lost sight of the staggering
riches of the illuminating vision of faith in the paradise story."[17]
Inasmuch as the literal rendering of the paradise story is wrong, there
is no difficulty in accepting the fact that man is a product of the
highest living organisms.[18] The latter view is much more beautiful to
Lever anyway.

Having rejected Biblical pictures of reality and accepted the
modern scientific picture of reality, Lever turns to the Christian faith
and its significance in life. "I simply take my stand on the most basic
Christian beliefs—that God is the creator of the entire earthly reality,
that mankind was infected with evil, beginning with our first parents,
and that the way to the Creator and to peace on earth can be found
in Christ in whom God has revealed himself."[19] But how has God
revealed Himself in Christ? What is the gospel of Christ to which
Lever would call us in an age of complexity and anguish and despair?
What hope does Lever give to a race that has usually, for some
unknown reason, used its freedom to rule in wrong ways? Lever's call
to the gospel is *urgent*. "If ever there was a time in which the gospel
of our Lord Jesus Christ is relevant, it is ours."[20] "Christ's message
can really assist us in our search for solutions to the great problems
of today and tomorrow."[21]

What is Christ's message?

> For Christ teaches us the universal equality of all men without dis-
> tinction of race or color. Christ teaches us social concern, love of
> neighbor, peaceableness and personal responsibility. Following him
> therefore means the arresting of aggression in all its forms, and the
> realization that brute force should be replaced by a real solidarity,
> each of us being prepared to make sacrifices to his fellow man.
>
> In Jesus, who has proved his teaching by his life and death, God, the
> creator of this entire reality, comes to mankind in a wondrous
> manner. He desires in forgiveness to liberate us from the evil that we
> individually and collectively have brought about on the earth, and he
> shows us a new way, the only right way.[22]

There is much in Lever's views that the Christian ought to disagree
with. He makes numerous incorrect assumptions and takes faulty

---

16. Ibid.   19. Ibid., p. 42.   22. Ibid.

17. Ibid.   20. Ibid., p. 58.

18. Ibid., pp. 36-41. 21. Ibid.

leaps in logic. One of Lever's major errors is to equate, in several instances, a Biblical writer's picture of reality with an interpretation that, in the past, may have been widely held by the Christian community. For example, there may in the past have been Christians who *believed* that the Bible teaches that the sun revolves around the earth and that the earth is flat. Such an interpretation of the Bible is erroneous, but it cannot be said that the picture of reality held by the Biblical writer was in error. The picture of reality of the interpreter, not the Biblical writer, is incorrect and must be rejected. There are no inspired statements in Scripture to indicate that the Biblical writers believed that the sun revolves around the earth. The Biblical writers were simply speaking colloquially, as we do, of the relative, or apparent, motions of the sun and the earth.

Similarly it is incorrect to identify with Moses' picture of reality the interpretation of Genesis 1 which posits that the six days of creation were of 24-hour duration. It is entirely possible that Moses' picture of reality included days of creation of very long duration. Different, equally plausible interpretations of the days of Genesis 1 are possible, and it is therefore an invalid procedure to identify one of those interpretations with the Biblical picture of reality and to claim that the Biblical picture of reality is wrong because one does not happen to believe that particular interpretation.

Again, who is to say that the Biblical picture of reality includes the idea of a very young earth? This idea is based on a very rigid *interpretation* of certain Scriptural data and may or may not be Biblical. Scripture nowhere specifically states that the earth is only a few thousand years old. How can we condemn a Biblical picture of reality when there is considerable doubt or uncertainty as to what that picture of reality is? Thus in many instances when Lever thinks he is judging Scripture, he is actually judging faulty *interpretations* of Scripture.

Lever also wrongly assumes that the Biblical picture of reality is nearly always rigidly literal. This would certainly appear to be the case as regards Genesis 1 and 2. Lever concludes that if we interpret Genesis 1 and 2 literally, we end up with internal contradictions. Therefore the paradise story is not intended to be read historically, that is, as a record of events that actually took place then and there. Here, however, Lever has incorrectly assumed the identity of the terms "literal," "chronological," and "historical." It is certainly true that Genesis 2, unlike the preceding chapter, does not present a chronological account of creation. Rather it presents a non-chronological, *topical* account of the offspring, the generations of the creation (Genesis 2:4), namely *man*. The account is concerned with man and with setting the stage for his temptation and fall, not specifically with creation. If aspects of creation are mentioned in Genesis 2, they are incidental to, or reinforce, the main theme of *man's* creation, temptation, and fall. But having said that Genesis 2 is not to be read in a rigidly literal, chronological way by no means justifies the assumption that the account is not concerned with *historical* facts and events. Lever has forgotten a cardinal principle of hermeneutics: exegesis is concerned with the sense or the meaning that the writer is trying to convey. Scripture conveys its meaning in many literary forms. Much of Scripture is poetry, and there are many poetical passages which speak of the foundations or pillars of the earth. But it is totally incorrect to say that the Scriptural picture of reality includes the idea that the earth rests on pillars or foundations. Only if the rigidly literal interpretation were the only possible interpretation could this be said to be the case. But the psalms are not to be read in slavishly literal fashion at all points. The psalms are poetry and we cannot forget this. Scripture wants us to interpret its poetical portions in a different manner from purely historical portions like the Book of Acts. We must also remember that Biblical history is often recorded in topical rather than chronological manner, but it does not thereby cease to deal with real events. Much of what Lever thinks is a Biblical picture of reality is a distortion of Scripture derived from a rigidly literal interpretation that Scripture cannot and did not intend to bear.

Lever also assumes that the Biblical writers were thoroughly absorbed and enmeshed in the picture of reality held by the pagan nations round about. He offers no evidence for this, and it is probable that there is not much evidence. Does the picture of reality of the Greek, Egyptian, Assyrian, Babylonian, and Hittite myths bear much resemblance to that of the Israelites? Such is not likely the case.

Despite these errors in Lever's views, we have not yet arrived at the fundamental weakness in his theistic evolutionist approach. The basic weakness in Lever's view is not faulty interpretations and faulty logic. The basic weakness, from a *Christian* standpoint, is that Lever holds to an unbiblical view of Scripture. This basic weakness leads of necessity to all the other errors and weaknesses of his position. Lever says that "the Bible definitely is not concerned with scientific knowledge." On what basis can he say this? Lever evidently does not derive this statement from Scripture. He is *driven* to the statement because, in principle, he holds to a standard of knowledge that is on a par with, and in the last analysis becomes elevated over, Scripture. Lever evidently believes that science is an independent source of knowledge over against which the statements of Scripture may be tested as being true or false. But Lever also thinks he believes in the authority of the Bible. Hence the Bible cannot be shown to be wrong in anything really important, that is, in anything religious. As a result Lever must twist Biblical interpretations around—it is his view that the Bible cannot say some of the things that it really does say. For Lever science has shown that man has evolved from animals. Therefore it must be so. But the Bible teaches that man was specially created. Since in Lever's eyes this is not true, the apparent doctrine of the special creation of man *cannot* be important and the Bible *cannot* really mean for us to believe this as a scientific fact. Thus for him the Bible is not, because it cannot be, concerned with scientific facts.

Lever does not obtain all of his beliefs about Scripture *from* Scripture. He approaches Scripture with principles from without and superimposes them on Scripture.[23] He holds the view that Scripture is not concerned with scientific matters, not because Scripture says so, but because in the last analysis *science* does. The principle of the self-interpretation of Scripture is denied. Now science will help us to

---

23. Lever's views with respect to the nature of Scripture strongly resemble those of existentialist and neo-orthodox theologians. As examples, the thought of both Dietrich Bonhoeffer and Alan Richardson employs extrabiblical ideas in coming to an understanding of the nature and message of the Bible. Bonhoeffer superimposes existentialist categories of interpretation on the Biblical data in such a way that he sees the first chapters of Genesis as having nothing to do with real space-time history (*Creation and Fall* [New York: Macmillan, 1959]).

As examples of Bonhoeffer's thought we note the following statements: "Hence every use of a causal category for understanding the act of creation is ruled out" (p. 14). "The heavens and the seas were not formed in the way he [the writer of Genesis 1:6-10] says: we would not escape a very bad conscience if we committed ourselves to any such statement. The idea of verbal inspiration will not do" (p. 26). With regard to the account of the origin of man in Genesis 1:26: "This has nothing to do with Darwinism . . ." (p. 34). Of Genesis 2:7 Bonhoeffer writes: "The anthropomorphisms become more intolerable. . . . This can surely not produce any knowledge about the origin of man! To be sure, as a narrative this story is just as irrelevant or meaningful as any other myth of creation. And yet in its capacity as the Word of God it is the source of knowledge concerning the origin of man" (p. 44). "Why can we not understand that God must reach out towards us with these ancient, magical pictures as well as

shred away the husks of erroneous pictures of reality in the Bible in order to arrive at the kernel of religious truth. Lever's position is a virtual denial that God can with authority and clarity reveal and identify a fact to man in the space-time world.

Lever's faulty view of Scripture quite naturally leads to an exposition of the gospel of Christ that is watered down and not fully Biblical. Lever's presentation of the gospel is very brief.[24] It may be somewhat unfair to attack a view of the gospel that is so brief, but I believe it is possible in two paragraphs to set the true gospel over against false gospels in crystal clear fashion. This Lever has not done. It is virtually impossible to distinguish Lever's gospel from a secularistic, humanistic, social gospel. It is not clear whether Jesus Christ was simply our example or if He is the Lord and Savior who died a substitutionary death on the cross on behalf of His elect people. Lever says nothing of sin, God's holiness, wrath, judgment, heaven and hell, repentance and faith, substitutionary atonement, justification and sanctification, and other themes that pervade the Scriptures. He tells us only of a bland gospel of love and human works.

Vague, incomplete, imprecise expositions of the gospel are characteristic of many of the exponents of theistic evolutionism. The vague gospel offered by theistic evolutionism is a logical outgrowth of the evolutionary view of man. But both the evolutionary view and the vague gospel are unchristian inasmuch as they ultimately derive from a failure to grasp the principle that Scripture is its own interpreter because it comes to us from God, the self-identifying, self-contained, self-attesting triune God who made heaven and earth. Principles of interpretation of Scripture derived from extrabiblical sources will *always* lead logically to the death of Christianity. Expressions of

---

with our technical, conceptual pictures, that he must teach us if we are to become wise?" (p. 48). "It is not the purpose of the Bible to give information about the origin of evil . . ." (p. 65).

Similar statements are made by Richardson in *Genesis I—XI* (London: SCM Press, 1953). For example, he believes that modern people are misled because they fail "to understand that the language of religion is the language of parable and poetry, and that ultimate truth can be expressed and communicated only by means of the images and symbols of the imagination, not by the exact prose of the scientific intellect" (pp. 18-19). I believe that none of these statements can be supported from the Bible itself. Rather they are presumptions about how the Bible ought to speak to men.

24. Lever, *Where Are We Headed?*, p. 58.

Christianity apart from the self-interpreting Scripture are always like the writhings of the dead snake before sundown. The evidences of life are only apparent.

Richard H. Bube

One of the leading exponents of theistic evolutionism in the United States is R. H. Bube, professor of materials science and electrical engineering at Stanford University. Bube has, in collaboration with several other scientists, produced a thought-provoking work entitled *The Encounter Between Christianity and Science.*[25] About half of the book was written by Bube; hence we have an extensive presentation of his views.

The heart of Bube's views may be found in his discussion of Biblical revelation (Chapter 4). Bube asks the question as to just what is the purpose of the Bible. He correctly notes that the purpose of Scripture is "centered upon the relationship of man with God and with his fellow man, through his relationship with Jesus Christ."[26] Bube goes on to discuss the interpretation of the Bible, and he observes that in order to determine the content of a passage we must always keep in mind this great purpose of Scripture. "One of the major principles of hermeneutics is that the revelational *content* of the Biblical message is to be derived insofar as possible in terms of the revelational *purpose* of the author."[27] "By the phrase 'revelational content' we mean the message that God intends that we receive from the Bible."[28] Furthermore, *"only those questions that are consistent with revelational purpose lead to the revelational content."*[29] Bube then suggests some guidelines by which to establish the revelational purpose of a Biblical author, inasmuch as the purpose is so important in determining the content. Among these guidelines Bube suggests that "the simple mention of a secondary detail of some sort in the development of the revelational message does not bestow upon this detail the status of scientific objectivity unless it is itself the *subject* of the message."[30]

---

25. R. H. Bube, *The Encounter Between Christianity and Science* (Grand Rapids: Wm. B. Eerdmans, 1968).

26. Ibid., p. 85.   28. Ibid., p. 93.   30. Ibid., p. 95.

27. Ibid., p. 90.   29. Ibid., p. 94.

Throughout this discussion Bube is leading up to some of the ticklish areas in the conflict between science and religion, and he wants to be in a position to show that matters in the Bible which may touch on scientific points are, after all, only secondary details.

> Or consider again what conclusion can be drawn from the words of Paul in Romans 5:14 when he writes, "Nevertheless death reigned from Adam to Moses." Does this statement of Paul constitute irrefutable proof that there was a unique first man by the name of Adam who experienced the events of Genesis in a natural historical sense? The New Testament authors were basically concerned with the theological import of Old Testament events, and with the revelation of God that came through them. Paul's reference to Adam as the head of the human race, as well as the words of Jesus in Matthew 19:4-9, may be taken as a revelational presentation of the truth of God inherent in the Genesis account, without necessarily giving sanction to the literal historicity of the details of that account. Paul had no better reference to summon up to present the truth of his argument—what better reference could he have than that which was supplied by the inspiring guidance of God through His revelation to the Old Testament prophets? Paul's use of the concept of Adam is indeed an important piece of Biblical evidence that must be weighed in forming a decision as to the literal historicity of the Genesis account, but it is not by itself a decisive one.[31]

Again Bube notes that

> the right questions are essentially theological questions, taking that term in its broadest sense to include questions about the nature of God, the nature of man, the relationship between God and man, and the relationship between man and man in fulfillment of the God-to-man relationship. The wrong questions are those that seek to establish natural mechanisms for God's activity by looking for these mechanisms in the Bible; there is no information in the Bible, for example, that is either in favor of or opposed to theories of organic evolution.[32]

It seems to me that Bube, like Lever, has approached the Bible with certain presuppositions as to how it ought to be interpreted. He has not permitted Scripture to provide its own rules of interpretation. That the Bible does not speak for or against evolution has not been determined so much by exegesis as by the principle that the Bible speaks only to religious matters and not to secondary matters of scientific or historical nature. Bube ought to have shown us *by exegesis of Scripture* that Scripture does not and cannot talk about

---

31. Ibid., pp. 96-97.   32. Ibid., p. 97.

science. The idea that secondary details are not too important has not been derived from Scripture. It has been superimposed on it.

The Bible clearly does contain information that opposes the idea of the evolution of man from animals, and much of that information is found in Romans 5. Obviously Romans 5 is concerned with theological matters, and that includes, according to Bube, the nature of man. But does not the nature of man bear on scientific matters? The passage is, of course, concerned *primarily* with the relationship between God and man, but how in the light of the central truths of Scripture the passage makes sense without also teaching that Adam was a unique first human being who fell into sin is not clear. Bube has avoided this point. Even though he has discussed the Romans text at length he has not suggested positively what the text *does* teach about the origin of man. The only alternative open to him is that Adam is a picture or representation of every man and the story of the fall is a picture of the struggle against evil within the heart of every man. But the whole New Testament seems very clear that Christ did not save us from this metaphysical kind of evil.

Bube's view of Scripture, like that of Lever, is ultimately inimical to Biblical religion inasmuch as part of his view is not derived from Scripture itself. Bube's exegetical interpretations of Scripture are poured into a mold of such a nature that they can never say anything about scientific questions. Bube's position assumes that in many instances secondary details in Scripture are unimportant or irrelevant to the central purpose of Scripture, and his position further assumes that man has the wisdom to know which elements of a text are secondary and which are not. Bube's approach to Scripture becomes dangerously subjective inasmuch as it virtually asks the reader to determine the primary purpose and message of Scriptural passages without due regard to the details.

Pierre Teilhard de Chardin

The discussion of the views of some theistic evolutionists concludes with a brief examination of the thought of the renowned philosopher-scientist-theologian, Father Pierre Teilhard de Chardin. Teilhard, as a Roman Catholic priest, was, of course, a deeply religious man, and one need only read *The Divine Milieu* to appreciate the depth of his commitment to the Christian religion. We need not trouble ourselves here with the question as to whether or not Teilhard's Christianity or Catholicism was orthodox. It is sufficient to say that his religious life was profoundly permeated by Scripture. He was anything but a materialist. We might then expect his Christian faith to influence his approach to science. Hence in *The Phenomenon of Man* we find him saying that

> the time has come to realize that an interpretation of the universe—even a positivist one—remains unsatisfying unless it covers the interior as well as the exterior of things; mind as well as matter. The true physics is that which will, one day, achieve the inclusion of man in his wholeness in a coherent picture of the world.[33]

"Co-extensive with their Without, there is a Within to things."[34] "Has science ever troubled to look at the world other than from without?"[35] Teilhard obviously is very concerned with consciousness and with that which is spiritual as well as with the material.

As a Christian scientist, however, does Teilhard view nature with principles that are derived from Scripture? Does Scripture have anything to say about science? About the nature of man? Evidently not. Teilhard does not even mention Scripture in building up his scientific world-view. Does he derive his view of man from Scripture? He does not. He is concerned to look at man solely as *phenomenon. The Phenomenon of Man* "may be summed up as an attempt *to see* and *to make others see* what happens to man, and what conclusions are forced upon us, when he is placed fairly and squarely within the framework of phenomenon and appearance."[36] Throughout *The Phenomenon of Man* Teilhard traces for us the development of the earth and its life as it works towards its culmination in man. This development is an *evolution,* an evolution not only of matter but also of consciousness. Time sees not only a progressive complexity of biological organization but also an associated progressive expansion of consciousness.

Was this evolutionary view derived from Scripture? It was not. It was derived from the phenomena. Apparently Teilhard did not even consider Scripture to be relevant to the matter. Yet there was for him absolutely *no question* that this evolution has taken place. "It may be said that the problem of transformism no longer exists. The question is settled once and for all. To shake our belief now in the reality of biogenesis, it would be necessary to uproot the tree of life

---

33. P. Teilhard de Chardin, *The Phenomenon of Man* (New York: Harper and Row, 1959), pp. 35-36.

34. Ibid., p. 56.   35. Ibid., p. 52.   36. Ibid., p. 31.

and undermine the entire structure of the world."[37] "One might well become impatient or lose heart at the sight of so many minds (and not mediocre ones either) remaining today still closed to the idea of evolution, if the whole of history were not there to pledge to us that a truth once seen, even by a single mind, always ends up by imposing itself on the totality of human consciousness."[38] "Is evolution a theory, a system or a hypothesis? It is much more: it is a general condition to which all theories, all hypotheses, all systems must bow and which they must satisfy henceforward if they are to be thinkable and true. Evolution is a light illuminating all facts, a curve that all lines must follow."[39] In man we finally have *"evolution become conscious of itself."*[40] Teilhard's views, even though for a time viewed as heretical within the Roman Catholic Church, plainly are informed by the scholastic nature-grace scheme of thought which controls the Catholic world-view. Teilhard, with Aquinas, feels that man, by his reason, and apart from Scripture, may rightly view the world in which he lives. Scientific reason is sufficient for obtaining knowledge in the realm of natural phenomena, but revelation is needed in the realm of faith and religion.

It is unnecessary to consider here Teilhard's view of an evolving, increasingly collectivized consciousness—the Omega point—in which man virtually becomes absorbed into the consciousness of Christ. It suffices only to note that Teilhard, as a theistic evolutionist, does not obtain support for his position from Scripture. Lever and Bube are at least *concerned* with Scripture in its relation to science because they to a larger extent than Teilhard consider the Bible to be inspired. They attempt to show that the Bible rightly interpreted doesn't deal with these scientific questions. To the extent that they are concerned with the Bible they show some Protestant influence on their thought. To a degree even greater than in Lever and Bube Teilhard's thought structure is based on principles not derived from Scripture. Man's reason is considered to be virtually autonomous in the realm of science and phenomena. There is no need to make reference to Scripture. For Teilhard it isn't even necessary to impose *unwittingly* upon Scripture some principle that is extrascriptural. Teilhard's synthesis of science and religion must therefore be unacceptable to Christians, for his synthesis gives no rightful place to Scripture as the absolutely authoritative Word of God.

---

37. Ibid., p. 140.   38. Ibid., p. 218.   39. Ibid., p. 219.   40. Ibid., p. 221.

The Basic Interpretation of Genesis

It has been pointed out that the position of theistic evolutionism as expressed by some of its proponents is not a consistently Christian position. It is not a truly Biblical position, for it is based in part on principles that are imported into Christianity. The view of the Bible involved in much of theistic evolutionism is not wholly derived from the Bible itself. Consequently the interpretations of those parts of the Bible that are critical to the whole discussion of origins are incorrect and inadequate. Naturally the first few chapters of Genesis are of extreme importance to the discussion, and it is vital that a correct interpretation of these chapters be presented in a genuinely Biblical approach to science. Lever maintains that the paradise story in Genesis 2 is not to be taken historically. The details of that story are unimportant. Bube's writings suggest that we do not have to take the Genesis account regarding Adam as literally historical. If the views of Lever and Bube are incorrect with respect to the crucial opening chapters of Genesis, it is necessary that due consideration be given to the correct way in which these chapters are to be understood.

While it is agreed by the majority of scholars that Genesis 12—50 purports to be reporting history, chapters 1—11 are commonly regarded as being of a different literary genre that need not be considered as reporting history. This point of view has obviously had some influence on the thinking of Bube and particularly Lever. The question of immediate importance is thus the question of literary genre, and hence the question as to whether or not Genesis 1—11 is to be viewed as reporting history, that is, ordinary, calendar-time history occurring in the physical space-time world. In order to answer this question correctly we must ask the Bible to tell us the answer. We cannot come to the Bible with some preconception based upon science, philosophy, or archaeology. In fact if we take a serious look at the overall structure of Genesis we will soon find out how Genesis 1—11 wants to be regarded and therefore how we ought to regard it.

The Book of Genesis is divisible into two major sections. The first major section comprises 1:1—2:3 and is the account of the creation. The second major section contains 2:4—50:26 and discusses "events" that have occurred since the creation. Whether or not these events were genuinely historical may be disregarded for the moment. The second section can be further subdivided into several subsections

TABLE 1

Occurrence in the Book of Genesis
of the Phrase, "These are the generations of . . ."

2:4	These are the generations of the heavens and of the earth . . .
5:1	This is the book of the generations of Adam.
6:9	These are the generations of Noah . . .
10:1	These are the generations of the sons of Noah . . .
11:10	These are the generations of Shem . . .
11:27	These are the generations of Terah . . .
25:12	These are the generations of Ishmael . . .
25:19	These are the generations of Isaac . . .
36:1, 9	These are the generations of Esau . . .
37:2	These are the generations of Jacob.

each of which is related to the phrase, "these are the generations of. . . ." A list of the eleven occurrences of this phrase in Genesis is presented in Table 1.

Is this oft-repeated phrase a subscription or superscription of the various subsections of Genesis? Some scholars think that it is a subscription or conclusion of the various subsections. In this view the expression "these are the generations of the heavens and of the earth" is seen as a conclusion to the account of creation. This opinion is said to be reinforced by the accompanying expression "in the day that the LORD God made the earth and the heavens" (Genesis 2:4).

Several considerations militate against the idea that the "generations" phrase is a concluding statement. In the first place the Book of Genesis does not close with any such statement. Furthermore usage of the expression in other parts of Scripture clearly indicates that it is a heading rather than a concluding statement. For example, in Ruth 4:18 we read the expression "now these are the generations of Pharez." It is clear that what precedes this verse has very little to do with Pharez. His name is mentioned in Ruth 4:12, but the preceding verses were not really talking at all about Pharez. The following verses (18-22), however, talk about the descendants of Pharez. It is clear that in this instance the expression is used as a heading, not as a conclusion. Similarly in Numbers 3:1, the expression "these also are the generations of Aaron and Moses *in the day* that the LORD spake with Moses in Mount Sinai" is more natural as a heading for what follows than as a conclusion to what precedes.

We come to the same conclusion when we examine usage of the expression elsewhere in Genesis. Look, for example, at the section 11:27–25:11, which is *headed* by the expression "these are the generations of Terah." What we find in these chapters is the story of Abraham, the son, the descendant of Terah. We are presented with a presumably historical narrative of the life of Abraham and Isaac. The heading of the section thus implies that what follows is a history of the descendants of Terah, for that is what we are given. To take another example, look at Genesis 37:2, "These are the generations of Jacob." What immediately follows is a discussion of Joseph, Jacob's son. Chapters 37–50 are quite evidently concerned to present us with a historical narrative of the life of Joseph. The expression is thus a heading which implies that what follows is a *history* of the generations or offspring or descendants of Jacob.

Let us look again at Genesis 2:4. Here we read the *heading,* "these are the generations of the heavens and of the earth." The heading should immediately suggest to us that what we are about to read is intended to be viewed as *history* in the same way that the stories of Abraham and Joseph are intended to be viewed as history. Not only is the account of 2:4–4:26 intended to be a history, it is intended to be a history of the *offspring* or *descendants* or *products* of the heaven and earth, namely man himself. It is *not* intended to be an account of creation but of the *product* of creation, man. And this is what we read, namely, an account of the early history of man. It seems clear from the overall structure of Genesis that the account of man's origin and fall is *intended to be considered as real history,* real space-time world events. In the same way the account of the flood is to be regarded as historical inasmuch as it is headed up by the key phrase, in 6:9, "these are the generations of Noah." The internal evidence of Genesis virtually insists that chapters 1–11 are intended to be historical (not necessarily purely chronological history) in the ordinary sense of that word. These stories are *not* intended to be myths, parables, or allegories. In general such literary forms are plainly identifiable in Scripture (cf. Judges 9, Ezekiel 17, Matthew 13). Hence we must reject Lever's conclusions with respect to the paradise story.

Having said that the Bible would have us regard these chapters as historical, we must not make the mistake of reading all the material in slavishly literalistic-chronological fashion. The chronological method of reporting history is characteristically western. The Biblical writers did not always report history in such fashion. Oftentimes they reported historical facts in thematic or topical arrangement. Obviously the Gospel of Matthew is intended to be a historical report of things that a real person, Jesus of Nazareth, actually said and did in the real world. The Gospel, however, although there is chronological development in it, commonly treats aspects of the life of Jesus in a *topical* rather than purely chronological manner. Hence we need not regard Genesis 2 as giving a *chronological* order of creation simply because it is historical. To reinforce this point, we can point out that Genesis 2 is not concerned primarily with creation anyway. We may not, however, say that when Genesis 2 talks about trees it is unimportant whether or not there really were any trees. If a historical narrative mentions trees or snakes, as in Genesis 3, it is evidently the intention of the writer that we should understand a real, physical, actual tree or snake.[41]

A fundamentally important position adopted in this book is that in order to attain a genuinely Christian, that is, a genuinely *Biblical* perspective on science and origins we must regard the Book of Genesis as providing us with genuine history. Hence, the account of the origin of man really deals with the origin of man. Only an exegesis of Genesis 2:7 which considers that text to be dealing with history can give us a true understanding as to whether or not the Bible says anything for or against the theory of the evolution of man. Similarly, the account of creation is a historical account that deals with activities that God really engaged in and the world experienced at the beginning of its existence. Genesis 1 is *history*.

---

41. E. J. Young, "What Shall We Believe About the Serpent and the Trees in the Garden of Eden?" in *International Reformed Bulletin* 11 (1968), pp. 42-48.

3

Mature Creationism
and Geology—A Collision Course

The thesis has just been developed that the Book of Genesis, and especially the first eleven chapters, was intended by its author to be viewed as reporting events that actually occurred in space and time. A truly Biblical approach to origins must therefore regard Genesis as *history* and not allegory or myth.

Merely stating that the opening chapters of Genesis are history by no stretch of the imagination solves all the problems of interpretation. The Christian is not automatically locked in to one exegetical view of, say, Genesis 1 simply because he regards that chapter as historical. Under the broad umbrella of "historical" there is considerable room for multiple interpretations of the *exact* meaning of the text of Genesis 1. The student of Genesis 1 must wrestle with the words and overall structure of the text to arrive at the correct meaning of the chapter. The question thus becomes, "Just what *did* happen *in history* according to Genesis 1?"

One "historical" interpretation of the chapter that is still widely accepted in the Christian community is the most literal interpretation. By this is meant that the term "day" is taken in its most literal English sense, that is, as a 24-hour day. The term "create" is taken in its most literal English sense, that is, as a purely miraculous,[1] in-

---

1. Throughout this book I use the terms "miraculous" and "miracle" in the

stantaneous act involving the production of something out of nothing. The rigidly literal interpretation of Genesis 1 envisages the formation of the entire universe by a series of purely miraculous acts of God in the time span of six successive 24-hour days. This view has been ably defended by many excellent theologians[2] and has enjoyed the support of large numbers of Christian people throughout the ages. I will refer to this particular interpretation of Genesis 1 as *mature creationism.*

It is important to realize that one may hold to mature creationism without being a neo-catastrophist. That is, one may believe that God created the universe in six ordinary days without accepting the idea of a geologically mammoth, catastrophic flood in the days of Noah. Conversely it is possible to believe that Noah's flood was a global flood that completely renovated the entire face of the earth without believing in a 144-hour creation. Hence a neo-catastrophist, or "flood geologist," need not necessarily accept mature creationism. As a matter of fact, however, Biblical flood catastrophism and mature creationism are very closely associated in the writings of many Biblical neo-catastrophists so that to undermine the position of mature creationism is also to undermine seriously the whole position of neo-catastrophism.

Mature creationism is a legitimate *Biblical* interpretation of the text of Scripture. However, other *Biblical* interpretations are equally (if not more) acceptable. Mature creationism is incompatible with sound geology and therefore it is less acceptable than the alternative interpretation of Genesis 1 that we will develop in chapters four through six.

The Exegetical Basis of Mature Creationism

Proponents of mature creationism have advanced several lines of argument in support of their position. Most fundamentally, the mature creationist position is based on the usage of the Hebrew word for "day," *yom.* It is vigorously asserted by mature creationists that the word *yom* refers to an ordinary 24-hour day unless the context

more or less popular sense of purely supernatural, instantaneous acts of God. This should by no means be taken to imply that this is the Biblical meaning of the terms.

2. For example, L. Berkhof, H. Hoeksema, H. C. Hoeksema, H. C. Leupold, C. F. Keil, J. C. Whitcomb.

clearly indicates otherwise. Thus C. F. Keil says that "if the days of
creation are regulated by the recurring interchange of light and darkness, they must be regarded not as periods of time of incalculable
duration, of years or thousands of years, but as simple earthly
days."[3] For Keil the context here demands that *yom* be taken as an
ordinary day. Not only that, but the last three days "were regulated
by the rising and setting of the sun."[4] H. C. Leupold notes that
"when the verse (Genesis 1:5) concludes with the statement that the
first 'day' (*yom*) is concluded, the term must mean a twenty-four
hour period."[5] J. C. Whitcomb and H. M. Morris observe that "since
God's revealed Word describes this Creation as taking place in six
'days' and since there apparently is no contextual basis for understanding these days in any sort of symbolic sense, it is an act of both
faith and reason to accept them, literally, as real days."[6]

Mature creationists also are concerned to point out that the word
yom rarely, if ever, means "period." Hence Leupold says, "There
ought to be no need of refuting the idea that *yom* means period."[7]
And Morris says that

> in the relatively rare occurrences of the Hebrew singular *yom* where
> it is meant to refer to an indefinite period of time rather than the
> literal meaning of "day" (a 24-hour period, or the day-light portion
> thereof), such a symbolic meaning is always clear from the context.
> But a straightforward reading of the Genesis account does not indi-
> cate any indefinite period.[8]

He also notes that "the Hebrew word *olam* (meaning 'age,' 'long,
indefinite time') should have been used instead of *yom* if a long
period of time were intended, or else the writer should have made it
clear that *yom* was being used figuratively."[9] Thus in the opinion of

---

3. C. F. Keil and F. Delitzsch, *Biblical Commentary on the Old Testament, I, The Pentateuch* (Grand Rapids: Wm. B. Eerdmans, 1949), p. 51.

4. Ibid., p. 52.

5. H. C. Leupold, *Exposition of Genesis* (Columbus: Wartburg, 1942), p. 56.

6. J. C. Whitcomb and H. M. Morris, *The Genesis Flood* (Philadelphia: Presbyterian and Reformed, 1961), p. 228.

7. Leupold, *Exposition of Genesis*, p. 57.

8. H. M. Morris, *Studies in the Bible and Science* (Philadelphia: Presbyterian and Reformed, 1966), p. 36.

9. Ibid.

the mature creationist school of interpretation the assignment of billions of years of uniformitarian geology to the days of Genesis 1 is an exegetical impossibility. To equate the six days of creation in some way with the geologic time periods would be to stretch sound exegesis beyond the elastic limit. The mature creationist, however, goes still farther. For him the matter is clinched by the fact that each day of Genesis 1 is said to be composed of an evening and a morning. Hence Morris states that

> the day-age theory cannot explain the reference to evening and morning at the end of each day's work, which seems unequivocally intended to refer to 24-hour days, and the light and dark aspects of them. Surely it is a gross misuse of language to understand "evening" as representing the beginning of an age, and "morning" its end, or any similar interpretation.[10]

Leupold says,

> Or again, to make this statement refer to two parts of a long geologic period: the first part a kind of evening; the second a kind of morning; both together a kind of long period, runs afoul of three things: first, that "evening" nowhere in the Scriptures bears this meaning; secondly, neither does "morning"; thirdly, "day" never means "period."[11]

Professor Homer C. Hoeksema of the Theological School of the Protestant Reformed Church defends the view of mature creationism very vigorously by appealing to the doctrine of the perspicuity, that is, the clarity, of Scripture. Mature creationism is said to be correct because it is *obvious*. In approaching the exegesis of Genesis Hoeksema says,

> Closely connected with the infallibility and authority of Holy Scripture, and also belonging to the basis on which we must proceed in our discussion of the creation record, is the truth that Scripture is *perspicuous*. It is not obscure, not dark, but clear, —so clear that any child of God can understand it. One need not be a theologian or an exegete or a scientist or some other kind of well-educated expert to understand the Scriptures; but any child of God can apprehend the truth that is revealed in them. This is fundamental. If Scripture is not perspicuous, then you must needs take the position that it is, for the most part, after all a closed book.[12]

10. Ibid., p. 37.

11. Leupold, *Exposition of Genesis*, p. 56.

12. H. C. Hoeksema, *In the Beginning God* (Grand Rapids: Protestant Reformed Churches in America, 1966), p. 35.

Hoeksema's position on perspicuity has so much truth in it that it is misleading, for it goes a bit beyond Scripture and the Reformed creeds to which he subscribes. For example, the Biblically-based Westminster Confession of Faith (Chapter I, Article VII) says,

> All things in Scripture *are not alike plain* in themselves, nor alike clear unto all: yet *those things which are necessary to be known, believed, and observed for salvation, are so clearly propounded,* and opened in some place of Scripture or other, that not only the learned, but the unlearned, *in a due use of the ordinary means,* may attain unto a sufficient understanding of them (italics mine).

The Westminster Confession's doctrine of perspicuity carries with it the idea that not all Scripture is equally clear and that even that which is clear requires some effort in the understanding of it. A specific Scriptural statement of the Apostle Peter (II Peter 3:16) maintains that in the Scriptures, with particular reference to the epistles of Paul, there "are some things hard to be understood." There are passages of Scripture that are difficult, that are obscure, that can be interpreted in different ways. The Christian cannot necessarily rest content with an obvious interpretation of Scripture. He must always very thoroughly compare one passage of Scripture with another in arriving at conclusions concerning the teaching of Scripture. Deeper investigation may reveal that the obvious interpretation is not necessarily the correct one.

As a simple example Matthew 1:8, a part of the genealogy of Jesus, says that Asa begat Jehoshaphat (Josaphat), that Jehoshaphat begat Jehoram (Joram), and that Jehoram begat Uzziah (Ozias). The *obvious* interpretation of this text is that Uzziah was the son of Jehoram, that Jehoram was the son of Jehoshaphat, and that Jehoshaphat was the son of Asa. This is the obvious interpretation in terms of the whole genealogy because it is known, for example, that Jesus was the son of Joseph, that Solomon was the son of David, and that Isaac was the son of Abraham. Matthew 1:17 says that only fourteen generations elapsed between David and the Babylonian exile. Only fourteen names are given between David and Jechonias (1:11). Hence it is obvious that Uzziah was the son of Jehoram (1:8). This is the obvious interpretation, but it is an incorrect interpretation. The correct interpretation can be made only in the light of the total Scripture, especially the books of Kings and Chronicles, and, most particularly, in the light of I Chronicles 3, which indicates that the names of Ahaziah, Joash, and Amaziah were omitted from the genealogy in Matthew. Hence the *obvious* interpretation may not always be the *correct* interpretation.

Therefore despite the fact that the view of mature creationism is the obvious view, serious consideration must be given, in light of the complexities of the religion-science issue, to whether or not the *totality* of Scripture *demands adherence to this view and this view alone.*

Creation as Divine Miracle Devoid of Process

Members of the mature creationist school typically maintain that the creative events of Genesis 1 are to be seen as divine acts and not as processes of nature. Inasmuch as these divine acts were accomplished within only 144 hours, the acts are viewed as being essentially instantaneous in nature. Scripture, according to the mature creationist, does not allow for anything much lengthier than a series of virtually instantaneous creations. Moreover, the language of Genesis 1 is said to imply instantaneousness. God said, "Let there be," and it was so. In the view of the creationist these statements cannot be consistent with millions of years for the accomplishment of the divine fiat. Rather the fiat is instantaneously fulfilled. Then, too, mature creationists often quote Psalm 33:6 and 9, "By the word of the LORD were the heavens made; and all the host of them by the breath of his mouth. . . . For he spake, and it was done; he commanded, and it stood fast." Does not Scripture clearly speak of the *instantaneousness* with which the creation obeys the Creator's voice?

The mature creationist can allow for as much as 24 hours for the fulfillment of a given fiat, but then this to him is essentially instantaneous, especially in comparison with billions of years. If just a slight amount of time is granted for fulfillment of the fiat, it is possible to admit the incorporation of some degree of process in the creative acts, but the process is indeed minor. The general tendency among mature creationists is to attempt to purge the concept of creation of any taint of natural process. Whitcomb and Morris[13] use the term "creative process" somewhat reluctantly, but it is clear that by this term they do not intend to talk about any natural processes such as could be going on today. Such processes were unique to the creation period.

---

13. Whitcomb and Morris, *The Genesis Flood*, p. 219.

R. J. Rushdoony, a Reformed writer, is perhaps the most insistent that creation be viewed purely as a miraculous divine act totally free of any natural processes whatsoever, whether primary or secondary, whether significant or trivial. Rushdoony fears that any ascription of process to the creation week is an assault on the sovereignty of God. Basic to the positions of creative evolution or progressive creationism,[14] he says,

> is the denial of the *creative act* in favor of a *creative process*. The six days of creation give way to the geological timetable, a substitute god of like creative power. But the moment creativity is transferred or to any degree ascribed to the process of being, to the inner powers of nature, to that extent sovereignty and power are transferred from God to nature.[15]

Elsewhere he declares somewhat more graphically that

> to affirm the *act* of creation is to affirm the sovereignty of God and the reality and priority of the eternal decree. No small stake is therefore at issue in this controversy. In every affirmation of process, the sovereign and transcendent God begins slowly and steadily to be enfolded by the mists of immanence in man's beclouded mind, and then to disappear into a continuous ocean of being in process.[16]

Rushdoony's fears are unfounded. An affirmation of process in itself certainly does not constitute an attack on the sovereignty of God. Scripture revels in the sovereignty of God in history, in day-to-day affairs, in the ordinary rising and setting of the sun. Process is going on all about us now, and God is every whit as sovereign as He was in the creation. The real issue is not the sovereignty of God, but whether or not the term "creation" in Scripture is totally devoid of any thought of process.

The mature creationist tends to fear any incorporation of process into God's creation. The events of the creation week are seen as a

---

14. The term "creative evolution" may be considered more or less synonymous with "theistic evolution" in that the universe undergoes a long-term evolutionary development under the hand of God. "Progressive creationism" may also be viewed as a long-term development of the world, but in this case God, as it were, interrupts the development of the world with special acts of creation such as the creation of birds on the fifth day.

15. R. J. Rushdoony, *The Mythology of Science* (Nutley, NJ: Craig Press, 1967), pp. 38-39.

16. Ibid., p. 64.

series of essentially instantaneous, miraculous divine acts involving virtually no processes. These events consisted in the formation of totally new structures; they were not the shaping or forming of pre-existent material. The appearances of the firmament, the seas, the grass, the sun, the animals, and man were thus not geological, biological, and astronomical events; they were purely the product of the miraculous work of the all-powerful God.

The Doctrine of Apparent Age

An extremely important facet of the mature creationist view of Genesis 1 is precisely the concept of *mature* creation, that is, the *creation of the appearance of age.* Inasmuch as the universe and its contents are extremely diverse and differentiated and structurally complex, it would seem that the universe or, more specifically, the earth has gone through an extensive history to arrive at its present highly differentiated state. Mature creationism, however, allows for a maximum of 144 hours of creative events. Therefore the differentiated state of the universe and of the earth must have been attained extremely quickly; "history" was accelerated. To say that, however, is tantamount to saying that the universe or the earth was created to look *as if* it had undergone a complex history. It was created with the appearance of age. The newly created Adam[17] may have thought that the plants in the Garden of Eden around him had been growing for several years, but in reality they had been created only three days before. The three-day-old plants simply looked old to Adam; they were created with an appearance of age. They were created in their *mature* state.

Viewing creation in this manner may give some readers the desire to ridicule the appearance-of-age theory. One tends to think of Adam as somehow being deceived by God if the plants around him simply *looked* mature. But it is at precisely this point that those who believe in the createdness of Adam must not treat lightly the apparent-age theory, for the question must be asked as to how old the newly created Adam was when he examined those plants. It certainly cannot be assumed that Adam was a one-hour-old baby. He was far more mature than that. He was at least mature enough to communicate

---

17. I am here assuming the correctness of the position that Adam was directly created by God. Argumentation in favor of this position is reserved for chapter seven.

intelligibly with his Creator. Adam was created in a mature condition, with the appearance of age, with the appearance of having developed through infancy, childhood, and adolescence. Adam may have looked 25 years old but he was in reality one hour old as he came from the hand of the Creator. Similarly the other creative events recorded in Genesis 1 were creations of mature geological structures or biological groups, according to the mature creationist view.

Therefore as study of the universe proceeds scientists must not be misled by the apparent fact that the radiation from some galaxies takes billions of years to reach the earth. The radiation must have been created on its way to the earth in such a position as to *appear* that it had left a particular astronomical body so many billions of years ago. Investigators must not be misled by the fact that the abundance of radioactive rubidium and strontium isotopes in an igneous rock from Ontario suggests that the rock crystallized from a liquid 1550 million years ago. God created the rock with the appropriate abundances of the elements rubidium and strontium so that it would appear to be 1550 million years old, and He also created the rock texture and field relations so that it would appear to have crystallized from a liquid magma.

Whitcomb and Morris have dealt with the doctrine of apparent age at great length. As an example of their thinking on this point:

> Plants, in order to continue to grow in the present economy, must have a soil, water, light, chemical nutrients, etc. The account has mentioned water and light, although in a somewhat different physical context than now provided, but the soil and nutrients must also be available. As now formed, a soil requires a long period of preparation before becoming able to support plant growth. But here it must have been created essentially instantaneously, with all the necessary chemical constituents, rather than gradually developed over centuries of rock weathering, alluvial deposition, etc. Thus it had an appearance of being "old" when it was still new. *It was created with an "appearance" of age!*[18]

Moreover plants and animals were created full-grown. The theory of radioactive age-dating of rocks is also viewed on the basis of the apparent-age idea.

> And this is exactly the situation we find in connection with these radioactive elements and with many other geochronometers. It is

---

18. Whitcomb and Morris, *The Genesis Flood*, pp. 232-33.

eminently reasonable and consistent with the basically efficient and
beneficent character of God, as well as with His revelation concerning the fact, that He would have created the entire universe as a
complete, operational, functioning mechanism. The grossly cruel and
wasteful processes of an almost interminable evolution leading up to
man's arrival as its goal, as usually envisioned by uniformitarians (or
at least by theistic uniformitarians), are on the other hand utterly
inconsistent with the character and wisdom of God! It is therefore
not ridiculous after all, but perfectly reasonable, to suppose that the
radiogenic elements, like all other elements, were created directly by
God.

The obvious question then arises as to whether the "apparent ages"
of the minerals so created, as indicated by the relative amounts of
"parent" and "daughter" elements contained therein, would all be
diverse from each other or whether they would all exhibit some
consistent value; and if the latter, what value of apparent age might
be implied.

In the absence of specific revelation, it seems impossible to decide
this question with finality. However, it is more satisfying teleologi-
cally, and therefore more reasonable, to infer that all these primeval
clocks, since they were "wound up" at the same time, were also set
to "read" the same time. Whatever this "setting" was, we may call it
the "apparent age" of the earth, but the "true age" of the earth can
only be known by means of divine revelation.[19]

To Whitcomb and Morris the doctrine of apparent age or mature
creation is extremely important. "We see, therefore, that when one
decides to reject the concept of real Creation, there is no scientific
stopping-point short of what amounts to atheism."[20] They note that
men often complain that God would be dishonest to create things
with an appearance of age, but

if God reveals how and when He created the universe and its inhabitants, then to charge God with falsehood in creating "apparent age"
is presumptuous in the extreme—even blasphemous. *It is not God
Who has lied, but rather man who has called Him a liar, through
rejection of His revelation of Creation as given in Genesis and verified by the Lord Jesus Christ!*[21]

Rushdoony, too, is insistent on the maturity of God's creation: "The
ultimacy of God is the issue in the concept of a mature creation."[22]

19. Ibid., pp. 345-46.

20. Ibid., p. 237.

21. Ibid., p. 238.

22. Rushdoony, *The Mythology of Science*, p. 73.

The Impossibility and Illegitimacy of Scientific Investigation on the Mature Creation Doctrine

Perhaps the most serious implication of the mature creationist view of Genesis 1, an implication that is bothersome particularly to the scientist who is a genuine Bible-believer, is that scientific investigation of the creation week is an impossibility. The very possibility of the scientific enterprise is undergirded by the assumption of the invariability through time of the "laws of nature."[23] Thus natural events that occurred in the past can be explained scientifically by the laws of nature and the processes which operate in accord with those laws. If it is temporarily assumed that the laws of nature have been the same since the absolute creation (Genesis 1:1) to this day, then the geologist may, in looking at a layer of so-called sedimentary rock and comparing the shape and composition of mineral grains within the rock with those that might be found on a beach or stream bed today, conclude that the rock was formed by the deposition of sediment under the influence of gravity in some sort of medium such as a river, stream, or ocean. If the laws of nature were essentially different during the creation week than they are now, then such a rock layer, if formed during creation week, could not be explained scientifically. First of all there would be no assurance that gravitational forces acted on mineral grains causing them to settle to stream bottoms during creation week. Then, too, there would be no assurance as to whether or not erosion and weathering could produce the shape and composition of mineral grains observed in the rock layer. Presumably an entirely different set of laws and processes could have generated the same product as gravity, erosion, and weathering can generate today. The difficulty is that the scientific investigator has absolutely no way of knowing what those laws and processes might have been; hence explanation of the formation of the rock would be an impossibility. The most he could do would be to describe the rock.

This is exactly the predicament into which the mature creationist position leads us. If the view is adopted that Genesis 1 records purely

---

23. I am here using the expression "laws of nature" in a very loose, non-philosophical way. For more rigorous discussion of the meaning of the "laws of nature" see, e.g., T. H. Leith, "What Do We Mean by the Uniformity of Nature?" in *The Gordon Review* 8 (1964), pp. 2-17, and S. Toulmin, *The Philosophy of Science* (New York: Harper and Brothers, 1953).

divine act with no process, then *no laws* were influencing the material being created. Laws of nature did not come into existence until the completion of creation. If the view is adopted that the laws of creation week were creative laws and creative processes, unlike those of today, then the laws of nature as we know them now did not begin to operate until after the fall of Adam. In either case the laws now in existence cannot be applied to the events of creation week, for they did not operate then. Therefore, according to the mature creationist position, to interpret the events of creation week in terms of present laws and processes is *an illegitimate procedure*.

Mature Creationism and Geology

The question may be raised at this point as to why this particular implication of mature creationism should be disturbing to the Bible-believing scientist. The really sincere Bible-believing scientist should be content simply to describe rather than interpret the products of creation if mature creationism is truly what Scripture teaches. The Bible-believing scientist should not presume to go beyond what Scripture permits for him. If Scripture really does teach unequivocally that the universe was miraculously created in 144 hours a few thousands of years ago, then I, as a Christian geologist, will be willing to stop scientific interpretation of the supposedly one-billion-year-old rocks of northern New Jersey which I have been studying for the past several years.[24] Obviously my only task now is to describe those rocks and to find valuable resources in them. If the mature creationist interpretation of Genesis 1 is correct, I am wasting my time talking about magmas and metamorphism inasmuch as these rocks were created instantaneously in place.

In many instances there is no attempt by mature creationists to evaluate geological phenomena in terms of their 24-hour-day creation theory. In general it is flatly asserted that the Bible teaches the miraculous creation of all things in 144 hours, and the Christian geologist is left to figure out for himself what this doctrine may mean with respect to geology or other historical sciences. Occasion-

---

24. D. A. Young, "Precambrian Rocks of the Lake Hopatcong Area, New Jersey," in *Geological Society of America Bulletin* 82 (1971), pp. 143-58, and "A Quartz Syenite Intrusion in the New Jersey Highlands," in *Journal of Petrology* 13 (1972), pp. 511-28.

ally negative criticisms[25] of current scientific thinking with respect to earth or solar system history are written but little is given in the way of positive theory. Fortunately, however, a fairly comprehensive view of earth history in terms of the 24-hour-day view has been presented by Whitcomb and Morris.[26] Many modern adherents of mature creationism have been favorably impressed and influenced by the Whitcomb-Morris theory of the earth, and careful evaluation of this theory in the light of Scripture, of geological facts, and of philosophical principles is in order. What is of interest is whether or not the Whitcomb-Morris theory is internally consistent and whether or not it explains the facts observed in nature. Is this theory a satisfactory solution to the great debate between religion and science?

Gross Structure and Composition of the Earth

Before the major emphases of the Whitcomb-Morris theory are outlined, the geologic structure of our earth must be discussed as briefly as possible. With this basic geologic background the reader will be able more effectively to evaluate the system developed by Whitcomb and Morris. The reader is also urged to consult some of the general texts in geology to reinforce some of the facts and concepts introduced here.[27]

In gross the earth may be considered to be like a gigantic peach in that it is thought to be composed of three major structures. These structures are diagrammatically portrayed in Figure 1. The innermost part of the earth is called the *core* and corresponds more or less to the peach-pit. The thin outer part of the earth which includes materials that are exposed on the earth's surface is termed the *crust*. The crust is something like the fuzzy skin of the peach. And in between the crust and the core of the earth is a large zone that has been

---

25. Cf. J. C. Whitcomb, *The Origin of the Solar System* (Philadelphia: Presbyterian and Reformed, 1964), and B. Davidheiser, *Evolution and Christian Faith* (Philadelphia: Presbyterian and Reformed, 1969).

26. Whitcomb and Morris, *The Genesis Flood.* See also J. C. Whitcomb, *The Early Earth* (Winona Lake, IN: Baker, 1972).

27. For example, L. D. Leet and S. Judson, *Physical Geology* (Englewood Cliffs, NJ: Prentice-Hall, 1971); C. R. Longwell, R. F. Flint, and J. E. Sanders, *Physical Geology* (New York: John Wiley, 1969); J. Gilluly, A. C. Waters, and A. O. Woodford, *Principles of Geology* (San Francisco: W. H. Freeman, 1968); R. J. Ordway, *Earth Science* (New York: Van Nostrand Reinhold, 1972); and B. Kummel, *History of the Earth* (San Francisco: W. H. Freeman, 1970).

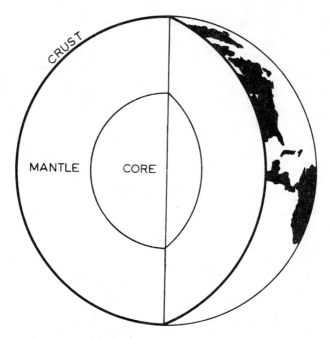

Figure 1. Cutaway of the earth showing simplified internal structure. The crust varies in thickness from five to sixty kilometers. The depth to the mantle-core boundary is about 2900 kilometers. Seismological studies have disclosed considerable detail of the lateral and vertical structure of crust, mantle, and core.

designated the *mantle*. The mantle corresponds to the major part of the peach, namely the sweet, edible fruit.

No one has ever seen the earth's mantle, let alone its core. The deepest holes yet drilled into the earth by man have penetrated only a few miles and remained in the outer crust of the earth. How then can it be said that the earth has a mantle and a core if these have not been directly observed? How do we know that the earth is not hollow?

Scientists are confident that they know something about the interior of the earth in at least a general way because of many indirect observations and inferences. In the first place the overall density of the earth, that is, the general amount of material or mass concentrated into a unit volume of the earth, is known. Both the total mass of the earth and its volume are known; hence its density can be calculated. Geophysicists have learned that the average density of the earth is about 5.5 grams per cubic centimeter. This may be compared with the density of water which, at room temperature and pressure, is about 1.0 grams per cubic centimeter. Thus one cubic centimeter of "average earth" is about 5.5 times as massive or dense or heavy as a cubic centimeter of water. The earth is thus quite a dense body and in fact is the densest of all the planets in our solar system. In addition to the overall density of the earth the density of the common rocks that are found near the earth's surface can easily be determined. It is found that the densities of most common rocks, such as granite or sandstone or basalt, range between about 2.5 and 3.0 grams per cubic centimeter. The surface rocks are much less dense than the average density of the earth. As a result scientists believe that the interior of the earth cannot be entirely hollow. There must be some material inside the earth whose density is far greater than 2.5 grams per cubic centimeter.

Geologists have observed the eruptions and the products of many volcanoes around the world. Various kinds of lava have been erupted, but in general the lava that is erupted in greatest quantity is basaltic lava. The volcanic rock that hardens from this kind of lava is termed *basalt* and is composed of very tiny crystals of the minerals olivine, pyroxene, and plagioclase feldspar. Minor amounts of other minerals as well as some glass, because of the quick chilling of the lava, may be present. Where did this lava come from? Obviously it came to the surface from deeper in the earth. And in order for liquid lava to erupt either the interior of the earth must be a mass of hot liquid or the lava must have been melted out of a solid interior. If it is assumed that the interior is essentially solid, then what kind of solid material would give rise to a basaltic lava upon partially melting? Obviously it is not just any kind of rock which would produce basaltic lava upon melting. Also the solid interior of the earth must be largely homogeneous in order to produce so much basalt in comparison to other kinds of lavas. Intelligent inferences about the nature of the earth's interior can be made by conducting laboratory studies of the melting behavior of basalt. Experimental petrologists, those geologists who study experimentally the behavior of geologic liquids, solids, and gases, have found, for example, that basalt cannot be produced by melting a granite, a shale, or a limestone. And no geologists really expected that it could. But it has been found that basalt liquids are produced by the melting of solids very rich in olivine and pyroxene and containing very minor quantities of garnet and plagioclase feldspar. These are essentially the same minerals that are present in basalt but the proportions are much different. There may be 40 to 60 percent plagioclase in a basalt, but very little needs to be present in the rock from which it is melted. Experimental studies suggest that the earth's interior is composed largely of the minerals pyroxene and olivine.

Interestingly enough the basaltic lavas that are erupted from many volcanoes (such as the Hawaiian volcanoes) contain solid chunks of rock that bear little resemblance to the surrounding rocks of the islands. Presumably these solid chunks incorporated in the lava were brought up with the lava from great depths. These chunks are composed largely of olivine and pyroxene with minor quantities of garnet and plagioclase. In South Africa there are some curious rocks known as kimberlites. The kimberlites are thought to be solidified volcanic rocks that are presently frozen into the pipes or throats of extinct, deeply eroded volcanoes. They came from considerable depths in the earth as evidenced by the presence of many diamonds. Experimental studies show that diamond, a natural form of carbon, can crystallize only under extremely high pressures. Otherwise graphite, the material used in lead pencils, will form. In addition to the diamonds the kimberlites contain chunks of rock like those in the lava flows, namely chunks made up largely of olivine and pyroxene with perhaps minor quantities of garnet and plagioclase.

Another line of evidence leads to the same conclusion. A great variety of meteorites from outer space have been collected on the earth's surface. It is believed that many of these meteorites may have been derived from the asteroid belt between the planets Mars and Jupiter. It is possible that the asteroids are the exploded remains of a planet that developed some kind of gross concentric structure similar to what we believe the earth has. In any case many of the meteorites are composed largely of pyroxene and olivine with minor amounts of other minerals.

One final line of evidence comes from the study of seismic waves, those vibrations or sound waves that are generated within the earth during an earthquake or large explosion. Studies of the velocity of these waves through the earth suggest that at least the outer part of the earth's interior is most likely composed of minerals such as olivine and pyroxene which transmit sound waves at approximately the velocities observed. The seismic wave studies indicate the size of this part of the interior and also the fact that it is predominantly solid and not liquid. Many lines of evidence converge to suggest that the outer 85 percent of the earth's interior is essentially solid material composed to a large degree of minerals such as olivine and pyroxene. This zone is the mantle.

The kind of material that is in the mantle, however, has an average density of about 3.3 to 3.5 grams per cubic centimeter. Hence the entire interior of the earth cannot be composed of this material. There must be within the deepest part of the earth a very dense material that will give the earth its average density of 5.5 grams per cubic centimeter. The study of meteorites discloses that many of them are composed largely of a metallic alloy of iron and nickel. Perhaps this material represents the core of a fragmented asteroid or planetesimal left over from the formation of the solar system. This suggests the possibility that the earth's core is also composed of very dense metal such as iron. Seismic and other geophysical studies have suggested that the core is composed of a liquid outer core that surrounds a solid inner core. It is possible that under conditions which may obtain in the earth's deep interior iron would be in its liquid state. The best guess at present then is that the core is chiefly a very dense liquid that may be composed essentially of the elements iron and nickel.

Far more is known about the crust than about the core or the mantle. Much of the crust is directly observable at the surface and much of the inside of the crust has been probed by mines and drill holes. It is chiefly from the crust that the earth's geologic history has been unraveled, for the simple reason that the crust is the most accessible part of the earth.

The crust is composed of two major types of material designated as oceanic crust and continental crust. Seismic studies indicate that crustal rocks at the bottom of the sea are only about five miles thick. The continental crust which underlies the continental landmasses, however, is much thicker. It varies roughly between twenty and forty miles thick. Both types of crust rest on top of the mantle and are separated from it by a boundary known as the Mohorovicic discontinuity or the Moho. The existence of the Moho has been determined by means of seismic studies.

The two types of crust differ not only in geographic distribution and thickness but also in general chemistry and type of rocks present. The oceanic crust is sometimes called *sima* because the two most abundant chemical elements along with oxygen are *si*licon and *ma*gnesium. This type of crust is composed chiefly of solidified basaltic lava flows and sheets and minor amounts of thinly-layered sedimentary rocks and loose sediment made up of fine clay or the remains of the "shells" or "skeletons" of exceedingly tiny one-celled oceanic organisms.[28] The rocks in the deep ocean basins are essentially undeformed. That is, the layers of rock have been formed by flowage of lava like a carpet over the sea floor or by slow settling of clay particles or hard parts of organisms. As such the layers are essentially horizontal, or parallel to the sea-floor surface, and have not been severely squeezed or squashed or folded or distorted, except near the boundaries between continental and oceanic crust.[29] Nor are sea-floor rocks metamorphosed. That is, the rocks have not since the time of their deposition on the sea floor been subjected to extreme heat and pressure. They retain the character original to them at that time.

The continental crust is sometimes referred to as *sial* because of the general abundance of the chemical elements *si*licon and *al*uminum. There is a great variety of rock types in the continental crust, far greater, so far as we know, than in the oceanic crust. All three of geology's famous rock categories (igneous, sedimentary, and metamorphic) are present in great abundance in the continental crust. The igneous rocks, those that have solidified from molten masses of liquid called magma, are present as large masses of rock that have squeezed or intruded their way into the surrounding rocks or as hardened flows of volcanic rock that have erupted through the vents of volcanoes or fissures in the ground. A great part of the Sierra Nevada Mountains in California and the White Mountains in New Hampshire are composed of intrusive igneous rocks. These rocks are thought to have solidified well underground and are now exposed at the surface after long periods of erosion. The entire area around the

---

28. Most of our present knowledge of the sea floors has been obtained through the JOIDES (Joint Oceanographic Institutions Deep Earth Sampling) deep-sea drilling program carried out by the research vessel *Glomar Challenger*. For brief summary reports of findings of the JOIDES program see the magazine *Geotimes*. Detailed reports are being published in *Initial Reports of the Deep Sea Drilling Project* (Washington: U. S. Government Printing Office).

29. The boundaries between converging slabs of oceanic crust and continental crust are known as Benioff or subduction zones. At these junctions oceanic crust is very gradually (a few centimeters per year) gliding downwards underneath the edge of the continental crust. Considerable rock deformation, earthquake activity, and volcanism take place at these locales. As an example, consider the volcanism and seismic activity where Pacific Ocean crust meets continental crust near Japan, Alaska, or the Andes of South America.

Columbia River in Washington and Oregon is composed of a thick pile of layered extrusive volcanic rocks, chiefly basalt.

Sedimentary rocks are those that have formed by the settling of rock or mineral particles to the earth's surface through some medium such as wind, glacial ice, or, chiefly, water. Accumulations of mud in river bottoms or sand at ocean beaches are examples of sediment which ultimately ought to be converted into layered sedimentary rock. Sandstone, shale, and limestone are the most common types of sedimentary rocks. Most of the layered rocks of the interior states such as Kansas and Nebraska are sedimentary rocks.

Metamorphic rocks also are present in great abundance in the continental crust. Originally igneous, sedimentary, or some other kind of metamorphic rock, these materials have undergone severe changes thought to be induced by recrystallization of the constituent mineral particles under the influence of extreme heat and pressure. It is believed by most geologists that these kinds of rocks must at one time have been very deeply buried in the crust, where they experienced extreme heating and distortion. The rocks of Manhattan Island, Philadelphia, and most of New England are metamorphic rocks. These are known chiefly as schist, gneiss, marble, and quartzite.

Fundamental Principles of Earth History

For the simple reason that the continental crust is more accessible than the oceanic crust, the study of earth history has been developed chiefly on the basis of the distribution, structure, and composition of continental rocks. In general how has the history of the earth been worked out from these data? Reduced to its very simplest terms, geologic history, in the sense of a relative sequence of geologic events, can be worked out by means of three principles inductively derived from empirical observations. These are the fundamental laws of geology: the law of superposition, the law of cross-cutting relationships, and the law of faunal succession.

The law of superposition states that in any undisturbed stack of layered sedimentary or volcanic rocks the layer which is at the bottom of the pile must be older, that is, it must have been deposited earlier, than the layer immediately above it. This can be observed in the deposition of present-day river muds. An obvious analogy is the layering in a stack of paper lying on a table. The sheet of paper lying at the bottom of the stack must have been placed on the table before

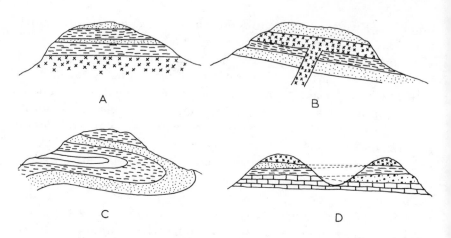

Figure 2. The law of superposition. **A.** Normal situation showing cross section of a mountain in which layered sedimentary rocks rest on top of igneous rock (crosses). In this case it is reasonable to assume that the closer the layers are to the top, the younger they are in terms of time of deposition. **B.** An igneous rock (crosses) formed by intrusion of hot liquid into sequence of sedimentary rocks. In this case the igneous layer was emplaced *after* the top sedimentary layer, i.e., it is *younger* than the layer above. **C.** The sedimentary layers have been completely overturned so that the layers are progressively *older* toward the top in the upper part of the mountain. **D.** The interlensing of layers indicates that superposition can be used to establish only a relative age sequence. In any given outcrop, layers representing a certain time interval may be entirely lacking due to erosion, nondeposition, or other factors.

the sheet lying on top of it. This event—"deposition" of the sheet of paper—is an earlier event than the "deposition" of the next sheet. Similarly, it is possible to obtain *relative* age sequences of layered rocks in a pile. There are, of course, exceptions to the law of superposition which must be noted carefully. Some of these exceptions are illustrated in Figure 2. Proper application of the law of superposition assumes that the entire stack of rocks has not been completely overturned so that it is now upside down. For example, throughout the central United States the sequence of layered sedimentary rocks is very nearly horizontal over thousands of square miles. There is no evidence of bending of rocks to suggest that they have been overturned. It is difficult, even for the most extreme catastrophist, to imagine that these thousands of square miles of rock could have been overturned *en masse* to a presently horizontal position without any signs of disruption. The geologist is fairly safe in assuming that the layered rocks of Kansas are in their original position rather than an inverted one. In addition, many sedimentary rock features like ripple marks or cross-bedding are indicators as to whether a rock or sediment layer is right side up. These kinds of features in Kansas rocks clearly indicate that the rocks are in their proper positions. To the west, however, as one approaches the Rocky Mountains, the rocks begin to show signs of deformation. The rocks have been cast into a series of great folds or warps which are most intense in the mountainous regions. Locally it is possible to observe sequences of layers that have been folded so intensely and severely that they have been turned completely upside down. It is possible, however, for the geologist to trace physically the normal sequence of layers into the upside-down sequence. Hence the geologist, by careful field mapping, is able to apply the law of superposition properly in this anomalous situation. Here he knows that the bottom layer is younger than the one above it for he knows that he is dealing with an anomalous situation. Overturned sequences of layered rocks are relatively rare, and in many (if not most) instances it is possible to identify such situations for what they are either by mapping or by noting such features as ripple marks.[30]

A second exception to the law of superposition occurs if a layer of intrusive igneous rock is sandwiched in between layers of sedimentary rock. In this case, assuming the rocks to be right side up, the igneous rock was intruded as a liquid between the sedimentary materials and crystallized there so that the geologist can say for sure that the igneous rock is younger than the rock beneath it but that it is also younger than the rock above it! It may also be younger than the next 100 or even 10,000 layers above it. Generally it is difficult to determine just when the igneous rock was intruded.

Another exception to the law of superposition is provided by thrust faults. In this case one mass of layered rocks is shoved physically by great stresses within the crust over the top of another mass of layered rocks along a great fracture known as a fault. Where these kinds of faults occur older rocks may well be shoved on top of younger rocks. This type of situation is sometimes difficult to identify, but geologic mapping, that is, physical tracing of distinctive layers of rocks across the countryside has shown that these fault situations do exist. Older rocks have been physically moved on top of younger rocks.

30. R. R. Shrock, *Sequence in Layered Rocks* (New York: McGraw-Hill, 1948).

Figure 3. The law of cross-cutting relationships. Sketch of an outcrop containing highly contorted layers of rock cut by a dike of igneous-looking rock. It may
be safely inferred that the dike material was emplaced or "intruded" into the
rock *after* the folding and contortion of the layered material took place. The
dike rock is *younger* than the folded rock.

One modification of the law of superposition ought also to be
noted. In most areas where layered sequences of sedimentary rocks
are exposed, some layers may be missing in one sequence but present
in another exposed five miles away. Hence in a given sequence a layer
superimposed on top of another layer was not necessarily formed
immediately after the layer below. There may well have been a gap in
time during which no deposition of sediment occurred, while five
miles away it is possible that a layer of sediment was being deposited.
The development of any relative sequence of geologic events must
therefore take into account the fact that not all events are necessarily
represented at one location.

The second principle of geologic interpretation is the *law of cross-
cutting relationships*. This principle simply states that any body of
rock whose borders transect the layering or other structures in surrounding rocks was emplaced in its present situation *later* than the
surrounding rocks. The principle is illustrated in Figure 3. A simple
analogy should again serve to demonstrate the validity of the princi-

ple. Imagine a box of fudge-ripple ice cream (or if you wish to perform and then eat your experiment, take a box of fudge-ripple ice cream from the freezer). Dig a spoon into the ice cream. The physical distribution of spoon and ice cream is now such that the borders of the spoon transect or cut across the swirls of fudge in the ice cream. This cross-cutting relationship is the result of the "intrusion" of the spoon into the ice cream. The obvious time relationship is that the pushing or intrusion of the spoon into the ice cream follows or is later than the formation of the ice cream. In the same way rocks that cut across others are *relatively* younger. Many igneous rocks show this kind of cross-cutting relationship. Apparently the rocks formed from hot liquid which forced its way into cracks in the surrounding rocks and then solidified. Using this principle it is possible to determine the relative ages of many igneous rocks with respect to other kinds of rocks.

Another observation has also been employed in the development of a relative sequence of geologic events. This observation has been formulated in the *law of faunal succession.* The law states that in general it is possible to determine the relative age of a given layer of fossil-bearing sedimentary rock on the basis of the assemblage of fossil plants and animals which it contains. Very closely related to this is the observation that successively younger sedimentary rocks generally contain progressively more complex types of fossil flora and fauna. The implication of the law is that during the time when a certain layer of sediment was deposited, the earth was inhabited by a certain population of living organisms which upon death were incorporated into the sediment. When a later layer was being deposited, the earth was inhabited by a different population of organisms. The organisms had changed through time. This by no means implies that many species could not have lived at both times. Nor does this observation necessarily imply the validity of the general theory of organic evolution. It implies only that the overall association or assemblage of species had changed.

The law of faunal succession is not the result of the theory of organic evolution, though it has been used in support of that theory. The law is an observation that derives from studies of sequences of fossiliferous sedimentary rocks to which the law of superposition may be unhesitatingly applied. In areas where there are thicknesses of thousands of feet of horizontal undisturbed sedimentary rock, the layers at the bottom contain relatively simple plant and animal fossils. The topmost layers typically contain more complex fossils such as mammals and reptiles. Fossils of man and manlike creatures have been discovered in the layers closest to the surface. As a generality, too, over wide areas a given rock layer or formation contains essentially the same fossils throughout. It is therefore often possible in places where a given rock formation cannot be physically traced for miles across the countryside from one place to another to identify that formation on the basis of its fossil content as well as its composition. Figure 4 illustrates the application of the law of faunal succession.

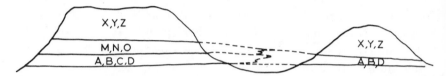

Figure 4. The law of faunal succession. The letters represent hypothetical fossil species occurring in layered rocks exposed in two hills. Fossils A, B, and D are characteristically found in the older, bottom layers whereas X, Y, and Z are found in younger layers. Discovery of these fossils in some other outcrop can be used to establish the *relative* age of the layers containing them. A certain group of fossils such as M, N, and O may be found in layers in one outcrop but not in another because of nondeposition in the one locality. Hence the inference may *not* be made that fossils X, Y, and Z lived at a time *immediately* after the time when fossils A, B, and D lived. This further establishes the fact that the use of specific fossils as time indicators must be built upon information obtained from numerous localities, not just one.

The application of these three fundamental laws along with some intuition has helped geologists to erect the famous geologic time scale. The time scale is a list of various periods of the geologic past whose events are now recorded in the rocks. The scale is one of *relative* ages. Even though absolute ages have been applied to the geologic periods, these have not been determined on the basis of the three fundamental laws and are subject to change. Even if the absolute numbers applied to the time scale were to be completely invalidated, the time scale would still stand in the sense that the relative ages or relative sequences of rocks have been well worked out on the basis of innumerable worldwide studies. It will thus generally be possible to study a rock of unknown age and refer it to a known geologic period by determining its relationships to rocks of known relative geologic age. This relative time sequence of rocks holds whether one is a uniformitarian or a neo-catastrophist. The uniformitarian simply believes that this relative sequence of events took place over very long stretches of time, whereas the neo-catastrophist thinks this relative distribution of rocks must have been produced in a very short time. Figure 5 serves to illustrate this point. Table 2, The Geologic Time Scale, should be studied thoroughly. The ages listed are the latest estimates as to when each of the periods began as far as uniformitarian geologists are concerned. Neo-catastrophists Whitcomb and Morris refer to these periods in their work; hence, the reader should be familiar with these names or refer back to the table.

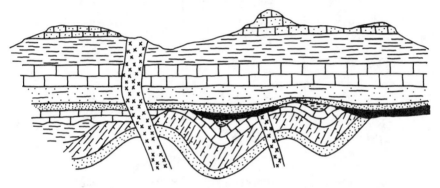

Figure 5. Relative sequence of geological events. The diagram represents a hypothetical cross section of rock units that might be observed in a well-exposed canyon wall such as the Grand Canyon. Basically the major events represented are folding of the bottom layers, intrusion of the right-hand dike, erosion, deposition of the flat-lying layers, intrusion of the left-hand dike, and final erosion. Both neo-catastrophist and uniformitarian would agree on the relative sequence of events, but the uniformitarian believes that substantial lengths of time were required for the events to transpire whereas the neo-catastrophist believes only a few days to a few months were required.

A Sketch of North American Geology

The general distribution of rocks in the United States and Canada is depicted in Figure 6. Most of eastern and central Canada is composed of highly-contorted metamorphic and igneous rocks. This very complex group of rocks is sometimes referred to as crystalline rock. There is presently little earthquake activity and no volcanic activity in that area. It is thus geologically stable and is commonly referred to as the Canadian shield. The distortion and metamorphism of the rocks suggest that the shield area was one of intense, vigorous geologic activity a long time ago. Radioactivity measurements suggest

TABLE 2

The Geologic Time Scale

Era	Period	Approximate Time Since Beginning of Period in Millions of Years*
Cenozoic	Quaternary	1.8
	Tertiary	65
Mesozoic	Cretaceous	136
	Jurassic	185
	Triassic	225
Paleozoic	Permian	280
	Pennsylvanian	320
	Mississippian	345
	Devonian	395
	Silurian	425
	Ordovician	500
	Cambrian	570
	Precambrian	4550

*According to uniformitarian geologists and based on radiometric dating.
These ages are subject to continuing refinement.

that these rocks are extremely old. The rocks are essentially devoid of any type of fossils. The rocks of the shield are believed to have been formed during the Precambrian period of the Paleozoic era. In the central United States and in the Hudson Bay region, the shield rocks are overlain by flat-lying, fossiliferous, layered sandstones, shales, limestones, and coal beds. This stack of layers varies in thickness from one area to another, but is generally only a few thousand feet thick. Rocks of the underlying shield or basement have been penetrated by drill holes in the search for extensive deposits of petroleum in the layered sedimentary rocks. It is clear that the undeformed sedimentary rocks of the central United States are younger than the rocks of

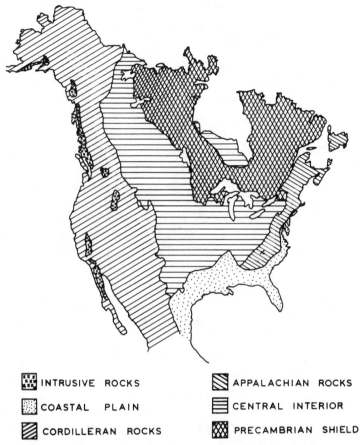

	INTRUSIVE ROCKS		APPALACHIAN ROCKS
	COASTAL PLAIN		CENTRAL INTERIOR
	CORDILLERAN ROCKS		PRECAMBRIAN SHIELD

Figure 6. Generalized geologic map of North America. The Precambrian shield consists of predominantly granitic rocks and mildly metamorphosed rocks. The central interior consists mainly of nearly horizontal sedimentary rocks that over-lie and are younger than rocks of the shield. The Appalachian rocks consist mainly of sedimentary rocks which are equivalent in age to the interior rocks but are greater in thickness and highly folded and faulted. Locally deep-seated meta-morphic rocks have been folded up with the sedimentary rocks and are now exposed at the surface. Local igneous rocks are also present. Much the same may be said of Cordilleran rocks except that the Cordilleras (the Rockies, Sierra Nevadas, and other mountains of the west) contain rocks that are younger than those of the Appalachians. The Atlantic and Gulf coastal plain consists chiefly of unconsolidated layers of sand, clay, gravel, and limestone that dip very gently seaward. These layers have been derived from and overlap older rocks in the Appalachians and the central interior. The intrusive rocks represent gigantic exposures of granitic rocks. Much smaller masses of intrusive igneous rock are found throughout most of North America, but are absent in the coastal plain and scarce in the central interior.

the shield, for they have been deposited on top of them. Rocks of Cambrian to Tertiary age are present in varying proportions in different parts of the central United States.

Westward and eastward from the central interior are mountainous belts. The Appalachian Mountains run the length of the eastern United States; the Rocky Mountains and the Sierra Nevada Mountains are present in the western United States. As the layered rocks of the interior are traced toward these mountain belts they become more and more disturbed. The rocks become folded and faulted, and in many instances the intensity of folding and faulting is greatest near the core of the mountain belts. In some places the Precambrian metamorphosed crystalline rocks of the underlying basement have been punched or domed up into the overlying deformed sedimentary rocks. In mountains, sedimentary rocks are present in thicknesses of tens of thousands of feet of highly folded material. Near the cores of some mountain chains the deformation of these fossiliferous sedimentary rocks has been so intense that the rocks have been converted into crystalline metamorphic rocks. So intense have been the heat and distortion that the original sedimentary appearance of the rock is commonly obliterated. It is typical, too, for the fossils to be thoroughly destroyed, although some fossils escape the heat treatment and are plainly recognizable despite being smeared out to some extent. Thus crystalline metamorphic rocks that are Cambrian to Devonian in age occur, for example, throughout virtually all of New England. Not all complex metamorphic rocks are Precambrian. The rocks of New England can be traced westward to less metamorphosed sedimentary material. The metamorphic materials of the intensely deformed cores of mountain chains commonly are accompanied by intruded igneous magmas that subsequently crystallized into great masses of granite and related rock. The igneous rocks are of various ages. The Palisades diabase of New Jersey is Triassic. The White Mountain granites are Cretaceous. Other igneous bodies in New England and New Jersey are Ordovician. Igneous activity occurs throughout the development of a mountain chain.

A Mature Creationist View of the Geological Events of Creation Week

Needless to say, this is a very simplified sketch of geological fact and principle, but it should suffice to permit proper evaluation of the

Biblical neo-catastrophic geological theory. John C. Whitcomb, professor of Old Testament at Grace Theological Seminary, and Henry M. Morris, a civil engineer who is now director of the Institute for Creation Research, have developed an especially comprehensive theory of geology in *The Genesis Flood*. The neo-catastrophist theory of Whitcomb and Morris revolves around three Biblical events of presumed catastrophic significance: the creation, the fall of man, and the flood. The whole theory is built around the Biblical record of these events. Geologically speaking, the theory is founded on two generalized observations. The first generalization is that the lower part of the crust, that is, the basement or shield, as previously noted, is composed chiefly of crystalline igneous and metamorphic rocks that are intensely deformed and devoid of fossils. On the basis of abundant radioactive age determinations orthodox uniformitarian geologists believe that these rocks were formed in Precambrian time. The second generalization is that over large parts of the various continents these crystalline rocks are overlain by sequences of layered, fossiliferous, sedimentary rock that are only locally deformed and metamorphosed. The neo-catastrophic theory seeks to integrate the three catastrophic Biblical events with these two geologic generalizations.

Neo-catastrophists, as a rule, are also mature creationists. Whitcomb and Morris see no reason not to accept the idea that creation occurred in the span of 144 hours. There must therefore have been a certain amount of geologic "work" accomplished during creation week by the Creator. The rocks created during creation week must have been created essentially in place. The rocks so produced cannot be studied by geologists in terms of the laws that are presently in operation, for the laws of the present are not the laws of creation. Neo-catastrophism, of course, realizes to some extent that it must tell us what rocks were produced during creation week, else the geologist would make the mistake of interpreting them in terms of inapplicable laws and principles. "We must approach a study of the work of the six days of Creation strictly from the perspective of Scriptural revelation, and not at all from that of a projection of present natural processes into the past."[31]

---

31. Whitcomb and Morris, *The Genesis Flood*, p. 228.

The so-called Precambrian crystalline rocks, as just noted, are structurally very complex and are without question among the most difficult of all rocks for geologists to decipher. Are uniformitarian geologists perhaps using the wrong principles to decipher them? Whitcomb and Morris believe that, for the most part, these so-called Precambrian crystalline rocks were formed during creation week. Clearly on the first day of creation light was created. Let there be light—and it was so. But also

> what physical activity and chemical reactions were stimulated by this impulse of light energy, in connection with the earth's heat and its primeval element, it would be pure speculation to try to say. It seems only reasonable that much of such activity then took place, particularly in the materials near the surface which now form the deeper crust, materials which everywhere give evidence of intense primeval activity—motion, deformation, pressure, metamorphism, etc. It is possible that many of those rocks now called Archaeozoic[32] received their characteristics largely during this time. These rocks, also known as the "basement complex" apparently underlie all other crustal rocks and are almost or entirely composed of igneous and metamorphic rocks, in extreme heterogeneity. These crystalline rocks have roots which are as yet inaccessible to man and are separated at their surface by a worldwide unconformity[33] from the sedimentary rocks that have been superimposed upon them at some later time or times.[34]

It is very interesting to note that Whitcomb and Morris could not resist the temptation to discuss the events of the first day of creation at least partly in terms of *present* processes, such as deformation and metamorphism.

"On the second day of Creation, the waters covering the earth's surface were divided into two great reservoirs—one below the firmament and one above, the firmament being the 'expanse' above the earth now corresponding to the troposphere."[35] D. W. Patten also finds the work of the second day especially important to his neo-catastrophic construction. On the basis of Genesis 1:6-7 Patten sug-

---

32. The term "Archaeozoic" has been applied to the most ancient rocks in the earth's crust, namely, those that were formed during the first half of Precambrian time.

33. An unconformity is an eroded land surface, generally expressed by somewhat irregular topography, that has become buried under newer deposits of rock material.

34. Whitcomb and Morris, *The Genesis Flood*, pp. 228-29.

35. Ibid., p. 229.

gests that there was always a water vapor canopy in the upper atmosphere until after the flood.[36] The water vapor canopy formed on the second day is said to be the source of the rainwaters which fed the great Noahic flood.

On the third day dry land appeared. "Thus is implied the first great 'orogeny' or 'mountain birth.' This seems to have been accomplished, at least in part, by differential sorting of the primeval surface materials in accordance with their weights."[37] Again the writers fall into the trap of talking about creation in terms of present processes. Also on the third day

> as the movements began and continued, the waters began to flow into the newly-formed basins and of course initiated erosion and deposition of sediments on a vast scale. It seems reasonable that many of the deeper sedimentary rocks may have been formed at this time, especially those now attributed to the Proterozoic Era.[38]
>
> The Proterozoic Era is thought to be the period between the Archaeozoic and the Cambrian. It is also known by the term "Algonkian." It is marked by nonfossiliferous rocks quite commonly typical sedimentaries except for this lack of fossils. As noted before, it is separated by a profound unconformity from the Archaeozoic Rocks below it, although quite often the latter are also found either at the surface or else directly below some fossil-bearing stratum, with the Proterozoic absent. This great unconformity at the top of the Archean rocks has, until recently, been attributed to a tremendously long period of erosion. This is very unlikely, if not impossible, however, because such a lengthy period of universal erosion must have produced somewhere great thicknesses of corresponding sediments, and these have *never been found.*
>
> It is much more likely that the Archean rocks were truncated in this way by a brief intense period of erosion in connection with the activities of the first three days of Creation. The rocks of the Proterozoic, of course containing no genuine fossils since life had not yet been introduced onto the earth, perhaps were then in part deposited during the orogeny of the third day.[39]

Here again are such words as "deposition" and "erosion," present-day processes. Perhaps to be truly consistent with their principle of an essentially mature or grown creation, Whitcomb and Morris

36. D. W. Patten, *The Biblical Flood and the Ice Epoch* (Seattle: Pacific Meridian, 1966), p. 197.

37. Whitcomb and Morris, *The Genesis Flood*, p. 230.

38. The term "Proterozoic" generally has been applied to rocks formed during the latter half of Precambrian time.

39. Whitcomb and Morris, *The Genesis Flood*, pp. 230-31.

should simply have said that these rocks were created *in situ*. In any case their belief is that the earth's Precambrian rocks were created during the first three days of the creation week, namely during a brief period of 72 hours. In effect all Precambrian basement rocks were formed during creation week and are therefore not susceptible to scientific study. The most one can do is to describe them and to mine them for their ores. The development of the rocks or of the processes which led to the ore-bodies cannot be interpreted scientifically, for the rocks were created.

The second great catastrophe in the Bible is the fall of man. According to Whitcomb and Morris there was at the time of the fall of Adam a cosmic shift in the laws of nature.[40] As a result of Adam's sinful disobedience to God the universe was cursed and began to undergo decay. Whitcomb and Morris believe that the first and second laws of thermodynamics came into effect at this time. The first law of thermodynamics expresses the conservation of energy. It states that neither matter nor energy can be created or destroyed; the various forms of energy are simply interchangeable. This would seem to be consistent with the Biblical teaching of a completed creation (Genesis 2:1). The second law of thermodynamics expresses the gradual degradation or decay of energy. It states that the energy of the universe is continuously being converted into heat. The result of this process is that progressively less energy remains which is capable of performing useful work. The universe is said to be running down. It is dying a slow "heat death." The physicist expresses the second law by saying that the entropy of the universe is always increasing, striving towards a maximum. Whitcomb and Morris see the second law as being consistent with the decay we see all around us.

One expression of the curse and of this universal decay is death. Death, according to neo-catastrophism, was unknown prior to the sin of Adam. Any kind of death, be it in plants, animals, or men, occurred only after the fall.[41] "Although the sentence of death was specifically pronounced only on man and on the serpent used by Satan as the vehicle of temptation, the most obvious implication is that this curse on the master of creation extended likewise to his dominion."[42] If, then, no animal or plant died prior to the fall of Adam, all fossil-bearing rocks must have been formed after the fall inasmuch as fossils are the remains of dead animals and plants, their

---

40. Ibid., pp. 454-73.   41. Ibid.   42. Ibid., p. 239.

parts, tracks, or impressions. "We feel compelled to date all of the rock strata which contain fossils of once-living creatures as subsequent to Adam's fall!"[43]

The larger part of the earth's surface is covered by fossiliferous sedimentary rocks. In the neo-catastrophist view, these rocks, typically assigned by uniformitarian geologists to such geologic periods as Cambrian through Tertiary, must have been formed since the time of Adam's fall. Moreover, these rocks cannot be tens or hundreds of millions of years old as believed by uniformitarians, for Adam was created only a few thousands of years ago.[44] These fossiliferous rocks themselves must be, at the most, a few thousands of years old. How then could these fossiliferous sedimentary rocks have been formed?

To be sure some of these rocks may have been produced by the processes of erosion and deposition as we see presently in operation at the seashore. Just as sea shells are being incorporated into beach sand today so may fossils have been formed during and after the lifetime of Adam. Whitcomb and Morris, however, feel that these processes are incapable of producing the staggering volume of fossiliferous rock covering the earth's surface if only a few thousand years were available.

> It seems likely, furthermore, that relatively few of these strata, if any, can be dated during the period between Adam's fall and the Deluge. This is primarily because geologic activity seems to have been very mild during that time and because such deposits as may have been formed then were most likely reworked during the Flood.[45]

Something spectacular is needed to produce all those fossiliferous rocks.

Something spectacular is available to Whitcomb and Morris in the form of the Genesis flood. They invoke a catastrophic, globe-encircling flood as the explanatory principle of the vast volumes of fossiliferous sedimentary rock. The fossils are themselves the remains of those creatures that were destroyed in the great flood. A fuller discussion and analysis of the flood aspect of the Biblical neo-catastrophist theory is given in chapter nine.

---

43. Ibid., pp. 474-89.   44. Ibid.   45. Ibid., pp. 239-40.

A Critique of the Neo-catastrophist View of Creation Week Geology

Whitcomb and Morris maintain that the present laws of physics and chemistry and the other sciences were not in existence during creation week, but that they have been in existence *since the fall of Adam.* This would mean that these present laws were in existence during the time of the flood. Whitcomb and Morris do not seem to be at all concerned to present the flood in terms of pure miracle.

This point is stressed because it is fundamental to criticism of neo-catastrophism. A basic difficulty arises in that it is virtually impossible, on the Whitcomb and Morris theory, for the Christian geologist to know which rocks he may legitimately study and which rocks he may only describe. The problem the practicing Christian geologist confronts while standing on a rock outcrop is: "Was this rock I am standing on created *in situ* or was it formed by natural processes since Adam's fall? Do I have any right to interpret this rock in terms of present processes?" Whitcomb and Morris do not think that this presents any particular difficulty. If the rock has fossils it is definitely post-fall. If no fossils are present, but the rock can clearly be shown to be sandwiched between (or lying above or intruded into) fossiliferous rocks, then again the rock is definitely post-fall. The geologist may properly interpret that rock in terms of the present laws of physics and chemistry.

But this does not solve the problem. For argument's sake, suppose that the rock outcrop upon which the Christian geologist is standing is highly metamorphosed and devoid of fossils. Also assume that uniformitarian geologists claim the rock is Precambrian on the basis of radioactive age measurements of approximately one billion years. Quite probably Whitcomb and Morris would assign this rock to the creation period and advise the Christian geologist merely to admire the scenery and see if any rare minerals worth collecting are present! But still, how *does* one know that *this* rock was created? Because it has no fossils? Because it is Precambrian?

Whitcomb and Morris believe that all fossiliferous rocks are post-fall. They seem fairly confident that there are virtually no fossils in so-called Precambrian rocks. They are willing to grant that a few fossils might be found in Proterozoic (Late Precambrian) rocks, but the presence of fossils would show that these rocks are not really Precambrian after all.

> The main criterion for recognition of the Proterozoic rocks, unless they are found deposited between systems which are evidently

Archean below and fossiliferous above, is that they be non-crystalline and non-fossil bearing. If crystalline, they would be called Archaeozoic; if fossiliferous, they would be identified as Cambrian or later, depending on the contained fossils.[46]

The facts, however, are that more and more fossils are being discovered in so-called Precambrian rocks as the rocks themselves are subjected to a more detailed investigation than ever before. Primitive kinds of fossils are being increasingly discovered in Newfoundland, South Africa, Australia, and Ontario.[47] Many of these fossils, such as the fossil micro-organisms from the Gunflint chert in Ontario are probably on the order of two billion years old. Some possible micro-fossils may be 3.5 billion years old.[48] These fossils occur in what are considered to be Precambrian rocks. These rocks must have formed *prior* to the obviously fossiliferous sedimentary rocks, for the latter can be demonstrated to overlie the former. Whitcomb and Morris must accept this conclusion if they believe the law of superposition. They would have to admit either that the flood produced considerably more rocks than they had anticipated or that these "Precambrian" rocks were formed prior to the flood but after the fall.

Now if these "Precambrian" rocks are viewed as having formed after the fall, on the grounds that they contain fossils, then they may legitimately be studied on the basis of presently-existing laws of physics, chemistry, and geology. If this is the case, the age of two billion years, obtained by radioactive dating, cannot be ruled out by claiming that it is the product of mature creation, that is, creation of apparent age. There is thus a good chance that this rock *really is* two billion years old, a conclusion clearly unacceptable to Whitcomb and Morris. The exact absolute age of this fossiliferous rock is immaterial to the discussion. What is important is that on the basis of radioactive studies and the application of the laws of superposition and cross-cutting relationships many so-called Precambrian rocks that are nonfossiliferous and intensely deformed and metamorphosed show solid evidence of being *younger* than these fossiliferous Precambrian

---

46. Ibid., pp. 231-32.

47. Several workers have been involved in the field of Precambrian life. The reader is referred particularly to the work of Barghoorn, Schopf, Glaessner, Cloud, and Misra.

48. A. E. J. Engel, "Alga-like Forms in Onverwacht Series, South Africa: Oldest Recognized Lifelike Forms on Earth," in *Science* 161 (1968), pp. 1005-08.

rocks. This means that many deformed Precambrian rocks were, if we follow the neo-catastrophic view, also formed after the fall and are therefore the legitimate objects of scientific study. Precambrian rocks cannot be considered to have been created during creation week simply because they are crystalline, nonfossiliferous, and apparently old and complex. Already very large areas of Precambrian rocks are the legitimate objects of scientific study if the neo-catastrophic theory is correct.

Now suppose that the outcrop on which the Christian geologist is standing has been radioactively dated at 2.5 billion years. Can he legitimately study that rock if it contains no fossils, or must he assign it to creation week? Clearly it is not possible to say. Geologists may eventually discover extremely old fossiliferous rocks that can, on the basis of clearly demonstrable geometric relationships, be proved to be older than the 2.5 billion-year-old rock. The desire of Whitcomb and Morris to assign a rock to creation may be directly related to geologists' ignorance of much of the early Precambrian period. The older the fossils found, the fewer the rocks that can be assigned to the creation week. And the great difficulty is precisely this: *the exact boundary between created rocks and post-creation rocks can never be identified.* As knowledge increases the boundary will only be pushed backward in time so that the amount of material assignable to creation continuously decreases. When the geologist is confronted with this predicament, it almost seems the better part of wisdom to interpret *all* the rocks in terms of the presently operating laws and processes of nature anyway. The Whitcomb and Morris theory, at least in its mature creationist aspect, is then subject to the criticism that *it cannot identify for the practicing geologist that part of the earth which was created during the six days. The theory cannot identify in rocks the point at which the earth was cursed (the fall of Adam).*

There are other alternatives for mature creationists. One alternative is to suggest that death occurred in animals and plants prior to the fall and that only man became subject to death at the fall. In this case many of the fossils might have been formed during creation week. The difficulty with this alternative is that during the 24 hours of the fifth day not only would God be creating fish and birds but they would be dying almost as soon as God made them. Hundreds of species would be extinct within minutes or hours after God had created them. No one has seriously proposed this alternative. It also faces the difficulty that it would still not be possible to identify in the rock record where the six days of creation stopped and human history began.

A second alternative is to say that during creation week not only were rocks created *in situ* but so also were their contained fossils.[49] In this view the fossils are not the remains of dead organisms; they only look that way. This view has no serious supporters. Everyone in this day and age seems to feel that fossils must have been alive at one time. This alternative, too, cannot show where in the rock record is the boundary between creation and post-creation.

The position of mature creationism, that is, the view that Biblical creation took place in 144 hours, leads the practicing geologist into insoluble problems in actually dealing with rocks. The boundary between creation and history cannot be identified, and the geologist cannot know how he ought to interpret the rocks. This point is stressed for the benefit of those who are very insistent about the truth of mature creationism, for such individuals are often not sufficiently aware of the practical difficulties of that position.

The existence of these difficulties, however, does not disprove the mature creationist interpretation of Genesis 1. In fact, given Biblical evidence alone, mature creationism is an acceptable interpretation of Genesis 1. I will never argue with the Christian who wants to hold to the view, but I am fully persuaded that Scripture permits other legitimate interpretations. The *Christian* scientific investigator ought first, last, and always to be led into the truth, not by his theories or his feelings or his practical difficulties, but by the infallible Word of God.[50] Therefore if Genesis 1 absolutely, unequivocally teaches the creation of the universe in six 24-hour days, then the Christian geologist must believe it wholeheartedly and carry out the logical, practical consequences wholeheartedly despite any mental anguish or tension it may produce. The difficulties noted, however, indicate that it is imperative that Scripture be examined much more thoroughly so that we may become more appreciative of what it really says about creation. The facts of geology are therefore useful in serving as a *stimulus* to renewed, deeper analysis of Scripture; that is, these facts may help us to ask questions in exegetical work that

49. Cf. M. Meeter, "Geology in the Dark or in Bible Light," in *International Reformed Bulletin* 38 (1969), pp. 27-29.

50. Hoeksema, *In the Beginning God*, p. 62.

we may not have thought to ask before. Christians ought to be doing this all the time. May God forbid, however, that interpretations of the text of Scripture be twisted simply in order to fit what men are "certain" are facts. Extrabiblical evidence may be of immense assistance in increasing our grasp and appreciation of Scripture, [51] but by all means the conclusion must be avoided that the extrabiblical evidence is *identical* to what Scripture says or that exegesis is based on extrabiblical evidence as much as it is on the text of Scripture. With these thoughts in mind and in a spirit of caution, let us take a closer look at the text of Scripture to see what we may safely learn about the history of the earth.

---

51. See, for example, the excellent work of M. G. Kline on extrabiblical covenants and their bearing on the structure and interpretation of Scripture: *Treaty of the Great King* (Grand Rapids: Wm. B. Eerdmans, 1963); *By Oath Consigned* (Grand Rapids: Wm. B. Eerdmans, 1968); and *The Structure of Biblical Authority* (Grand Rapids: Wm. B. Eerdmans, 1972).

4

The Basic Structure
of Genesis 1

Thus far aspects of two major approaches to the problems of origins
and earth history have been presented as they are viewed by groups
within the Christian world. I objected to the view of theistic evolutionism inasmuch as it often approaches Scripture with extrabiblical
presuppositions, often makes no serious attempt to exegete Scripture, and in some instances seriously distorts the meaning of
Scripture. Many theistic evolutionists have developed incorrect interpretations of the first chapters of Genesis. Specifically these chapters
have not been regarded as *historical.* I also objected to Biblical neo-
catastrophism in regard to its mature creationism, that is, the view
which sees the creation of the world as a series of miraculous divine
acts which transpired in six successive 24-hour days. This particular
view raises nearly insurmountable obstacles for geological practice
and theory. In addition, although mature creationism correctly views
the first chapters of Genesis as history, it has failed to recognize the
viability of alternative interpretations that are Biblically based.

Against the background of this negative critical approach, I will
now begin to develop more positively my own views. In the following chapters are presented the exegetical considerations of the relevant Scriptural texts that bear on the problem of origins and earth
history. Only if this exegetical work is done can the Christian scientist have any assurance that his approach to these problems is truly
Biblical.

81

It has been seen that many Christian scholars insist that the days of Genesis 1 must be taken as ordinary 24-hour days. The proponents of this view have argued that the primary meaning of *yom*, the Hebrew word for "day," is an ordinary day; it is not a long, indefinite period of time. The use of the formula "the evening and the morning" is seen as clinching the fact that Genesis is talking about ordinary days.

In the previous chapter it was indicated that there should be no quarrel with the Christian who wants to hold to the 24-hour day view inasmuch as it seems to be a legitimate Biblical interpretation of Genesis 1. What is of importance is whether or not it is *necessary* to hold this view. Is there any other possible interpretation of *yom* in Genesis 1? Does Scripture demand this view?

It was also demonstrated that a Christian scientist who must adhere to the 24-hour theory runs into some insoluble problems when tackling the interpretation of earth history. Can he be relieved of this dilemma? Holding to the 24-hour view, the earth scientist might as well give up earth science and turn to some other field. Is there any possible legitimate interpretation of Genesis 1 that will permit the Christian to pursue earth science without these difficulties?

It may now sound as if I want to twist Scripture a bit to conform to the demands of science, but the twisting of Scripture is abhorrent and must be avoided at all costs. Indeed, if it can be demonstrated beyond all doubt that Scripture demands a 24-hour view of the days, then the Christian scientist must accept that and, in effect, give up geological science and turn to something else. If he is consistent in his faith in Scripture, he must do this. Scripture, *not* science, must determine our beliefs of the world and its history. Science may help us ask new questions of Scripture, but Scripture still provides the answers.

A century ago Charles Hodge, the great Princeton theologian, in discussing creation and the word, *yom*, said that "it is of course admitted that, taking this account by itself, it would be most natural to understand the word in its ordinary sense; but if that sense brings the Mosaic account into conflict with facts, and another sense avoids such conflict, then it is obligatory on us to adopt that other."[1] No doubt this statement sounds like a compromise with science, but

---

1. C. Hodge, *Systematic Theology*, Vol. I (Grand Rapids: Wm. B. Eerdmans, n.d.), pp. 570-71.

Hodge was as solidly Scriptural as anyone. He was a theologian and not a scientist and therefore not especially interested in preserving any pet scientific ideas. Moreover, science, and geology in particular, in Hodge's day were far less influential and authoritative than they appear now. It is doubtful that Hodge was interested in conceding anything to science. The point is twofold. In the first place Hodge saw that the word *yom* does have more than one sense, and secondly, it is therefore unnecessary to insist that the ordinary meaning is the only meaning.

Other theologians with no interest in rescuing science or conceding to it felt that 24-hour days were not necessarily in view. E. J. Young maintained that "the length of the days is not stated."[2] He also said that "if the word 'day' is employed figuratively, i.e., to denote a period of time longer than twenty-four hours, so also may the terms 'evening' and 'morning,' inasmuch as they are component elements of the day, be employed figuratively."[3]

The Structure and Significance of Genesis 1

The matter of understanding Genesis 1 correctly can be resolved only if the overall structure of the chapter and its significance in the totality of the Scriptures are grasped. First of all in Genesis 1 we are not dealing with a certain number of days that stand somewhat in isolation. Rather Genesis 1 presents a specified collection of days, namely a unit of seven days, a creation *week*, as it were. The significance of the week must therefore be understood if the significance of the individual days is to be understood. In particular this week is composed of two parts. The first part contains six days of creation, and the second part contains the seventh day, a day specifically blessed by God, a day of rest and not of creation. Genesis 1 thus presents to us a creation week with the scheme of six days plus one day.

Scripture explains the significance and purpose of this week. The creation week clearly bears a close relationship to man's activities. It is the pattern for man's week. This is made very clear in the fourth commandment. "Remember the sabbath day, to keep it holy. Six

---

2. E. J. Young, *Studies in Genesis One* (Philadelphia: Presbyterian and Reformed, 1964), p. 104.

3. Ibid.

days shalt thou labor, and do all thy work: but the seventh day is the
sabbath of the LORD thy God: in it thou shalt not do any work,
thou, nor thy son, nor thy daughter, thy manservant, nor thy maid-
servant, nor thy cattle, nor thy stranger that is within thy gates: for
in six days the LORD made heaven and earth, the sea, and all that in
them is, and rested the seventh day: wherefore the LORD blessed the
sabbath day, and hallowed it" (Exodus 20:8-11). The commandment
makes clear the regulative nature of the creation week. It serves to
establish the nature of man's activities. The human week is a replica
of the creation week. As God worked six days, so does man. As God
rested one day, so does man. Creation week is therefore the great
divine prototype of the human week.

The mature creationist might argue with some cogency that inasmuch as the six to one ratio in the human week is patterned after the
six to one ratio in the divine week, so, too, the 24-hour nature of our
days is patterned after the 24-hour nature of the divine week.

W. G. T. Shedd, however, has argued quite convincingly against
this kind of reasoning. He states that

> the seven days of the human week are copies of the seven days of
> the Divine week. The "sun-divided days" are images of the "God-
> divided days." This agrees with the Biblical representation generally.
> The human is the copy of the Divine; not the Divine of the human.
> Human fatherhood and sonship are finite copies of the trinitarian
> fatherhood and sonship. Human justice, benevolence, holiness,
> mercy, etc. are imitations of corresponding Divine qualities. The
> reason given for man's rest upon the seventh solar day is, that God
> rested upon the seventh creative day. Ex. 20:11. But this does not
> prove that the Divine rest was only twenty-four hours in duration;
> any more than the fact that human sonship is a copy of the Divine,
> proves that the latter is sexual.[4]

The Seventh Day

Moreover, it can be established from Scripture that there is only
one divine week, the creation week. The entire sweep of all God's
activities with respect to His creation may be subsumed within the
one week. God operates with respect to His world for a period of one
week, a week that still has not been concluded! That this is the case
may first be suggested by posing the question, "What did God do on

4. W. G. T. Shedd, *Dogmatic Theology*, Vol. I (Grand Rapids: Zondervan,
1971), p. 477.

the eighth day? or the ninth?" That God did not resume creative activities after the seventh day, the day of rest, is clear from Genesis 2:1, which tells us that the work of creation was finished after six days. Did God continue resting on the eighth day? If so, then the question can be posed as to why God does not Himself observe further the six and one pattern of activity-rest that He has already established. Of course, this is a somewhat speculative way of looking at the matter, but this speculation does help to show that God "experiences"[5] only one week with respect to creation, or more correctly, the universe experiences only one week of the activity of God.

That this speculation is correct is borne out by Scripture itself. An obvious indication of this is seen in the account of the seventh day in Genesis 2:2-3. In reading that account we note significant differences between the seventh day and the preceding days. One difference, of course, is that the seventh day receives a particular blessing and so serves as the model for man's blessed sabbath. Moreover, there is no recording of the statement "and the evening and the morning were the seventh day." Such a statement occurs after the description of the preceding six days, but is lacking here. The omission of the statement immediately does raise the question as to whether or not the seventh day has ended. The account seems to give us a hint that it has not. Hence the proper answer to the previous question, "What did God do on the eighth day?" is that there was no eighth day. And if there was no eighth day the problems raised above in connection with the eighth day do not exist.

The idea that the seventh day of creation week and therefore creation week itself has not yet ended is much clearer in the New Testament. The first relevant text is found in John 5. In this passage is an account of Jesus' healing an infirmed man at the pool of Bethesda on the sabbath day. The Jews accused Jesus of breaking the sabbath by performing an act of healing on that day (John 5:10), and later they tried to kill Him. Jesus' reply to the Jews (John 5:17-19) provides some insight into the way God acts on *His* sabbath day. God's resting on His sabbath day is not an abstract resting, implying total cessation from all activity. Rather it is a rest that

---

5. The term "experience" is here used in a very loose sense, for God, who is infinite, eternal, and unchangeable, is not subject to time and undergoes no succession of moments.

involves kinds of activity different from creative activities. On God's sabbath day He heals, shows mercy, and indeed upholds the world. God does not totally abstain from all activity. As God the Father does, so must Jesus, God the Son, do also. Jesus, too, must rest on the sabbath day, but healing and the forgiving of sins are seen as consistent with the resting of God. It seems that both the Jews and Jesus here understood that God is *still* resting on His own seventh (sabbath) day ("my Father worketh hitherto"). Hence there is here an indication that the seventh day of Genesis 2:2 is still in progress and that creation week has not ended.

This idea is even more obvious in Hebrews 4. In this passage the writer is urging his readers to enter into the rest of God. This rest for the people of God (Hebrews 4:9) is seen to be the same as God's resting.[6] In attempting to establish from the Old Testament Scriptures the existence of this rest for God's people, the writer appeals to Genesis 2:2 and the rest of God following the six days of creation. One commentator states that "the fact that He is never said to have completed His rest and resumed His work of creation implies that His rest continues still, and may be shared by those who respond to His overtures with faith and obedience."[7] Hebrews 4 thus tells us that the seventh day is still in progress and therefore cannot have lasted 24 hours.

Genesis 1–A Figurative Creation Week

The Biblical evidence is indicative of the fact that one divine week includes the totality of God's activities with respect to His creation. The seventh and concluding day of the week has not yet ended, and, in fact, will continue into the eternal state. The divine week has therefore not yet ended. Inasmuch as the seventh day is seen as a long, indeterminate period (it is really a *figurative* day), there is no pressing reason to conclude that the six creative days were other than long, indeterminate periods of time. The seventh day is therefore the key to understanding the creation week. Creation week is best seen as a figurative week, a figurative divine week which serves as the pattern for man's ordinary, repetitive 168-hour weeks.

---

6. F. F. Bruce, *The Epistle to the Hebrews* (Grand Rapids: Wm. B. Eerdmans, 1964), p. 73; see also *Minutes of the Fortieth General Assembly* (Philadelphia: The Orthodox Presbyterian Church, 1973), pp. 102-03.

7. Bruce, *The Epistle to the Hebrews*, p. 74.

The suggestion that the creation week of Genesis 1 is best interpreted as a figurative week does not mean that the days and the week
are allegorical or mythological or symbolical. It is absolutely imperative that it be understood that this week is still a historical week, a
real week in which the events described for the various days are
actual events that occurred in space and time. Genesis 1 is still a
historical account of genuine occurrences. The day-structure is
figurative only in the sense that these days are not identical to our
days, but rather indeterminate stretches of *real, historical time.*

The Biblical data regarding the seventh day indicate that the days
and the creation week of Genesis 1 are best interpreted in this figurative manner. If this interpretation is correct, one comes to the conclusion that the total length of the creation period is indeterminate.
This leads to the further conclusion (of importance to the geologist)
that the Bible does not tell us the age of the universe and that a
hypothetical age of the earth of 4.6 billion years is *not* incompatible
with the Bible. This Biblically-based interpretation of Genesis 1 gives
the scientist great freedom in attempting to unravel the ages of various events in earth history. This Scriptural interpretation of Scripture, however, does not necessarily solve the problem as to whether
or not it is legitimate to interpret the results of creation week in
terms of laws and processes that are currently in operation. There is
other Biblical evidence that does indicate that a uniformitarian approach to earth history is basically permissible. For now, however,
the figurative interpretation of creation week solves any *time* problems we might have with respect to the universe.

The Framework Hypothesis

Now that a figurative view has been adopted a new problem arises.
Shall the days be taken in sequential fashion or not? Is chronological
succession really important in Genesis 1 if the days are figurative
days? A number of theologians have developed the so-called framework hypothesis.[8] This view

> regards the chronological framework of Genesis 1 as a figurative
> representation of the time span of creation and judges that within

---

8. The framework hypothesis has been elaborated by A. Noordtzij, *Gods
Woord en der Eeuwen Getuigenis* (Kampen: J. H. Kok, 1924); N. H. Ridderbos,
Beschouwingen over Genesis I (Kampen: J. H. Kok, 1963); and M. G. Kline,
"Because It Had Not Rained," in *Westminster Theological Journal* 20 (1958),
pp. 146-57.

that figurative framework the data of creation history have been arranged according to other than strictly chronological considerations.[9]

The semipoetic or epic nature of the chapter and the apparent topical treatment of the material have suggested that the events recorded need not have transpired in chronological sequence. For example, it has been pointed out that days one and four seem to dwell on the same topic. So do days two and five, and days three and six. Days one, two, and three seem to treat of realms or kingdoms within creation, and days four, five, and six seem to treat of the rulers over those realms. Day one treats of the realm of light. Day four treats of the sun and moon, the rulers in the realm of light. Day two treats of the firmament and the waters under the firmament. Day five treats of birds and fish, the rulers of the firmament and the waters. Day three treats of the dry land. Day six treats of the higher animals and man, the rulers of the dry land. Hence there is said to be a parallel structure in Genesis 1 which treats material topically rather than according to strict chronological development. The six days of creation are definitely taken as a time block, but within that time block there is room for variable opinion as far as the actual sequential development of creative events.

The framework view is a brilliant way of looking at Genesis 1, but I am unable to accept it. There are a number of considerations which indicate that the seven days ought to be taken as chronologically sequential. The fact that our own week is sequential certainly suggests, but does not prove, that the days of the divine week were also sequential. Of more weight is the fact that the days are numbered in Genesis 1—day one, day two, and so on. The numerical sequence certainly implies real sequence in the creation. To be sure, there are similar numerical sequences in Scripture in which time sequence is lacking. For example, the seven seals or the seven trumpets or seven bowls of Revelation are sequentially numbered visions which do not correspond to any historical time sequence (Revelation 6—11; 16). Revelation, however, is so full of imagery and symbolism (the seven Spirits of God!) that unlike Genesis 1 it clearly is not to be read as a historical report. In addition to the sequential numbering of the days is the fact that the events of the seventh day, God's resting, *do*

---

9. Kline, "Because It Had Not Rained," p. 154.

follow the events of the preceding days. It is also agreed by all that man is the climax of creation and that therefore his appearance on the sixth day must follow the events of the preceding days. Day five certainly must follow day two. There must already be a firmament in order for birds to fly in one. It is also generally agreed that the appearance of light shining out of darkness (day one) preceded the other creative events. Moreover, the fact that there may be some topical arrangement of material by no means precludes the possibility of chronological sequence. It has also been pointed out that the supposedly very close topical relationship between days one and four, two and five, and three and six is not as close as might appear at first glance. An excellent discussion of the weaknesses of the framework idea has been given by E. J. Young.[10]

In conclusion I believe that the best interpretation of the Biblical data is that which regards Genesis 1 as a historical account of real events that occurred in the chronological sequence in which they are reported over the span of seven successive figurative days of indeterminate duration. The sequence of actual events of earth history ought therefore to correspond to the sequence of events reported in Genesis 1.

―――――――

10. Young, *Studies in Genesis One*, pp. 43-76.

5

What Is Creation?

The interpretation of Genesis 1 just proposed is based only on the data of Scripture and indicates that the creation of the universe may have occurred over vast stretches of time. This interpretation sets no limit on the age of the universe or on the amount of time that transpired between the initial appearance of matter and the initial appearance of man. Naturally, as a geologist, I am quite delighted with this interpretation, for I have become accustomed to thinking in terms of billions of years! It is still necessary, however, to resolve further problems. A Biblical neo-catastrophist could quite legitimately point out that in Genesis 1 we are dealing with *creation*, not providence, so that I still can not look at rocks with the goal of interpreting them in the light of present-day laws. After all, he might say, the laws and processes of the present did not exist during creation. In creation we are dealing with pure divine miracle so that all I have really gained is a collection of instantaneous divine miracles separated from each other by so many figurative days of indeterminate length. If my friend is right, then I have not gained very much as a geologist. Time alone does not help me out with the problems raised in chapter three.

In most discussions of the interrelations between Scripture and earth history, there is little (if any) attention given to the usage of the word "create" (Hebrew *bara*) in Scripture. The typical Christian, like the neo-catastrophist, probably thinks of creation as an essentially miraculous act of God that took place instantaneously without any processes being involved. This creation, of course, is likely to be viewed as a creation "out of nothing." This common assumption is carried over into the writings of various Christian scholars. It was indicated that Whitcomb and Morris, Hoeksema, and particularly Rushdoony are insistent that creation is a purely divine act that is virtually instantaneous and virtually free of process and development. Even neo-orthodox theologian Alan Richardson seems to accept uncritically this view of creation when he says, "Creation in the biblical sense is *creatio ex nihilo*—out of nothing."[1] In the light of this widely held view of the nature of creation it is incumbent upon us to look much more closely at the way in which the terms "create," "creation," "creator," and "creature" are used throughout the Scriptures. Only then can the Christian be in a position to evaluate more correctly the meaning of Genesis 1.

When the Christian thinks of creation, his thoughts almost automatically are turned toward Genesis 1. This is, of course, natural, for it is precisely here in the Bible that the whole idea of creation is presented with such force. Then, too, the creation of the heavens and the earth is without question the foundation or substratum upon which all other creations are constructed. What the student of Scripture must realize is that *there are other creations* in the Bible and that these other creations can help us to understand the great fundamental creation of Genesis 1.

Creation in Genesis 1:1

The Hebrew word for "create," *bara,* is used in the very first verse of the Bible. "In the beginning God *created* the heaven and the earth" (Genesis 1:1). That this text rules out the eternity of the universe or any part thereof is clear from the remainder of Scripture.[2] Given this fact, there are two alternative interpretations of

---

1. A. Richardson, *Genesis I—XI* (London: SCM Press, 1953), p. 41.

2. "Through faith we understand that the worlds were framed by the word of God, so that things which are seen were not made of things which do appear" (Hebrews 11:3). The prophecy of Isaiah, with its great stress on the absolute sovereignty and self-sufficiency of God, clearly rules out the eternity of the universe and therefore argues for an initial creation out of nothing. Cf. E. J. Young, *Studies in Genesis One* (Philadelphia: Presbyterian and Reformed, 1964), pp. 1-14.

Genesis 1:1. In one view the verse describes the initial creation-out-of-nothing of the primeval material from which the fully organized universe was subsequently formed by God during the six days.[3] An alternative view is that the verse is essentially a summary of the entire section which follows and explains the creation in detail.[4]

If the second alternative is adopted, then the term *bara* in Genesis 1:1 cannot refer to an instantaneous act that is devoid of all time and progression. The verse, according to this summary view, is referring to the creation of the fully organized universe. Six days, a stretch of time, were required for the creation to unfold. Thus the *initiation* of creation could be instantaneous, but not the entire creation, for the *fully developed* universe did *not* appear instantaneously. Some duration, namely six *yom* of whatever length, was involved.

The first alternative is adopted here, namely, that Genesis 1:1 is referring chiefly to the creation of the primitive, unorganized material of the universe. The usage of the phrase "in the beginning" (cf. Proverbs 8:22-23; John 1:1-3) seems to refer more specifically to the first moment of time rather than to the total span of creation time. If this alternative is adopted, then the term *bara* in Genesis 1:1 certainly can be viewed as referring to an instantaneous act, but it cannot be stretched to include the development of the fully or-

---

3. See A. Heidel, *The Babylonian Genesis* (Chicago: University of Chicago, 1951), pp. 90-91. Heidel observes that "elsewhere in the Old Testament the phrase 'heaven and earth' denotes the *organized* heaven and earth, the *organized* universe, the cosmos. This alone, however, does not prove that it must of necessity have the same meaning in the opening verse of Genesis, which introduces the account of how heaven and earth were created and organized. Elsewhere also the word 'earth' denotes the organized earth, but in Gen. 1:2 it undeniably refers to the earth 'in its primitive, chaotic, unformed state.' This usage clearly decides the signification of 'earth' in the preceding verse; and that, in turn, determines the sense in which 'heaven' is to be taken in the same verse. This fact and the circumstance that the following verses describe the elaboration and completion of heaven and earth justify us in concluding that in the initial verse of Genesis the phrase under discussion designated heaven and earth as first created out of nothing in a rude state but in their essential or basic form."

4. Young, *Studies in Genesis One*, pp. 9-11. According to Young the first verse "is a broad, general declaration of the fact of the creation of the heaven and the earth. . . . Then follows a detailed account of how God brought the well-ordered universe from the original material into its present form. In this detailed account, however, there is no explicit statement of the creation of the primeval material from which the universe we know was formed." Young takes verse 1 as a summary inasmuch as the phrase "the heaven and the earth" does refer, as Heidel indicated (see n. 3), to the organized universe.

ganized universe, for terms other than "create" are typically used in conjunction with that development.

Creation in the Old Testament

The term *bara* occurs many times elsewhere in the Old Testament, and the usage of the term must be examined in order to gain insight into the Genesis account of the creation of the universe.[5] Particularly helpful in this regard is the usage of the term in the Book of Isaiah. To be sure, Isaiah employs the term in regard to the creation of the universe (40:26, 28; 42:5; 45:12, 18), but he also uses it in regard to *new* historical (or future) events (41:20; 45:7-8; 54:16; 57:19; 65:17-18).[6] Isaiah also employs the term in describing the relationship between Yahweh and His people, Israel. Isaiah says that Yahweh has created Jacob (43:1).[7] Isaiah says that He has created

---

5. For the Old Testament texts, exclusive of those in the Book of Isaiah, which employ the idea of creation in contexts other than those of the origination of the universe or of man, see Exodus 34:10; Numbers 16:30; Psalm 51:10; 102:18; 104:30; Ecclesiastes 12:1; Jeremiah 31:22; Ezekiel 21:30; 28:13, 15; Amos 4:13; and Malachi 2:10.

6. With reference to Isaiah 41:20, E. J. Young, *The Book of Isaiah*, Vol. III (Grand Rapids: Wm. B. Eerdmans, 1972), pp. 94-95, notes that *bara* "points to the utterly new and marvelous character of the work God will accomplish. It is a work so radical and all-changing that it may be described with the very verb that depicted God's first work of creation." Commenting on Isaiah 48:7, Young says (p. 250) of the term "created" that it "indicates the startlingly new character of the *new things*, which have been kept by God until now." Of the creation of the smith and the waster in Isaiah 54:16 he writes (pp. 371-72), "This verb *bara'* (*create*) is used not only of the original creation and of the new heavens and earth but also of contemporary events. At the same time the thought may be that God has brought the very art of making weapons into existence."

7. "But now thus saith the LORD that created thee, O Jacob, and he that formed thee, O Israel, Fear not: for I have redeemed thee, I have called thee by thy name; thou art mine" (Isaiah 43:1). In commenting on this verse, Young states (*The Book of Isaiah*, p. 138): "The participle *creator* suggests creation out of nothing. Yahweh chose the nation at Sinai, created it out of nothing, and made of it the theocracy." That Young does not mean creation out of nothing in some sort of metaphysical sense and that his view of the creation of Israel is fully compatible with that sketched out by the present writer is evident from further statements, for example (p. 139): "How is one to explain the ancient nation of Israel? It did not grow of itself, and attempts so to account for it are doomed to failure. Nor did it become a theocracy merely because it thought that Yahweh had chosen it. The only explanation that satisfies is that Israel's God, who is the true God, created Israel out of nothing. Its coming into existence is so remarkable that Isaiah can employ a word used of the original creation. The

the dispersed sons and daughters of God for His glory (43:7).[8] And it is stated that Yahweh is the creator of Israel (43:15).[9] It is also helpful to note that the terms "form" and "make" are used somewhat interchangeably with "create" in describing this relationship between Yahweh and Israel (43:1, 7, 21; 44:2, 21, 24).

In what sense is Israel the creation of Yahweh? It seems fairly obvious that Scripture is not here talking of Israel as being created in the sense that the nations of the world have been formed through the providential control of God in history. It is certainly true that God establishes kingdoms and plucks them up; they indeed owe their existence to Him.[10] But the whole Bible bears eloquent testimony to the fact that Israel bore a unique relationship to God that no other nation had. An understanding of this relationship will help in grasping what is meant by the creation of Israel.

The creation of the nation Israel was obviously not an instantaneous *ex nihilo* act. God did not suddenly create out of nothing a large body of people at Mount Sinai, where the nation was first officially constituted. Rather Israel underwent development and growth. It is perhaps legitimate to speak here of a creative process. This process of creating Israel extended over a period of hundreds of years. It was initiated with the calling of Abraham out of Ur of the Chaldees, and it continued with the sojourn of the patriarchs in the land of promise, the Egyptian bondage of the twelve tribes, and the Red Sea deliverance from that bondage. The creation of the nation therefore involved a *history*, a *development*. This creation was not an instantaneous act, and it was not an *ex nihilo* act.

Nor was the creation of Israel a *purely* supernatural act. Many ordinary means were involved in the creation of Israel. For example,

---

word points to the complete distinctiveness of the theocracy. Israel and Jacob are the creation of God in a sense that is true of no other people. In their creation, sovereign, efficaceous grace was at work."

8. "Even every one that is called by my name: for I have created him for my glory, I have formed him; yea, I have made him" (Isaiah 43:7). Of this text Young says (*The Book of Isaiah*, p. 146): "Isaiah is speaking of an utterly new and supernatural work, the creation from an Israel that was such in name only and hence no Israel, of an Israel that is one in deed and truth. To compare this work with the original work of creation is to stress its magnificence and importance."

9. "I am the LORD, your Holy One, the creator of Israel, your King" (Isaiah 43:15).

10. Cf. Daniel 4:17; Isaiah 10:5-19.

ordinary biological laws applied to the conception, gestation, birth, and growth of the patriarchs, although there is an obvious exception in the case of the conception of Isaac. The children of Israel were ordinary men in that they were subject to the same laws of nature as the surrounding pagans. They had to eat and sleep. *There were, therefore, many aspects of natural processes involved in the creation of Israel.* The creation of Israel did not necessarily preclude ordinary natural processes controlled by ordinary biological, chemical, and physical laws such as are operating today.

What then is unique about the creation of Israel that makes it a creative phenomenon rather than a strictly providential phenomenon? The formation of Israel was a creation in that it was an entirely new fundamentally supernatural occurrence. Never before had there been a single nation chosen by the living God to be His own special, covenant people. *The nation of Israel could not possibly have been produced by the ordinary course of world events, even if those events were totally providentially controlled.* If God had not intervened into human history in a unique, supernatural way, no such nation as Israel could possibly have arisen. The very existence of Israel was due to God's supernatural revelation of Himself to it through the patriarchs, Moses, and the prophets. No ordinary nation could possibly receive such a revelation unless God chose to reveal Himself to that nation. In order to be a creation, then, Israel required supernatural workings of God. These are seen in the initial call to Abraham to leave Ur of the Chaldees, the conception of Isaac, the choosing of Jacob, the Red Sea deliverance, the entrance into Canaan, and the speaking of the prophets. Such phenomena do not belong to the realm of ordinary providence. The formation of national Israel thus was a creation in that it was a new supernaturally initiated and undergirded development. This creation, however, was not instantaneous (although its *initiation* at the calling of Abraham may be viewed as such); it was not *ex nihilo* (Abraham was already a real man, albeit perhaps unregenerate when God called him); and by no means did it exclude historical development and natural processes.

An examination of other texts in the Old Testament leads to similar conclusions about the nature of creation. For example, Psalm 102:18 refers to a future people who will be created in order to praise Yahweh. Clearly this text does not mean to say that at some future time God will miraculously populate the earth with a group of individuals who have appeared out of nowhere. Rather the thought seems to focus on the *regenerate* people of God. This regeneration is viewed as a supernatural work of God that is unique and is not included in the ordinary processes of history. The creation of a new heart in the adulterous David (Psalm 51:10) is a reflection of exactly the same thought.

Jeremiah 31:22 speaks prophetically of the birth of the Messiah, referring to it as the creation of a new thing. Again in the total light of Scripture this must be regarded as a supernatural work of God inasmuch as Christ was born of a virgin, but by no means do we need to rule out process. After all Christ was in the womb for nine months and experienced the same biological influences as do other babies in the womb.

The great majority of the "creation" texts in the Old Testament seem to involve some degree of supernatural activity on the part of God, but instantaneousness and lack of process are by no means implied by the term. As a rule the stress seems to be on the idea of *radical newness*. Alexander Heidel expresses these thoughts nicely when he writes that the "Hebrew *bara* has about the same meaning as *asa*, with this difference, that *bara* contains the idea of a new and extraordinary or epochal production, never necessitating toil on the part of the Creator. . . ."[11] Heidel also notes that the term *bara*, in and of itself, by no means necessarily expresses the concept of creation out of nothing.[12]

A few texts, however, do employ the term *bara* in a very bland and general sense. In these cases supernatural activity does not appear to be necessarily involved. For example, Isaiah 54:16 says that God has created the smith that blows the coals in the fire and that He has created the waster to destroy. There is clearly no intention on the part of this text to say that in the eighth century B.C. God miraculously out of nowhere created some individuals with the

---

11. Heidel, *The Babylonian Genesis*, p. 90.

12. "This concept (creation out of nothing), however, cannot be deduced from the Hebrew *bara*, 'to create,' as it has been done. For although this term is invariably employed to designate the creative activities of God and 'never takes the accusative of the material from which a thing is made, as do other verbs of making, but uses the accusative to designate only the thing made,' there is no conclusive evidence in the entire Old Testament that the verb itself ever expresses the idea of a creation out of nothing" (Heidel, *The Babylonian Genesis*, p. 89).

ability to do the work of the metalsmith. All that need be implied is that God has providentially brought forth the makers of weapons for this particular time in history. Conceivably this verse could be referring to the idea that God did place this particular ability into the structure of the human race at the beginning of the world,[13] but this is not the primary thrust of the text.

A similar case is found in Amos 4:13, which tells us that God creates the wind. We know that all winds throughout history are the result of the movement of air masses in response to certain providentially-controlled meteorological conditions. No miracles are involved in the creation of the wind. As in the previous text the thought may here be expressed that the wind, like all other things, owes its existence, in the ultimate analysis, to the original creative activity of God at the foundation of the universe, but this again is not the primary thrust of the text.

Two very instructive texts are found in the Book of Ezekiel. Here the term *bara* is applied in connection with the people of Ammon and Tyre. God threatens to judge Ammon in the place where it was created (Ezekiel 21:30). In what sense was the nation of the Ammonites created? It would seem, despite its close kinship to Israel, that Ammon was not a unique nation in the sense that Israel was. Ammon was not a special people of God. Ammon was not a people blessed with supernatural revelation from God. The origin of Ammon could perhaps be evaluated in terms of the ordinary providentially-controlled processes of history. It owed its origin to the disgraceful relationship between Lot, Abraham's nephew, and his younger daughter (Genesis 19:30-38). The creation of Ammon may be traced to this event, a perfectly natural, nonmiraculous, noninstantaneous event in which ordinary processes (especially the faulty wisdom of men) played the major role. The only way in which the creation of Ammon can be regarded as a supernatural event is by tracing its ultimate origin, like that of Israel, to the call of Abraham. If this is the case then we must be led to the conclusion that the ultimate supernatural origin of Ammon (the call of Abraham) *preceded* the creation of Ammon (the first descendants of Lot and his daughter). It is, then, very difficult to see in the creation of Ammon any miraculous act of God that is instantaneous and devoid of natural process.

---

13. Young, *The Book of Isaiah*, pp. 371-72.

Much the same conclusion can be drawn in regard to the creation of Tyre (Ezekiel 28:13, 15). The text speaks of the day in which Tyre was created. Tyre is evidently being compared to Adam in the Garden of Eden in his originally perfect condition. And just as Adam fell, Tyre also has fallen into great wickedness. The creation of Tyre then is used in an analogy; hence it may be well not to press any conclusions too hard. If we were to speak of the creation of Tyre we could do so only in terms of the ordinary nations. Tyre was not formed supernaturally as was Israel. So once again we see that creation may be used in the Old Testament in a completely non-miraculous sense.

To summarize the Old Testament evidence, a creation is generally an event that may have a miraculous beginning and in which many supernatural activities of God are involved. The total creative event is not necessarily instantaneous, although its beginning may be; nor is creation by definition an event or act that is devoid of all natural processes. In some instances a creation may be an entirely ordinary event, that is, the type of event that regularly occurs in terms of God's providential work. Creations in the Old Testament generally carry the idea of *newness*.

Creation in The New Testament

In the New Testament the Greek word *ktizo* is translated "create." The word *ktizo* is applied in several instances to those who believe in Christ. The "new man" in Christ is said to be created in the image of God (Ephesians 4:24; Colossians 3:10). The believer is said to be the workmanship of God, created in Christ Jesus unto good works (Ephesians 2:10). The man in Christ is said to be a new creation (II Corinthians 5:17; cf. Galatians 6:15).

In these instances regeneration is viewed as a creation or re-creation. The idea of *newness* is strikingly obvious in these texts. Certainly the whole tenor of Scripture indicates that this kind of creation, this quickening of the dead sinner to new life in Christ, is an impossibility apart from the special supernatural working of the Holy Spirit in man's heart. It simply is not an outworking of the ordinary course of nature, providentially controlled though it is. A supernatural work of God is required in this kind of creation, just as in the creation of Israel.

It is questionable whether this creation of the new man, however, can be construed as creation out of nothing, inasmuch as it is the old man that was operated on by the Spirit. A pre-existent object is involved here. The term *ktizo,* then, does not necessarily mean to create out of nothing, just as *bara* does not necessarily mean to create out of nothing. It is possible, however, to view this creation, that is, the transition from the unregenerate to the regenerate state, the transition from wrath to grace, as being instantaneous. Indeed there seems to be no evidence in Scripture that regeneration or conversion to Christ is anything other than an instantaneous occurrence even though there may be much preparatory work, for example, calling, involved. The question, however, might be raised as to whether the creation here is to be construed as exhausted by God's act of regeneration or if it is to be viewed as being *initiated* by the regeneration but encompassing the total process of producing the ultimately sinless man through the stages of sanctification and glorification. This question probably cannot be answered satisfactorily, but at least the creation here does carry the two ideas of newness and the impossibility of the production of the new structure or state of affairs through purely natural processes and outworkings.

Creation is also used in a much more general sense in the New Testament. Ephesians 3:9 says that God created all things by Jesus Christ. Colossians 1:16 reaffirms and amplifies this by noting that by Jesus Christ "were all things created, that are in heaven, and that are in earth, visible and invisible, whether they be thrones, or dominions, or principalities, or powers: all things were created by him, and for him." I Timothy 4:3 notes that meats were created by God and are to be received with thanksgiving. It is clear that these are extremely general statements that in no way imply that *every* thing, even such broad categories as dominions, was instantaneously created out of nothing and involved no ordinary processes of history or nature. In the category of "all things," or more specifically in the category of "dominions," Paul was very probably thinking of the Roman Empire. Surely Paul would envisage the Roman Empire as the outworking and development of providentially-controlled natural historical processes involving a long history and lacking an instantaneous beginning. The only sense in which Paul could have envisioned the Roman Empire as being created would be by tracing its roots either to the initial creation (Genesis 1:1) or to the creation of man (Genesis 2:7), when the foundational laws and principles of human structures and history were implanted into the very structure of the world. In essence then these verses say nothing more than that

the *initial* stuff and laws of the universe, whether physical or historical, were formed supernaturally by God and that all that is subsequent to that initial stuff is the outworking and development of it.
The word for "create" in these verses cannot preclude time and
process, *but virtually demands them.* But again the general idea of
creation is seen as something that ultimately must find its source in a
supernatural work of God. The "all things" of Ephesians 3:9 and
Colossians 1:16 cannot be the natural development of some sort of
"non-being" which could be viewed as coexisting with God before
Genesis 1:1.

Scripture Is God-Centered

Before returning to a closer examination of Genesis 1, let us
examine the possible reasons why creation has so commonly been
viewed as an essentially instantaneous divine act devoid of all
process. Perhaps the prime factor that has led to regarding the creative acts in Genesis 1 as instantaneous divine acts devoid of natural
process is the *brevity of the account.* Repeatedly it is recorded that
God said, "Let there be—and it was so." This very conciseness conveys the impression of instantaneousness. Psalm 33:6-9 conveys a
similar impression. This impression, however, is not necessarily correct. Moses obviously was not interested in giving a long, detailed
account of creation. He was not interested in discussing orogenies,
metamorphism, speciation, and erosion. Moses was a religious writer;
his prime purpose was religious, as was that of all Biblical writers.
Moses was not so much interested in drawing attention to nature as
to God, the Creator. The entire Bible is interested primarily in drawing attention to God in order that man may properly glorify Him.
Genesis 1 is thus a record of *God's* creation, and of the ease and
power and sovereignty with which He created. Whether or not creation involved laws, Moses was not especially concerned. He was concerned to point out that the universe did not just somehow happen
to come into existence out of non-being, out of its own accord.
Moses was concerned to show that God—the sovereign, personal
God—has created the universe so that His creatures might behold His
power and worship and adore Him!

It is also well to remember that Scripture always finds the source
of things that are perfectly natural and ordinary in the activity of
God. B. B. Warfield notes several Scriptural instances in which elements of nature such as rain and sunshine are described as being

totally under the control of God.[14] Scripture never says, "It rained," notes Warfield, as the weatherman might today. Instead *God sends* the rain. But such references,[15] although teaching the absolute control of God over nature, by no means rule out secondary causes such as the laws of nature. Surely weather patterns could have been analyzed by mathematical methods as much in Biblical times as they are now. In view of the fact that Scripture is so God-oriented, there is a rather strong temptation to assume that all activities of God are done instantaneously simply because God does them; this must be resisted! Only careful exegesis can demonstrate the occurrence of pure divine miracle in one instance or another; preconceived opinion of the way in which we think God must have acted because He has all power cannot demonstrate miraculousness. This is the mistake that has often been made in regard to creation. It has more or less been taken for granted throughout the ages that a creation, especially since creation is a work that only God can do and not man, must automatically be a pure, instantaneous miracle devoid of process. A careful examination of the Scriptural usage of the term "create" has shown that this by no means need be the case.

Creation in Genesis 1

Against this background let us return to the first chapter of Genesis to attempt an analysis of the meaning of *bara* in that chapter. First of all, in the account of creation the word *bara* is used only three times. Verse 1 speaks of the creation of "the heaven and the earth"; verse 21 speaks of the creation of whales, sea creatures, and birds; and verse 27 speaks of the creation of man. The remainder of the chapter uses vague, less colorful terms such as moving, calling, making, setting, dividing, saying. There is nothing in these verbs that conjures up the idea of the miraculous in quite the way that the verb *bara* does. It is therefore perhaps significant that *bara* is used so sparingly in Genesis 1.

The initial report is of the creation of "the heaven and the earth." This first verse probably refers chiefly to the formation of the primitive material from which the more organized universe was developed. The term *bara* in this context should convey two major thoughts.

---

14. B. B. Warfield, "Predestination," in *Biblical and Theological Studies* (Philadelphia: Presbyterian and Reformed, 1952), pp. 270-333.

15. See, for example, Matthew 5:44-45; Job 38:22-29, 34-35; Amos 4:7.

The first is the announcement of the formation of a totally *new* structure, a totally new state of affairs. What is new is the universe. Prior to this, God alone existed. The universe did not exist before the beginning. The universe is a completely new thing. The creation signals a new state of affairs. Now God and the universe exist.

The second thought conveyed is that the universe, this new structure, cannot be brought into existence spontaneously or gradually through the agency or outworking of some "thing" other than God. That is, there is no sort of being or non-being alongside God which gives rise to the universe. The universe does not somehow come out of the void. It would be doubly difficult for the universe to be produced in this way inasmuch as the Scripture allows no room for any sort of being or non-being to coexist with God prior to creation. God is eternally self-existent and self-sufficient. Thus the universe or *any* new structure, for that matter, *must* be created, if it is to come into existence at all. It cannot evolve or develop spontaneously. It must come into existence by an act of God that is purely miraculous. But only the initial material from which the fully organized universe developed need have been formed miraculously. This much must have been miraculous. But the creation of the universe need not have involved any miraculous events after the initial miraculous event. This is not to say that it did not, but that it need not if we consider only Genesis 1:1. This is entirely consistent with what is said about creation elsewhere in Scripture.

Therefore, given the fact that Scripture speaks of the creation of the heaven and the earth, and *temporarily ignoring other data,* a theistic evolutionist might conclude that this verse simply indicates that God miraculously, entirely apart from law or process, called into being the initial material of the universe, but that the subsequent development of the universe into its fully organized state could have followed laws and processes created by God at the initial moment. The development of the universe could thus be viewed as purely uniformitarian; that is, scientific investigation of the creation, based on the laws in operation today, would be perfectly feasible and legitimate. No miracles would have to be invoked in a study of the past history of the earth. One could even conceive of total biological evolution of all life including man. In all of this development, however, God controls and upholds the laws that He created at the initial moment. Geological uniformitarianism must thus be viewed as divinely ordered and evolution must be theistic evolution.

This viewpoint was developed *solely* on the basis of Genesis 1:1, while temporarily ignoring the rest of the chapter. A look at the remainder of the chapter, however, shows that other data do suggest that there were at least some miraculous events in the development of the organized universe. For example, Genesis 1:21 states that "God created great whales, and every living creature that moveth, which the waters brought forth abundantly, after their kind, and every winged fowl after his kind. . . ." The creation (*bara*) of these life forms on the fifth day strongly implies the appearance of something radically new, namely, sea creatures and birds. The fact that these life forms were created also strongly suggests that their formation could not have been brought about either suddenly or gradually from pre-existent life or matter or nothingness by any powers, processes, or laws implanted into and resident in nature up to that time, even if those powers, processes, or laws are viewed as God-created and God-controlled. What would seem to be suggested here is a supernatural activity of God in bringing into existence the first sea creatures and birds. If this is the correct interpretation, birds and sea creatures cannot be a part of any evolutionary scheme in the sense that the first birds and sea creatures (fish are no doubt mainly in view here) could not have gradually developed from nonbirds and nonfish. The fact that birds and sea creatures were created, however, does *not* preclude extensive natural biological modification or evolution of these groups *after* their initial appearance so long as it is recognized that such variations took place within the limits of "after their kind."

While the interpretation just sketched is highly probable, it cannot be insisted upon dogmatically. In light of the usage of *bara* in Amos 4:13, where God creates the wind, and in Isaiah 54:16, where He creates the smith and the waster, it must be recognized that *bara* need not *always* involve the miraculous. Hence a possible interpretation of Genesis 1:21 might view the creation of birds and sea creatures on the fifth day as implying nothing more than the appearance of those forms at that time. Miraculous formation of these life forms on the fifth day might not be any more implied by this text than miraculous formation of the smith is implied by Isaiah or of the wind by Amos. If this interpretation is possible, then it is conceivable that the text might permit some evolutionary development leading up to, say, birds, but the text indicates that they could not have evolved from sea creatures. Sea creatures and birds are in any interpretation not directly related to one another.

The final instance in which a creation occurred during creation week was the appearance of man. Verse 27 makes this plain: "So God created man in his image, in the image of God created he him; male and female created he them." Here again is an account of the appearance of something new—man. Man did not exist before the sixth day.

Now the totality of the Scriptural data regarding the origin of man is completely incompatible with the theory of biological evolution of man from that which was not man. This Biblical incompatibility with human evolution cannot, however, be established on the basis of the word *bara* in Genesis 1:27. If we confine ourselves, for the time being, to the evidence of this one text, it can be suggested that man, in that he was *created,* is a new special being. Given the usage of *bara* elsewhere in Scripture it is unlikely that man's appearance on earth could be construed *solely* in terms of the outworking of biological processes that had been implanted into nature by God, but it could be construed *in part* in those terms. That is, considering only the word *bara* in Genesis 1:27, one could legitimately adopt a view which sees man's body as having evolved.

This thought is perhaps made clearer if we keep in mind the uniqueness of man, that is, the fact that he is an image-bearer of God, the bearer of spirit as well as body.[16] If man is "split" into a spirit-body complex, *it is possible to view man as being created in the sense that his spirit was that part of man miraculously formed by God and without which man would not have been man.* Thus the body of pre-man could be viewed as evolving in accordance with divinely-controlled biological laws and processes up to a point at which the spirit was miraculously formed in this pre-man. The being in view would suddenly be constituted man. This miraculous in-breathing could be the divine miraculous initiation that is required to bring man, the new structure, into existence.

Lest there be objection to this usage of creation, remember the sense in which creation is used in the New Testament with respect to

---

16. It is important to realize that a careful study of the Biblical data renders untenable the theory that man is a composite of a spiritual substance, the spirit or the soul, and a material substance, the body. The stress of the Bible is rather on the unity of man. The term "soul," or "psyche," very commonly refers in Scripture to the total man inclusive of the body. For a helpful discussion of this problem see G. C. Berkouwer, *Man: The Image of God* (Grand Rapids: Wm. B. Eerdmans, 1962), pp. 194-309.

the new birth. In Ephesians 2:10, 4:24, and Colossians 3:10, the new man in Christ is said to be created. It is obvious that this creation has nothing to do with biology. The body of the man being regenerated undergoes no miraculous change; rather it is the heart of man that is affected. The new creation is a miraculous transformation of man's heart that cannot be effected through the ordinary course of nature. The special saving grace of God is required. It is therefore legitimate to say that Adam's creation as described *only* in Genesis 1:27 could be viewed as being concentrated on the miraculous appearance of his spirit in a pre-existent evolving animal body. Indeed this is the view that has been entertained by many theistic evolutionists, and it is a legitimate view if one has in mind only the meanings of the term *bara* and *ktizo*.

However, much other evidence regarding the origin of man is given in Scripture. These other evidences render absolutely untenable the idea of a biological evolution of man from animals. These evidences are discussed in detail in chapter seven. No one must get the impression that I accept the evolutionary origin of man or that I believe such a view is compatible with the total weight of Scriptural data. It is compatible *only* with the term *bara*.

In summary, the creation account, as far as the word *bara* is concerned, is not incompatible with a *generally* uniformitarian approach to earth history. In view of the evidence presented thus far, the Christian scientist is not compelled to reject the concept of the general development of the universe in accordance with physical, chemical, geological, and biological laws and processes formed by God at the very beginning and continuing to the present time. On this basis it is legitimate to project present laws and processes into the past and to study the earth and the cosmos in a scientific fashion. Explanation as well as description is possible. Nor does the usage of words for "create" put any time limit on God's operations. It is possible that the entire creation was a full-blown instantaneous achievement, but this is not required by the usage of the word *bara* in Scripture.

Providence During Creation Week

Another line of evidence from Scripture quite clearly corroborates the idea that the creation period of Genesis 1 was not a period utterly devoid of processes and laws like those of the present time.

The account of the origin of man in Genesis 2 provides in a topical manner a great deal of background material that is relevant to a consideration of the behavior of the world during creation. Genesis 2:5 (American Standard Version) reads, "And no plant of the field was yet in the earth, and no herb of the field had yet sprung up; for Jehovah God had not caused it to rain upon the earth: and there was not a man to till the ground." Some theologians have considered that this verse reflects on a total lack of vegetation on the whole planet and therefore has in view the beginning part of the third day of creation. It is more likely, however, that the text is reflecting, not on the whole earth, but on the wilderness conditions in the immediate area where the Garden of Eden was to be planted for man's abode. It is noteworthy that the text provides reasons why there was no vegetation, namely lack of rain for natural growth and lack of man to irrigate and tend the vegetation. Kline has noted that this text affirms "that at a point prior to the creation of man and, therefore, within the creation era the absence of certain natural products was attributable to the absence of the natural means for their providential preservation."[17] He also concludes that the "unargued presupposition of Genesis 2:5 is clearly that the divine providence was operating during the creation period through processes which any reader would recognize as normal in the natural world of his day."[18] The evidence from this text suggests at the very least that there were normal, providential, nonmiraculous occurrences on the sixth day of creation prior to the appearance of man. It also lends further credence to the idea that normal laws and processes occurred throughout the creation period. Hence the creation period need not be viewed as a period consisting exclusively of pure miracle.

Our investigation of the usage of the term "create" and of the evidence of Genesis 2:5 leads to the conclusion that it may be a legitimate procedure to interpret most, though not necessarily all, of the events of Genesis 1 in terms of physical laws and processes or analogues of processes that are in operation today. It cannot be demonstrated conclusively from Scripture that such a procedure is illegitimate. But it is important to note that the legitimacy of the procedure is qualified by the word "most." There are some events in

---

17. M. G. Kline, "Because It Had Not Rained," in *Westminster Theological Journal* 20 (1958), p. 150.

18. Ibid., pp. 149-50.

the record of Genesis 1 which probably cannot be interpreted in terms of present laws and processes. A strict, thoroughgoing geological uniformitarianism or theistic evolutionism is unbiblical. If there is room for a large degree of uniformitarianism or evolutionism in the record of Genesis 1, that uniformitarian or evolutionary development has been interrupted or punctuated by some miraculous acts of God. One might thus speak of *punctuated uniformitarianism* as being a view of origins or creation that is Biblically permissible. For example, it is permissible to interpret the events of the third day in terms of present laws and processes. Uniformitarianism is valid for the third and fourth days inasmuch as the text does not require us to believe in any purely miraculous acts of God. The text does speak of God's activity and His speaking and indeed indicates His power and sovereignty, but it does not necessarily imply purely miraculous workings. God's activity was simply accomplished without any interference.

Quite possibly it is not legitimate, however, to apply completely uniformitarian thinking to the fifth day. There may have been a great deal of geological activity on the fifth day. If so, Scripture does not mention it. If such activity did occur, there certainly is no Scriptural reason for rejecting a uniformitarian interpretation thereof. In the realm of biology, however, the theory of theistic evolutionism probably breaks down at this point, for on the fifth day God *created* whales, birds, and sea creatures. These organisms are wholly new creatures that quite probably, given the text, could not have been produced by the outworking of biological laws through time. They most likely required a miraculous act of God for their existence. It is probable that the *first* birds and sea creatures were supernaturally created by God. They did not evolve from pre-existing animals through time. But there is no reason to doubt that the original birds and sea creatures could have undergone a gradual change or evolution that was consistent with reproduction after their kind.

Theistic evolutionism may be incorrect in that it believes that birds and sea creatures evolved from pre-existent forms of life. In particular the evolutionary view would have the birds ultimately derive from primitive fish ancestors. This position would appear to be incompatible with the Biblical data in view of the prevailing use of *bara* in Scripture, and in view of the distinction made between these groups. Birds and sea creatures were most likely created supernaturally.

Genesis 1 and Paleontology

What are the implications of the position of punctuated uniformitarianism for scientific investigation on the part of the Christian investigator? How might the Christian paleontologist approach his discipline? Would his approach differ to any significant degree from that of the non-Christian paleontologist? Would the Christian paleontologist make hypotheses in a significantly different way from the non-Christian in regard to a certain group of fossils?

In order to answer these questions the following remarks are confined to the study of fossil fish. The work of the fifth day included not only the creation of birds and fish, but also large swimming creatures and no doubt a great variety of aquatic organisms which might be classed biologically as mollusks, reptiles, mammals, or something else again. It would appear from the text of Genesis 1:20-21 that the birds and the fish (among the other sea creatures) were separate creations, that is, they cannot properly be conceived of as having evolved in any way from one another. They are of independent origins. Now then, how does the Christian paleontologist apply the idea of the createdness of fish to the fossil record? How can he ever identify a supernaturally created being in the fossil record? Could he ever look at a species of fossil fish and state with a high degree of confidence that that species had been supernaturally created on the fifth day of creation?

The Christian paleontologist would show a great deal of wisdom by answering the last question in the negative. It would, for example, be a very unwise procedure to suggest in a leading paleontological journal that fossil fish species X was a species that was specially created by God. Perhaps there is some reason for the Christian to think that species X was created. Perhaps species X is the oldest known fish in the entire fossil record. Perhaps there is no other species of organism known in the fossil record that could possibly serve as an ancestor for species X. Even if these conditions were met, it would be a very unsound procedure to suggest that species X was created. It would be a much wiser practice to indicate that the origins of species X are presently unknown.

There are several reasons why it would be unwise to suggest that a given species of fossil fish was created. In the first place Scripture speaks in very general terms. It speaks only of sea creatures, a category far more general even than fish. It does not tell us what species of fish were created on the fifth day. Imparting such detailed information would have been far removed from Moses' (and God's) purpose in writing Genesis 1. Scripture does not tell what the first fish looked like or what their habits were. Perhaps the original sea creatures created on the fifth day by no means resembled modern fish. Perhaps they were the ancestors of modern fish. We simply do not know. It is the business of paleontology to unravel slowly and meticulously the history of sea life, to discover what were the most primitive types of fish, and to disclose what sort of variations fish may have undergone throughout time.

There is a second reason why a Christian paleontologist would be placed in a rather embarrassing position by suggesting that a certain fish species had been created by God. Later paleontological research might eventually disclose the existence of an earlier, more primitive type of fish which, by reproducing after its kind, had gradually developed into species X. Should this be the case species X obviously was not supernaturally created! There simply is no way for the Christian paleontologist to know what were the initial fish species or sea creature species created by God. Once the paleontologist declares a certain species to be created, further research may prove him wrong and probably will!

A similar conclusion should be drawn regarding the question as to whether or not a Christian paleontologist should suggest in a scholarly paleontological journal that birds, or fish, *as a class,* were created and did not have evolutionary origins. This would be rather difficult to do in a scientific journal inasmuch as Scripture does not discuss the nature of birds or fish as a class when first created by God.

This conclusion may come hard for many a Christian, but it simply is not possible to demonstrate supernatural, direct creation from the fossil record. Christian paleontologists can make guesses and perhaps the guesses would improve after many more years of research, but the danger always remains that new fossil material will be found which will disprove a presently-held Christian theory of special creation. No Christian needs to be troubled that special creation cannot be proved from fossils. Special creation is an article of faith. If Scripture really teaches the special creation of certain creatures on the fifth day, Christians should believe it even though all the implications of that belief cannot be understood. No Christian ought to worry if science does not or cannot corroborate all the teachings and data of Scripture. Such an attitude of worry betrays a lack of confidence in Scripture and Scripture's God as well as an unhealthy opinion of science. Science is hardly infallible. It is always changing. It is based on discoveries ever new. There is no need for distress if science does not always agree with Scripture. Such a situation may simply mean that science has not come far enough. All the facts may not yet be in, and, indeed, for science they never will.

6

An Excursion
Through Genesis 1

To this point we have seen that Scripture fully permits the interpretation that the creation week of Genesis 1 is a figurative week
consisting of figurative days. According to this view the account is
not concerned with the question of the duration of the creation
period, and the Bible does not tell us the age of the earth. The
Christian geologist may therefore pursue his work unfettered by the
false notion that the Bible teaches that the world is only so many
thousand years old.

A number of considerations were also adduced to indicate that the
creation by no means needs to be seen throughout as a purely divine
miracle that is either an instantaneous act or a series of instantaneous
acts totally devoid of process. Rather it was pointed out that there is
considerable evidence that, after the formation of the initial stuff of
the universe, the laws and processes of the present time may very
well have been in operation during creation week. On this basis it
becomes a legitimate procedure for the Christian geologist to interpret the rocks formed during creation week in terms of laws that
now characterize the world.

It was also pointed out that Genesis 1 evidently views the creation
in terms of a chronological sequence, that is, the events reported on
actually transpired in the order given. At this point our attention

113

may be directed to the matter of how well the sequence of events in Genesis 1 corresponds to the sequence as postulated by geological science. Is there a harmony between Genesis and geology?

Some neo-catastrophists have argued that the correspondence between the events of Genesis and the events of uniformitarian geology is very poor indeed, and therefore the view of Genesis 1 which sees the days as long periods of time is incorrect. Now in the first place the overall correspondence is by no means exact or perfect, but it is surprisingly close. More importantly, even if the correspondence were very poor, that would not constitute a very solid argument against the long-day or figurative-week view. It must be stressed that the correctness or legitimacy of the figurative-week view rests not on the basis of its presumed correspondence with the data of geology but on the basis of the data of Scripture. The figurative-week view cannot be proved or denied on the basis of science, although it certainly can be made to look more or less attractive. The truths and data of Scripture are independent of the opinion of science. The Christian must always be careful to remember that science is susceptible to change as new discoveries are made. There is no reason to doubt that at some point in the future geology may want to change its opinion regarding the relative sequence of events of earth history. If such a change were to occur, it certainly would neither prove nor disprove the figurative-week interpretation of Genesis 1. Such a change certainly *would* indicate that *the Christian has no right at any point in time to expect or insist upon complete agreement between Scripture and the available facts of science.* It is unreasonable to expect complete harmony until *all* facts are in.

In the light of these thoughts, the adherence of the Christian scientist to a particular interpretation of Genesis 1 should not therewith drive him to forcing his science into the Biblical mold. If he believes, for example, that fruit trees appeared before fish, he should not frantically begin searching for fossils of fruit trees that are older than fossils of the earliest fish. Scientific discovery and knowledge simply cannot be expected to expand in this particular fashion. In short the Christian ought to be willing to let science advance in its own way and in its own time, that is, to develop naturally as new discoveries are made. One cannot force scientific thinking to advance along a particular line. On the other hand the Christian does have the right to expect science to be less dogmatic than it has been in areas where science is dealing with theory and not fact.

Now whereas we need not expect complete harmony between the records of Genesis and geology even in terms of the chronological interpretation, it is of interest to see just how close the actual harmony or correspondence is at this particular stage in our scientific understanding of earth history. In order to do this let us survey the days of Genesis 1, commenting on the events of each day and on the events of earth history which, as interpreted by geologists, may possibly correspond with them. It will be seen that this correspondence is generally quite close.

This excursion through Genesis 1 must be prefaced by a few further remarks about the nature of the Genesis account. The chapter is speaking of historical events that transpired in the realm of nature. These events occurred in an essentially chronological order over a period of six consecutive *yom* of indeterminate length. The account of each day describes genuinely physical events that occurred in space and in time either on the earth or with respect to the earth. The six days of creation therefore deal with events of *geological, biological,* and *astronomical* significance.

Keep in mind, however, the brevity and conciseness of Moses' account. Because of his economy of expression, the mistake of believing that only that which is recorded in the chapter occurred during the creation must be avoided. Moreover, Genesis 1 is a generalized description of major events. The great Scottish journalist and naturalist of a century ago, Hugh Miller, commented very pertinently that "the inspired writer seized on but those salient points that, like the two great lights of the day and night, would have arrested most powerfully, during these periods, a human eye. . . ."[1] The account is concerned with major events, the highlights of creation.

The understanding of Genesis 1 would be greatly aided if the chapter were viewed as a concise report of the events of the week. If, for example, someone were to ask a friend what he did last week, the reply might be somewhat as follows. "Monday I worked in my back yard, Tuesday I painted my living room, Wednesday I wrote letters, Thursday I graded exams, Friday I read a book, etc." Clearly this reply is a summary of the activities of the week. It is a report of the highlights of the respondent's week. The answer is not intended to mean that only that which was reported on was done. For example,

_____

1. H. Miller, *The Testimony of the Rocks* (Boston: Gould and Lincoln, 1872), p. 171.

when the reply is given that "Wednesday I wrote letters," this does not mean that the respondent did not engage in any activity other than letter-writing. Also the answer given by no means implies that the activities mentioned were completely restricted to the day with which they are connected. When we are told, "Friday I read a book," we are not required to believe that the respondent sat down early Friday morning, opened the book at page one and completed reading the book on Friday evening. It is entirely possible that the reading of the book started Thursday evening or even Wednesday evening. Maybe the respondent read a few pages each night of the week and then had sufficient time available on Friday to read the bulk of the book. It is certainly possible, too, that the book was actually completed on Saturday morning. None of this is inconsistent with the statement, "Friday I read a book." All that is implied in the statement is that book-reading was the major activity (or one of the major activities) of the day and that quite probably a lot more reading of the book occurred on Friday than on any other day. Seen in this light, the activities of the various days of the week may show considerable *overlap*.

Genesis 1 should be regarded in the same way. We have a concise report of major activities that occurred in general sequence, but we do not need to rule out overlap. Hence when we read of the sixth day that the earth brought forth cattle we are not compelled to believe that *some* of this kind of activity could not have *preceded* the sixth day. Perhaps a few beasts were actually made on the fourth day. Some of the activity of the sixth day may overlap to earlier days. All we are compelled to believe is that in comparison with other activities the sixth day was pre-eminently the day of creation of beasts and man and that the great bulk of beasts and creeping things were formed on the sixth day. It is a great mistake to insist that not a single animal could possibly have been created before all the plants were created simply because the third day reports on plants and the fifth and sixth days report on animals. To insist on this kind of conclusion is to overlook the fact that Moses is speaking very generally. He is speaking in terms of very broad, large-scale phenomena and not in terms of precise, scientific, technically describable phenomena. We are therefore on good grounds in maintaining that we should be able to observe in nature the *general* sequence of the events in Genesis 1. While we have no right to argue that *all* plants were created before *any* animals, we do have the right

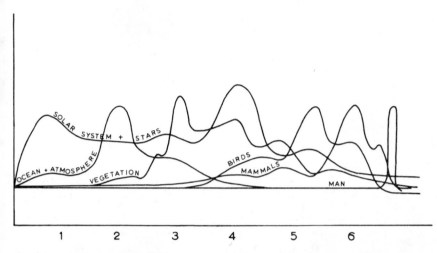

Figure 7. Schematic diagram of the creative events of the six days of creation showing possible (hypothetical) overlap of events. For example, day five records the creation of birds. It is clear that the creation of birds was a major event of that day, and that the day was pre-eminently one of bird formation as illustrated by the peak on the "bird curve." The curve as drawn, however, suggests that some lesser bird creation could have occurred, say, on days four and six as well. The curve for man has a sharp peak inasmuch as man was created on day six. For days one through five, however, the curve labelled "man" shows no peaks at all, indicating that no processes relating to the creation of man were in operation until day six. These curves should be used only to visualize how overlap of creative events might have occurred, but are *not* intended to set forth any definite pattern of overlap (assuming such overlap really existed).

to argue that the creation of plants generally preceded the creation of animals. In Genesis 1, then, there is not only a chronological sequence of days, but also a partially overlapping sequence of events. This view is schematically illustrated in Figure 7.

The First Day

Verse 1 probably describes the creation of the initial material of the universe, the unorganized heaven and earth. Many theologians have noted the fact that the burden of verse 1 is the heaven and the earth, that is, the entire universe, whereas the earth is the focus of the remaining verses. Leupold, for example, says in connection with verse 2:

> Of the two parts of the universe mentioned the author abandons the first, "the heavens," as lying outside the sphere of the present investigation, for of its creation we need not know or perhaps could

not understand its details. Moses definitely limits himself to the second of the two parts by emphatically setting "the earth" first in the sentence. This yields a shade of thought which our translation above tries to reproduce by saying: "And now, as far as the earth was concerned." Or one might render: "Now this earth," etc. As has been remarked, from this point onward the point of approach may be said to be geocentric.[2]

It is important then to stress that the events spoken of in verse 2 and thereafter are events that took place with reference to the earth. Even the cosmic events, such as the formation of the sun, moon, and stars, recorded as occurring on day four, are events that are important to life on earth. Even these cosmic events have reference to the earth. It is therefore a safe generalization to say that Genesis 1 is not concerned with the totality of cosmic events in themselves. The chapter does not discuss stellar events for their own sakes, but only from the point of view of their effect on the earth. As evidence of this generalization, in spite of the fact that God obviously created the various spiritual beings, the angels, the cherubim, the seraphim, Satan himself, nothing whatsoever is said in Genesis 1 about the origination of these heavenly beings. The theme of Genesis 1 is the creation of the planet earth.

The account of day one refers to several aspects of the proto-earth. We are told of the waste and void of the earth, the darkness on the deep, and the activity or brooding of God's Spirit. This condition is changed by the appearance of light. Verse 2 begins with an already existent earth. This primitive earth, however, is not yet in a fully developed and fully organized condition. It is rather "without form, and void," but it is an earth, a mass of matter. How long a time elapsed between the initial creation of matter and energy out of nothing and the appearance of the earth in the condition as described in verse 2 is not stated. Nor is it stated how long the earth was "without form, and void," but we do know from Scripture that the earth is not eternal. It did have a beginning. Some Old Testament commentators have spoken of this primitive void earth as a chaos, as something totally unstructured. Genesis 1:2, however, is not describing a chaotic, totally unstructured mass. Rather it sees earth as a structural entity, a partially organized body that at the moment is not a completed product. The primitive earth is unfit for life and

---

2. H. C. Leupold, *Exposition of Genesis* (Columbus: Wartburg, 1942), p. 45.

habitation. That this is the case is suggested by Isaiah 45:18.[3] The primitive earth is barren and desolate at the moment, but it is destined and intended to become inhabited. The Lord did not create the earth in vain. He did not create the earth for it to remain a waste, a desert, a void.

This initially desolate, uninhabited earth is dark, for darkness is upon the face of the deep and the command for light to spring forth has not yet been given. There is no light on the earth, and so it is not in a fit condition for the support of life. Geological science has long held that the earliest stages of earth history were characterized by a total absence of even simple forms of life.

Verse 2 speaks also of the deep. The primitive earth had a great deal of water, or some kind of fluid, on its surface. There was a primeval ocean. Geological science has long speculated on the origin of the oceans. Geologists have generally felt that from virtually the very beginning of the planet's history there has been an ocean, although there is considerable disagreement about the size of the primitive ocean, the rate at which the ocean changed from its primitive size to its present size, and the mechanism by which the ocean waters have accumulated. On this point, as with the absence of life in the first stages of earth history, current scientific theory and the particular interpretation of Scripture offered here are in agreement.

Next verse 2 speaks of the "hovering" or "moving" or "being borne" of the Spirit of God over the face of the waters of this primitive ocean. From what is learned of the activity of God's Spirit elsewhere in Scripture perhaps there is some warrant for suggesting that the Spirit was doing the preparatory work for the transforming of the wild, desolate, barren earth into the vibrant, dynamic, inhabited earth.[4] Leupold, for example, concludes

> that His work in this case must have been anticipatory of the creative work that followed, a kind of impregnation with divine potentialities. The germs of all that is created were placed into dead

---

3. See the discussions of Isaiah 45:18 in E. J. Young, *The Book of Isaiah*, Vol. III (Grand Rapids: Wm. B. Eerdmans, 1972), pp. 210-12, and *Studies in Genesis One* (Philadelphia: Presbyterian and Reformed, 1964), p. 18. An extended discussion of Genesis 1:2 is given by G. C. Berkouwer, *Sin* (Grand Rapids: Wm. B. Eerdmans, 1971), pp. 79-91.

4. The activity of the Holy Spirit has been dealt with at great length by A. Kuyper, *The Work of the Holy Spirit* (Grand Rapids: Wm. B. Eerdmans, 1956). See especially pp. 27-31 for a discussion in reference to Genesis 1:2.

matter by Him. His was the preparatory work for leading over from
the inorganic to the organic. . . . We should not be averse to holding
that the foundation for all physical laws operative in the world now
was laid by this preparatory activity.[5]

The preparatory work of the Spirit was followed by the formation
of light. Two observations are in order with reference to this light. In
the first place the formation of this light is in sharp contrast to the
initial darkness *of the earth*. It is the earth that for the first time
receives light in order that the earth may now be in the proper
condition to receive the inhabitants for which it is intended. The text
does not necessarily indicate that no light existed elsewhere in the
universe; no light fell on the earth until this fiat. In the second place
it is improper, as has so often been done, to view this creation of
geocentric light (verse 3) as the initial creation (the initial creation
has been treated in verse 1) or as the creation of energy. Christians
ought not to correlate the creation of light with the great explosion
of the popular Big Bang hypothesis of cosmogenesis. That such an
equation of light and the Big Bang is an improper interpretation of
the text is evident from the fact that the earth—a chunk of the
matter-energy presumably originated in the Big Bang—already existed
prior to the light of verse 3. Hence the light of day one is light or
radiant energy *falling on the earth's surface* for the first time. There
seems to be little compelling reason to doubt that this light had its
source in some light-emitting object in another part of the universe.
Perhaps at this point in time the light first reached the earth from
that distant light source or sources. This is speculation, but a speculation not inconsistent with the text. Many theologians[6] have spoken
about light apart from light sources, but this seems to be unnecessary, especially as verse 1 has spoken of the creation of the
heavens. The text certainly does not require us to think of light apart
from sources in spite of the fact that at this point it mentions only
light (but not light sources).

Science ought to be granted the freedom to investigate the earliest
history of the earth and cosmos with all the data and tools at its
disposal. What science already believes about the earliest history is
hardly at great odds with what are said to be the events of the first
day. Early earth was desolate and lifeless, and there was a primitive

---

5. Leupold, *Exposition of Genesis*, p. 50.

6. Ibid., p. 52; see also Young, *Studies in Genesis One*, p. 88.

ocean.[7] Moreover, whether or not the surface of the early earth was devoid of light for a time is still a debatable point as far as science is concerned.

The Second Day

With the advent of light on the earth, the planet is in a better position to uphold and maintain life, but all is not ready yet, for there must first transpire the events of the second day. Day two includes the formation of the firmament by means of the separation of the waters. The waters beneath the firmament are separated from waters above the firmament. This division of waters is brought about by God's activity. God is said to make the firmament and to divide the waters. The usage of these words by no means implies the purely miraculous or rules out God's using natural laws and processes that He had already implanted into the structure of creation. The work of God here is not a creation in the sense that the work of the initial creation or of the fifth day is. There is therefore no exegetical reason to rule out a uniformitarian approach to the study of the events of the second day and of the transition between the first and second days.

The products of the second day may be considered under three heads. First, the firmament; second, the waters under the firmament; finally, waters above the firmament. The term "firmament" in Hebrew conveys the idea of something that is hammered or spread out, so that the firmament may be referred to as an expanse. Genesis 1:8 states that this firmament is heaven. This heaven is not the nebulous, spiritual, ethereal dwelling place of God, but rather it is a *physical* heaven, namely the sky. That this physical heaven does not refer to the total expanse of outer space is clear from verse 20. The formation of the firmament was accomplished early in earth history for the specific purpose that the earth might be a more suitable or proper place for some of its future inhabitants to live. Note that according to verse 20 the fowls, the birds, fly in the firmament of heaven. From this it is evident that the term "firmament" refers

---

7. See W. W. Rubey, "The Geologic History of Sea Water—An Attempt to State the Problem," in *Geological Society of America Bulletin* 62 (1951), pp. 1111-48; and H. D. Holland, "The Geologic History of Sea Water—An Attempt to Solve the Problem," in *Geochimica et Cosmochimica Acta* 36 (1972), pp. 637-51.

essentially to the sky, which owes its appearance to the development
of earth's gaseous atmosphere. This is not contradicted by verses 14,
15, and 17, which speak of the lights in the firmament. Quite obviously the sun, moon, and stars are in outer space and not in our
atmosphere. Yet this does not mean that the firmament refers to
outer space; the text simply indicates that as far as the observer on
earth is concerned these heavenly bodies appear to be in the sky.
Their light is transmitted to us through the atmosphere. Thus verses
6-8 report for us the initial development of earth's sky and its atmosphere.

The formation of this sky is accomplished by a division of waters.
Originally the earth was surrounded by a nebulous watery fluid in
which life would have been virtually impossible. Now the boundary
between ocean and atmosphere is more sharply delineated. The
waters collected under the firmament clearly refer to the oceans or
seas, for in verses 9-10 we read that these waters are separated from
an emerging dry land and are gathered together and called seas.
Hence the text is suggesting that the earth's primeval ocean
mentioned in verse 2 simply took on a more definitive character as
ocean at this time.

A final feature produced on the second day is the waters that are
above the firmament. Do the waters above the firmament refer to the
clouds in the sky or are they some more ethereal waters that are
totally beyond the reach of the earth? Or do these waters refer to a
thick canopy of water vapor that originally surrounded the earth's
primitive atmosphere but was destroyed at the time of the flood?
Many opinions have been offered on this subject.

E. J. Young, for example, is "unable to accept the opinion that
the waters above the expanse refer to the clouds, for this position
does not do justice to the language of the text which states that these
waters are *above* the expanse."[8] He does not, however, advocate
either the canopy theory or the extraterrestrial theory. It is of interest to note that there is increasing scientific evidence of various
forms of water in outer space[9] so it certainly is not impossible that
Genesis 1:7 refers to extraterrestrial waters. The extraterrestrial

---

8. Young, *Studies in Genesis One*, p. 90.

9. E.g., M. M. Litvak, "Hydroxyl and Water Masers in Protostars," in *Science*
165 (1969), pp. 855-61; and M. L. Meeks et al., "Water Vapor: Observations of
Galactic Sources," in *Science* 165 (1969), pp. 180-84.

water theory is here rejected, however, on the basis of other Scriptural data, particularly in the Psalms. Psalm 104 is a psalm of creation. It reflects on the various activities of the days of creation of Genesis 1. Psalm 104:2 is a reminiscence of the creative activity of day one and the formation of light. God clothes Himself with light as with a garment. Verses 3-6 are a reminiscence of the work of the second day. Verse 3 says that God lays the beams of His chambers in the waters and makes the clouds His chariot. The statements of verse 3 do not seem to be referring to any cosmic, extraterrestrial waters. The use of the word "clouds" leads us to think of the atmospheric clouds. But perhaps the waters in which God's chambers are located are some kind of heavenly, cosmic waters. This possibility is ruled out by Psalm 104:13, where we read that God waters the hills from His chambers. The waters of God's chambers are clearly *rain waters* and therefore ordinary atmospheric clouds. The divine commentary of Psalm 104 on Genesis 1 seems to indicate quite plainly that the waters above the firmament are the clouds, the ordinary atmospheric rain clouds. The term "above" may be used simply to indicate that clouds are very high up in the sky. Indeed they are well above the space in which most birds are wont to fly. The same conclusion is corroborated by Proverbs 8:28, a passage of Scripture which also reflects on the work of creation.

A comment is also necessary with regard to the interpretation of Genesis 1:6-7 which maintains that the waters above the firmament were a unique antediluvian water vapor canopy which was the source of the flood waters at the time of Noah. The canopy theory has been advocated by a number of neo-catastrophists, particularly Patten.[10] The canopy is said to have been a thick globe-encircling envelope of water vapor that shielded the primitive earth from harmful rays of the sun and rendered the earth's climatic conditions uniformly mild and pleasant. At the time of Noah's flood, however, this canopy was drained of its water and disappeared. The sluice gates of heaven were opened and it rained for forty days and nights. It is said by neo-catastrophists that ordinary clouds could not produce that kind of torrential rain for such an extended period of time. The waters of the

---

10. D. W. Patten, "The Pre-Flood Greenhouse Effect," in *Symposium on Creation II* (Grand Rapids: Baker, 1970), pp. 11-41, and *The Biblical Flood and the Ice Epoch* (Seattle: Pacific Meridian, 1966), pp. 194-224; see also J. C. Whitcomb and H. M. Morris, *The Genesis Flood* (Philadelphia: Presbyterian and Reformed, 1961), pp. 240-42.

old canopy are said to be located at present in the ocean basins. The text of II Peter 3:5-6 is appealed to in support of this interpretation. Here we read that "by the word of God the heavens were of old, and the earth standing out of the water and in the water: Whereby the world that then was, being overflowed with water, perished." Obviously the waters above the firmament as well as the oceans are in view here as a source of flood waters.

Attractive as the vapor canopy theory may be, Scripture does not lend support to it. We have already seen that Psalm 104 indicates that the waters above the firmament are ordinary rain clouds. Moreover, Psalm 148 flatly rules out the vapor canopy idea. Psalm 148 is a psalm of praise. In it the psalmist calls upon the creation to praise its Creator God. In verse 4 the psalmist commands the *waters that be above* the heavens to praise God. The reference is clearly to Genesis 1:6-7. Obviously the psalmist, writing long after Noah's flood, understood that the waters above the heavens still existed. It would be rather odd to ask them to praise God if they no longer were in existence. Clearly then the waters above the heavens cannot refer to a water vapor canopy which was destroyed at the onset of the Noahic flood. Verses 5 and 6 of the psalm corroborate the above conclusion. God has created these things and "established them for ever and ever: he hath made a decree which shall not pass." The waters above the firmament still exist. They are the clouds.

What then might the events of the second day mean in terms of earth history? Isn't Moses here giving a sweeping, general account of the formation of the earth's atmosphere as a distinctive entity that encircles the planet, an entity that is now sharply delineated from the surface of the oceans? Interestingly current scientific thought also views the development of the atmosphere and oceans as a very early event in the history of the earth.[11] It is thought that gases have gradually accumulated around the earth primarily by means of the leakage of gaseous elements from the earth's interior as, for instance,

---

11. See P. Brancazio and A. G. W. Cameron, *The Origin and Evolution of Atmospheres and Oceans* (New York: John Wiley and Sons, 1964). See also F. P. Fanale, "A Case for Catastrophic Early Degassing of the Earth," in *Chemical Geology* 8 (1971), pp. 79-105. In contradistinction to the majority opinion favoring gradual accumulation of the atmosphere and oceans by degassing of the earth's interior, Fanale proposes that most of the material of the atmosphere and oceans was degassed from the interior at a very early stage in the earth's formation.

during eruption of a volcano. The chemical composition of the early atmosphere is believed to have been considerably different from what it is now, in fact, sufficiently different that virtually no life could exist. Genesis 1, we note, has not yet directly mentioned the appearance of any life. The early atmosphere is thought to have been rich in gases such as carbon dioxide and hydrogen and to have gradually changed to the present nitrogen- and oxygen-rich atmosphere. Genesis 1 does not say that the composition of the early atmosphere was the same as that of the present. Firmament is the appearance of sky produced by a gaseous expanse. There seems to be no textual reason to say that its chemical composition could not have been different from what it now is. The term "waters" would seem to put restrictions on the composition of the atmosphere, but we must remember that Moses is using nontechnical language of a prescientific age and that the waters refer to the clouds, not the firmament itself.

The Third Day

The third day sees the separation of the ocean from the dry land and the formation of various kinds of plants. With the appearance of dry land the earth will be ready to be populated by complex organisms. Verse 9 suggests that on the third day the waters under the firmament, that is, on the surface, were localized. The implication is that prior to the third day these waters essentially covered the entire face of the globe and no continental land masses existed. Perhaps small islands were present, but the general impression is that at the onset of the third day the surface of the earth was essentially covered by a global ocean. The third day, however, sees the appearance of dry land. Leupold says that the term for "dry land" really refers to the continents.

Psalm 104:6-9 describes poetically the work of this part of the third day: "The waters stood above the mountains. At thy rebuke they fled; at the voice of thy thunder they hasted away. They go up by the mountains; they go down by the valleys unto the place which thou hast founded for them. Thou hast set a bound that they may not pass over; that they turn not again to cover the earth." Gradually dry land appears and is drained of its watery covering.

We noted in chapter three that continental crust differs greatly from oceanic crust. Continental crust is different in chemistry and in density from oceanic crust. Because continental crust is less dense than oceanic crust it must be thicker than the oceanic crust in order to maintain a balance of stresses on the mantle below. This extra thickness of continental crust causes it to be elevated much higher than the oceanic crust; hence it appears above the level of the ocean water. Although geology is still puzzling over the means by which the original continental crust was developed, there is a great deal of evidence to indicate that the continental crust was formed very early in the earth's history. It is fairly certain that the continental crust preceded the appearance of life. A current estimate is that the continental crust is at least 3.5 billion years old.[12] It is not known *scientifically* how the primitive ocean, atmosphere, and continental crust are interrelated in terms of sequence of time, but it is believed that all these features of the earth are *extremely old.* Is there not thus in this verse another substantial agreement between Genesis and current geological thinking? Do not both teach the antiquity of the continents?

With the appearance of dry continental land masses the earth is now ready for substantial populations of living organisms. The account mentions the formation of three categories of plant life. The grasses refer, according to Leupold, "to the fresh green plants that are likely to grow in well-watered spots and may include such things as mosses and other carpeting plants."[13] Keil speaks of "the young, tender green, which shoots up after rain and covers the meadows and downs."[14] Also produced is herbage, which is described as "seeding" or "yielding seed." Leupold suggests that these are plants in which seed pods may be a more obvious feature than in the grasses. He further suggests that it is the herbage which man and cattle eat and therefore the term probably refers to such things as vegetables and grains. The third class of vegetation that is produced consists of fruit-bearing fruit trees. Leupold suggests that this class includes "both trees that bear fruit as well as trees yielding nuts and cones and, surely, all bushes yielding berries."[15]

---

12. Rocks 3.6 to 3.9 billion years old have been reported from Greenland.

13. Leupold, *Exposition of Genesis*, p. 67.

14. C. F. Keil and F. Delitzsch, *Biblical Commentary on the Old Testament, I, The Pentateuch* (Grand Rapids: Wm. B. Eerdmans, 1949), p. 55.

15. Leupold, *Exposition of Genesis*, p. 67.

The kinds of vegetation that are described here are fairly complex types of vegetation. Whether or not Moses intends for us to understand that *all* vegetation first appeared on the third day is not known, for Moses was not giving a technical description or a modern botanical classification of plants. He simply intended for the reader to understand that the third day was generally a day of plant production and that most plant materials were formed at this time. We do not know, for instance, whether bacteria or other one-celled or very primitive plants were formed at this time. Moses likely was unaware of their existence. Whether any one of the three plant categories listed includes such primitive plants is doubtful. It certainly is possible that some of these very primitive life forms appeared with the hovering activity of the Spirit in verse 2.

It is appropriate at this point to raise the question of the origin of life. Inasmuch as it cannot be determined from the text of Genesis 1 whether or not the most primitive forms of life, or, specifically, of plant life, were formed on the third day, it cannot be shown from Scripture either *when* life first appeared on earth or exactly *how* life first appeared on earth. The idea that God miraculously created the first life form cannot be supported dogmatically from the Bible. It is possible that the first, simplest organisms developed from inorganic material by means of natural processes. By no means does this lead us to any materialistic philosophy. The Christian surely must believe that God divinely upholds and directs any process or law in nature (Hebrews 1:3).

In any case the third day was a day when a lot of plant species were originally produced. The fact that general categories or classes of plants are mentioned indicates that an evolution of plants of one class from those of another is ruled out. The use of the term "after his kind" also suggests an independence of botanical classes that is incompatible with a general plant evolution; but when we look at fossil plants, there is no solid way in which to put into practice a disbelief in general plant evolution, for only very general information is given us in Scripture.

What does the science of paleobotany have to say about the history of plants on the earth? So far as is presently known only very simple types of plants such as seaweeds, algae, and bacteria existed during Late Precambrian and early Paleozoic time. Not until the Silurian and Devonian periods did more complex types of plants appear. The first seed plants appear in Devonian beds. Not until

Pennsylvanian times did the first trees, in the modern botanical sense, such as cycads and conifers, appear. The Mesozoic era was the time when these plants particularly flourished.

Some difficulties are readily apparent in correlating Genesis with paleobotany. For one thing different categories of plants seem to have arisen over widely-spaced times. Perhaps this is not as serious as it first appears if we remember that verses 11 and 12 are not necessarily referring to instantaneous events. There is nothing which says that grasses could not have come first, followed by herbs at some later time, and followed by fruit trees at yet a later time. Nor need we understand these organisms as being produced in their most fully developed state. The term "fruit trees" could well refer to the primitive ancestors of modern-day or even Cenozoic flowering deciduous trees.

Another more serious difficulty is that Genesis seems to indicate that, as a class, plants appeared before animals. The fossil record, however, seems to suggest that plants are simultaneous with a great variety of animals. In fact, primitive fish appear in rocks that are older than rocks containing evidence of the most primitive trees! This difficulty is an apparent contradiction but it need not cause any worry, for further scientific research will yield new information on the history of plants. Plant fossils are more difficult to preserve and to find than are animal fossils. Hence our record may be quite incomplete. Another important fact is that many fossiliferous rocks, especially of Early Paleozoic age, are of marine character and contain abundant marine animal fossils. We do not expect to find land plant fossils to any significant degree in marine rocks. Perhaps the record of plant history is somewhat biased by the nature of the rocks now available. Let science pursue its work and in time the difficulty may be resolved.

The Fourth Day

On the fourth day was the formation of the sun, moon, and stars. The making of these bodies has specific reference to the earth. The function of these bodies with respect to the earth is more in view in this section than is the absolute origination of these bodies. It is not necessary to think that the sun, moon, and stars are receiving their existence for the first time at this point. Rather at this point the sun, moon, and stars come into a particular relationship to earth. Keil's words are very instructive on this point:

> We are not taught here that on *one* day, viz. the fourth, God created all the heavenly bodies out of nothing, and in a perfect condition; on the contrary, we are told that in the beginning God created the *heaven* and the earth, and on the fourth day that He made the sun, the moon, and the stars (planets, comets, and fixed stars) in the firmament, to be lights for the earth. According to these distinct words, the primary material, not only of the earth, but also of the heaven and the heavenly bodies, was created in the beginning. If, therefore, the heavenly bodies were first made or created on the fourth day, as lights for the earth, in the firmament of heaven; the words can have no other meaning than that their creation was completed on the fourth day, just as the creative formation of our globe was finished on the third; that the creation of the heavenly bodies therefore proceeded side by side, and probably by similar stages, with that of the earth, so that the heaven with its stars was completed on the fourth day.[16]

Leupold concurs, "Heavenly bodies were in existence, but from this point onward they begin to serve a definite purpose in reference to the earth."[17] E. J. Young says that "the origin of heaven and earth, however, was simultaneous, but the present arrangement of the universe was not constituted until the fourth day."[18]

The specific function of these bodies is to serve as light-bearers for the earth. Whether or not the light of verse 3 was somehow related to the sun is not known. Perhaps the sun was the light-bearer; perhaps other heavenly bodies. The point seems to be that at this time the earth comes into its present and final relationship to the sun so that *now* the sun and moon can serve as *time regulators* for the earth. Verse 14 indicates that these light-bearers, obviously referring to sun and moon, are to divide day from night and to be for signs, seasons, days, and years. No doubt any phenomenon of a regulated, recurrent nature is in view here, such as springtime and harvest, as well as months, light and dark. The lights are given in order that man, who is yet to appear, may order his life in accordance with divinely appointed regulators or chronometers. Psalm 104:19 says that the moon has been appointed for seasons. The months are based on earth-moon relationships. The seasons of the year are based on earth-

16. Keil and Delitzsch, *The Pentateuch*, pp. 58-59.

17. Leupold, *Exposition of Genesis*, p. 71.

18. Young, *Studies in Genesis One*, p. 96.

sun relationships. Daylight and darkness and their duration are based on the earth's rotation at a given speed in the light of a light source.

The Fifth Day

The fifth day was discussed at some length in chapter five when we noted the difficulties of applying the idea of the creation of fish to the fossil record. Hence there is no need to enter into too detailed a discussion of the work of the fifth day. What was created on the fifth day includes winged fowl that fly in the open firmament of heaven. Leupold suggests that this category includes not only birds but perhaps also every type of being that has wings. In addition swarms of sea creatures, not only fish, but all aquatic creatures both small (the living creature that moveth) and large (great whales or, more properly, sea monsters), were created on day five. It is quite probable that these categories of sea creatures include some of the more primitive types of marine animals such as corals, sponges, jelly-fish, and anemones as well as more complex beings like crabs, octopi, squid, fish, and eels, but it is not wise to be dogmatic on this matter.

The fact that many marine invertebrate animals such as corals and trilobites appear in the fossil record prior to land plants implies a contradiction between Genesis and geology. We must, however, keep in mind the incompleteness of the plant record and our lack of knowledge as to the exact limits of the categories described in verses 20-22. It is important to point out that the major groups in view here, that is, birds, most fish, swimming reptiles such as crocodiles or the extinct mosasaurs, flying reptiles like pterodactyls, seals and whales, do appear later in the fossil record than most land plants. As a generality such is the case. Birds first appear in the Jurassic period, fish are well-developed from Ordovician onwards but proliferate in the Tertiary, complex marine and aerial reptiles are Mesozoic, and large swimming mammals are Tertiary.

One more consideration may be helpful at this point. These various forms of life were created on the fifth day, but does this neces-sarily mean that all these creatures first came into existence on the fifth day? Or could it possibly mean that the earliest of these creatures were formed prior to the fifth day and that the birds and fish came into their fullest development on the fifth day? In support of the possibility of this interpretation recall that in reference to the work of the fourth day several Old Testament scholars said that the sun and the moon did not necessarily first miraculously appear on that day. Rather their formation may well have begun prior to the fourth day and their completion with respect to their main purpose for the earth have been effected on the fourth day. If the sun was made or created on the fourth day but also existed in a less developed condition on prior days, we may also suggest that even though birds were created on the fifth day, nevertheless, the most primitive birds or original bird ancestors were miraculously formed on a day prior to the fifth day. Hence the data of Genesis 1 actually allow for some overlap of the events of the days. If such overlap exists, then all apparent discrepancies between Genesis 1 and science would fall away.

The Sixth Day

These comments on Genesis 1 conclude with a consideration of the work of the sixth day. We learn first of all of the formation of the beasts of the earth, the cattle, and the creeping things. After these animals appeared, man was created.

According to Leupold, the term translated "cattle" in the Authorized Version may better be translated "domestic animals." In some cases the word may be used in reference to all animals, but here it refers to domestic animals in contrast to beasts of the earth. Presumably the term is referring to animals such as sheep, horses, pigs, goats, and cows. Obviously these animals would not be created in the domesticated state, for man did not as yet exist. In addition there is a second class of animals, the wild, truly wild animals, those that cannot be domesticated. This category certainly includes what are generally classified as mammals, for example, lions, deer, antelope, elephants. The third class of animals is called "creepers" in the Authorized Version. Leupold suggests that in this category may be included "everything . . . large or small, that moves upon the earth or close to the earth, having but short legs."[19] Reptiles and smaller forms of life may be included. Keil suggests that worms and insects may be in view here.

Again these animals are said to reproduce after their kind and wide varieties were formed. These assertions seem to rule out the possibility of a general theory of evolution, although specific evolution of

---

19. Leupold, *Exposition of Genesis*, p. 84.

a type of animal, such as the horse, does not seem to be ruled out. We need not review the difficulties that confront the Christian paleontologist in applying the facts of Genesis to the fossil record. The Christian paleontologist is always confronted by the problem of knowing exactly *what* was created on day six and by the problem of not knowing whether the gaps in the fossil record are real or apparent.

Day six describes chiefly the formation of higher animals, mainly the mammals. The evidence available from the fossil record likewise indicates that mammals are a very late development. Not until Tertiary time do the mammals proliferate in the fossil record. Again there seems to be a general agreement between Genesis and geology.

Man is created after the other animals have been formed. Man is the crown, the culmination of creation. Paleontology has discovered the same. Man is a very recent inhabitant of earth. His fossils are found only in deposits of the Pleistocene and Recent ages; he appeared after the mammals were flourishing. Again there is no conflict between the Bible and science.

In summary, there are a number of difficulties in integrating Genesis and the geological record. These difficulties ought not to lead to a discrediting of the Bible. Rather the difficulties appear far less serious if only we understand both the Bible and science. It is difficult to know exactly how to interpret Genesis 1. It seems clear from the internal evidence of the Bible that Genesis 1 purports to be a historical account. It does claim to report real space-time events. But whether this history took place in 144 hours or over a long period of time cannot be answered definitely from Scriptural data. Internal Scriptural arguments can be given which lend support to either view. The view a Christian holds would seem to be a matter of individual conscience. The 144-hour view, even though a Biblically possible interpretation, presents extremely difficult practical problems for the geologist. It makes the practice of geology virtually impossible. The practicing Christian geologist then is likely to opt for the long-day interpretation of Genesis 1, which likewise has Biblical support and is therefore a legitimate option.

There is general agreement between the long-day theory of Genesis 1 that I have proposed and the known data of geological science. The Christian must be content with this general agreement. It is incorrect to reject the long-day interpretation simply because there are some points of apparent disagreement, that is, because there is not perfect agreement with science. There are several reasons for this conclusion.

In the first place Genesis 1 was not written as a technical document. It was written for ordinary people in common language. When it talks of animals, it talks in terms of broad "common-sense" groupings that were familiar to ordinary people, not in terms of a technical biological taxonomy. Hence the Christian scientist has the problem of determining exactly how the common-sense classification should be related to a technical paleontological classification. No one will *ever* be able to define *exhaustively* what species of plants and animals are in view in the generalized language of Genesis 1. Moreover, it is not known whether the classifications of plants and animals in Genesis 1 were *intended* to be exhaustive of *all* plants and animals. We do not know if amoebae and bacteria were in view during the writing of the account.

Secondly there are problems with the interpretation of Genesis 1. There is a very strong possibility that some of the events described may have overlapped a number of creation days. Recall, for example, the case of the formation of the sun. If there was such an overlapping of events, it cannot be insisted that *every* plant species that ever existed was created before any animal species came into existence. The extent of any possible overlap cannot be determined exegetically.

In the third place *science cannot be forced to agree with Genesis all at once*, even if Genesis had given us an exhaustive technical description of creative events. To insist that science should agree perfectly with Genesis 1 is to misunderstand the nature of science. In developing this thought let us note first that Genesis is infallible and inerrant. It gives us an absolutely correct description of the events of creation. Thus the *real facts* do agree completely with the account of Genesis. But *we have no human interpretation of Genesis 1 that is infallible*. The long-day theory with its successive overlapping creative days may be an approximation of the truth, but it is by no means infallible. Thus until an interpretation of Genesis 1 can be developed that is as accurate and trustworthy as, say, the Westminster Confession's doctrine of God or election or the person of Christ, we make a grave mistake in insisting on full agreement between Scripture and science, for the Christian community is not sure exactly what that agreement should be. Moreover, *scientific interpretations are by no means infallible and never will be*. Science is a picture of the world that is ever growing and changing shape, always altering its hues and textures. It changes as new facts are continuously discovered. But the facts are not discovered in such a way as to lead linearly ever closer to the truth. Science is always based on partial evidence. Sometimes the partial evidence may be such as to yield interpretations that are very close to the real situation. Sometimes the facts that are discovered may temporarily lead in the wrong direction or give a false impression of the truth until a new group of facts is discovered. If we insist that science at all points agree with Genesis, we forget that only some of the facts are presently available to science. We forget that science is not a finished product. We forget that science is always a progress report. There is therefore need for caution on the part of scientists. They should avoid dogmatic statements. Science should be cautious and tentative, not dogmatic. It is improper to say that Genesis and science disagree and that Genesis is therefore wrong. Science has not said its last word. New facts will be discovered.

7

Whence Man?

The discussion now focuses sharply on the creature who appeared on the sixth day of creation after all the other plants and animals were made. The mode of origin of this creature, namely man, has been the subject of considerable emotional debate not only between Christians and non-Christians, but also between different groups of Christians. It has already been noted that theistic evolutionists believe that man has gradually evolved from apelike ancestors. Moreover, they believe that this idea does not do any damage to the Christian faith. Other Christians insist that man is a special creation of God and that the meaning and vitality of the whole Christian religion depend on the truth of that special creation.

The following comments of Christian scientists should suffice to indicate the sharp divergence of opinion among Christians on the question of the origin of man. Richard Bube, for example, states that "the answers to evolutionary questions are not to be found in Genesis"[1] and also that "the reliability of the Bible and the vitality of a life with Jesus Christ do not depend in any way on the proof or the disproof of even the general theory of evolution."[2]

---

1. R. H. Bube, *The Encounter Between Christianity and Science* (Grand Rapids: Wm. B. Eerdmans, 1968), p. 105.

2. Ibid., p. 106.

Geologist F. D. Eckelmann concludes that we may view Genesis

as a literary vehicle through which shines the truth that God is Lord
and Creator. Such an approach does not involve viewing the creation
story as cosmology or cosmogony. Nor does it necessitate insisting
on a historical Adam or a historical fall. Adam can be seen as representative of all men and the fall as representing universal sin and
imperfection in humanity.[3]

Davidheiser maintains a diametrically opposite position. He claims
that "if man evolved, Christ was just a reformer and not the
Redeemer; He was a martyr and not the Savior."[4] Davidheiser insists
on man's special creation. Whitcomb and Morris also are very insistent that there were a real Adam and Eve and that they were
specially created by God.[5]

Biblical Evidence Regarding the Origin of Man

To obtain a genuinely Christian solution to the problem of man's
origin one must turn first of all not to the paleontological evidence
but to the Bible. It must first of all be determined whether or not the
Bible has anything at all to say about the origin of man. If the Bible
says nothing about the origin of man or if it has no definite position
on this question, we may then go to science for our answers. But first
the Christian goes to Scripture.

In the course of the discussion on the interpretation of Genesis 1
it was observed that man made his first appearance on the sixth day
of creation. "So God created man in his own image, in the image of
God created he him; male and female created he them" (Genesis
1:27). Obviously the Bible says *something* here about the origin of
man. The matter cannot now be passed off lightly. It is necessary to
probe more deeply into Scripture to determine exactly what is
taught about the origin of man.

It should be noted that Genesis 2:7 also seems to deal with the
origin of man. This text cannot be dismissed (as Lever has done) as
not reporting events occurring in space and time. It has already been

---

3. Ibid., p. 107.

4. B. Davidheiser, *Evolution and Christian Faith* (Philadelphia: Presbyterian
and Reformed, 1969), p. 10.

5. J. C. Whitcomb and H. M. Morris, *The Genesis Flood* (Philadelphia: Presbyterian and Reformed, 1961), pp. 455-57.

demonstrated that the structure of the Book of Genesis indicates plainly that Genesis 2 is *history*—space-time, real-world history. A good starting point is thus the text of Genesis 2:7, the most detailed text which evidently alludes to the origin of man. This text is to be interpreted as reporting a historical event, but does it settle the question as to whether man evolved or was specially created?

The text reads, in the Authorized Version, "And the LORD God formed man of the dust of the ground, and breathed into his nostrils the breath of life; and man became a living soul." Again the notion should be dispelled that simply because God forms, there must be a pure miracle or a special creation at this point. Many of God's activities are not miraculous. A firsthand impression of the text is that man is a two-part being. He has a body formed of the dust of the ground. He has a soul that is imparted by God's breath of life. The text does not say how much time elapsed in the formation of man's body from the dust of the ground. Perhaps considerable development through time has occurred in man's body. Perhaps God used some pre-existing creature, and permitted it to develop through time into a human body. When the body became sufficiently *human,* God breathed a soul into the body so that man became truly man.

The argument just outlined is sometimes used in support of theistic evolutionism. The argument assumes that man's *body* has evolved whereas his *soul* or *spirit* was created directly, miraculously implanted into his body by God. This interpretation is consistent with a possible interpretation of Genesis 1:27 suggested earlier. It was noted that the creation of man does not necessarily mean that his body was specially created. Ephesians 4:24 and Colossians 3:10 speak of the new creation of man's heart or spirit. Could not then the original creation of man refer to the miraculous implanting of a soul or spirit into a previously evolved body so that that evolved creature then became, miraculously and dramatically, *man?* Such an evolutionistic interpretation of the Biblical data on the origin of man is intriguing, but it is fallacious in that it is a misunderstanding of Genesis 2:7. It also fails to take into account other relevant data from Scripture.

First notice that the evolutionistic view is based on a misunderstanding of Genesis 2:7. This misunderstanding centers largely around the word which is translated "soul" in the Authorized Version. The translation "soul" is a perfectly valid translation of the Hebrew word *nephesh*—a translation which, in fact, is very commonly used throughout the Old Testament. But the word "soul" can cause difficulties if we are prone to thinking in terms of the scholastic dichotomy which views the soul and body as two substances set sharply in contrast to one another. In order to gain a more accurate understanding of the word "soul," it is necessary to turn again to Genesis 1. The word *nephesh* occurs four times in Genesis 1. In verse 20 it is translated "the moving creature that hath life." In verse 21 it is the "living *creature* that moveth." In verse 24 it is "the living creature," and in verse 30, "every thing . . . wherein there is *life.*" In all these instances *nephesh* is simply a living creature, an animated being, a creature with soul as its animating source or principle of life. The animals created on the fifth and sixth days could thus be viewed as souls. This would not imply that they possessed souls in distinction from their bodies, but that they *were* souls; they were animated, living creatures.

This usage of *nephesh* in Genesis 1 gives us the key to the interpretation of Genesis 2:7. This text might more helpfully be translated "and man became a living *creature."* The idea here is that when God breathed into man the breath of life, man became *alive,* he became a *creature.* It does not mean that he had a soul added to an already living body. The body that was prepared by God from the dust of the ground was *lifeless,* but the divine inbreathing suffused life, the animating principle, into it. Prior to the divine inbreathing man was not alive in any sense. Man was *not* any kind of a creature prior to the divine inbreathing; then and only then did man become alive. Thus that which constitutes man as a living being also constitutes man as man. The text clearly rules out the origination of man from pre-existing animal life.

A second Scriptural consideration leads also to the conclusion that the idea of the evolution of man is utterly foreign to the Bible. This second line of evidence also comes from Genesis 2 and finds support in texts in the New Testament. The plain reading of the text of Genesis 2:18-25, in light of the historical nature of Genesis 2, would seem to indicate that there was a lapse of time between the first appearance of Adam and the appearance of the first woman, Eve. The two sexes were not created simultaneously, despite the preliminary impressions given by Genesis 1:27. Genesis 2:18-25 is thus an amplification of Genesis 1:27. Moses provides considerable detail in the account concerning the creation of Eve. If he did not intend the account to be understood as ordinary history, it is a bit perplexing as to why he should provide such detail. It is Moses' obvious intent to teach that the female of the human species did not appear when the first male of the human species appeared. It is also his obvious intent to point out the miraculous appearance of the first female. It is difficult to see how the story of the rib could be compatible with an evolutionary view. It is also Moses' intent to point out the purpose of woman. The woman is *for* the man. She was specially prepared for the male to be a help meet for him.

The literal-historical interpretation that is presented above would seem to be supported by the Apostle Paul. Hence the Christian, whose every view is to be formed and framed by the words of Scripture, has an infallible interpretation of the Genesis account. Paul speaks of the relationship of men and women in a number of places but two texts are of special importance. In I Corinthians 11:8-9 Paul says, "For the man is not of the woman; but the woman of the man. Neither was the man created for the woman; but the woman for the man." The female is *of* and *for* the male. In I Timothy 2:12-13 Paul says that he will not allow "a woman to teach, nor to usurp authority over the man, but to be in silence. For Adam was first formed, then Eve." Paul accepts a kind of subordination of woman to man. In the latter text he plainly indicates that in time sequence the female of the species appeared later than the male. In the former text he corroborates Moses' teaching that woman exists and was made for the purpose of supplementing the man. She is *for* the man.

Any theistic-evolutionistic view of man that would claim to be genuinely Christian must come to terms with these Biblical data. But how this can be done without giving up the evolutionary view is hard to see. There seems to be no way that an evolution could produce a first male human before a first female human. Rather the sexes obviously must be evolving simultaneously from animal to man. There is no temporal priority of either sex in evolution.

The evolutionistic view must also account for the stress which Scripture lays on the idea that woman is *for* the man. In what sense can this be true in evolution? Is there a sense in which the female gorilla is *of* and *for* the male? Does the male gorilla have a *metaphysical* priority or superiority? In what sense could evolution lead to anything other than a pure equality between the sexes?

Another line of Scriptural evidence that bears on the question of man's origin is the statement that man was created in the image of God. In reading the account of creation in Genesis 1, we are impressed in verse 26 by God's determination to produce a creature *in His image*. We are struck by the *uniqueness* of this creature, for no other creature can lay claim to being made in the image of God. In fact nowhere in Scripture is any creature other than man ever spoken of as God's image. Man, however, receives this or a similar designation several times. In Genesis 5:1 man is said to have been made in the likeness of God. Genesis 9:6 speaks of the validity of capital punishment on the basis of man's creation in the image of God. The image of God is spoken of in the New Testament also. The Christian is to be conformed to the image of Christ (Romans 8:29). Man need not cover his head inasmuch as he is the image and glory of God (I Corinthians 11:7). Colossians 3:10 speaks of the new man being renewed in knowledge after the image of God. James condemns believers for blessing God and cursing those made in the similitude of God (James 3:9).

How is the image of God to be understood? How does it distinguish between man and other animals? Theologians have for centuries grappled with the problem of the meaning of the image of God.[6] Proper understanding of the expression rests in part on the meaning of the term "image." Hebrews 1:3 speaks of Christ as being the express image (character) of God's person. II Corinthians 4:4 speaks of Him as the image (ikon) of God. Commentators have generally said that this designation virtually implies identity of Christ and God. Christ is an exact reflection of God's person. Man as image, then, is a reflection of the nature and person of God. Man is a creature that is like God, expressive of the character of God. He is a finite replica of God. He is as much like God as a created being can be. It is to some extent difficult to know precisely what characteristics of God are in view inasmuch as Scripture speaks only in general terms. Colossians 3:10 relates knowledge to the image, and, by implication, Ephesians 4:24 speaks of holiness and righteousness. The term may suggest original immortality as well. There is danger of speculation on the point. Scripture, however, does view man as being like God, whereas other animals are not like God.

The usage of the term "image of God" thus implies a difference in kind between man and other animals. There is not a continuity between them. If the evolutionary hypothesis is true, we must visualize

6. G. C. Berkouwer, *Man: The Image of God* (Grand Rapids: Wm. B. Eerdmans, 1962), pp. 67-118.

a gradually increasing Godlikeness in the evolving animal. Through time the image of God in the evolving animal becomes sharper and more clearly defined. In the evolutionary view the image must progress and develop. The implication is that in all animals there is a tiny part of the image. Only in modern man has the image come to its full expression. The problem for theistic evolutionists is to point out where in the evolutionary sequence a creature first possesses or is the image of God. This identification of man as God's image sharply differentiates him from the other animals and renders impossible the idea of a common origin of men and animals.

Another extremely important Biblical text that bears on the origin of man and clinches the entire matter from Scripture's point of view is Romans 5:12-21. The central point of this great text is given in verses 12, 18, and 19. Verses 13-17 form a parenthesis in Paul's argument. The text presents an analogy between Adam and Jesus Christ in regard to the manner in which they affected the human race in their capacities as *representatives* of the race. The conclusion of the argument is stated in verse 19: "as by one man's disobedience many were made [that is, constituted or regarded as] sinners, so by the obedience of one shall many be made righteous." This text can be interpreted and understood properly, that is, Biblically, only if the Biblical teaching concerning the relationship between Jesus Christ and the people who belong to Him is properly grasped. Jesus Christ is the one by whose obedience the many are constituted righteous.

The New Testament writers regarded Christ as the eternal Son of God but also as a real, historical, individual human being. He was, for them, directly identical to Jesus of Nazareth, a Jew, a carpenter's son who lived and died in Palestine during the days of the Roman Empire. The Biblical writers regarded Jesus as an individual living in the space-time world just like themselves. For them Jesus was a human being, not a symbol, or an ideal, or a myth.

How, in the eyes of the New Testament writers, did this Jesus *represent* His people? How was the righteousness of His people related to Jesus and what He did? It is evident that the writers of the Bible had both a very high and a very low opinion of men. They had a high opinion in that they believed that man is made in the image of God and that he can have fellowship and communication with God. On the other hand they had a low opinion of man in that they believed he is a sinner who hates God and who is incapable of doing what is right in God's eyes.[7] In short, man was not regarded as being *righteous,* as being right with God. Not only this, but the Biblical writers did not think that this state of affairs could be rectified by human means alone. They did not think that men are capable of changing their ways simply by willing or desiring or trying harder to be better.[8] What is necessary is the grace of God. God must change man's evil heart, in fact give him a new heart, a new desire to do that which is proper in God's eyes.[9]

Jesus was seen as God's appointed representative on earth through whom He would give new hearts to His people. Jesus was not sent simply to be an example as to how to live. He was sent to be a deliverer from sin and death. Jesus represented His people before God by obeying God as they should have and by dying the God-accursed death that they justly deserved.[10] When therefore Paul says that through Jesus' obedience many are made righteous, he is claiming that for the sake of Jesus, God regards, declares, or constitutes a certain class of unrighteous people *as righteous.* God treats these sinful people as if they were righteous because of what Jesus, their representative, did for them.

How then does this relationship between Jesus and His people bear on the relationship between Adam and his people? It suggests first of all that Paul believed that Adam was a distinct, historical individual whose actions had an effect on the people he represented. It further implies that the disobedience of the individual, Adam, was a historical act, a real disobedience in space and time. Through this act the descendants of the individual were treated as, regarded as, constituted *sinners* even though they were not yet born and had not committed any transgressions of their own. The human race thus participated in the representative work of the historical individual, Adam.[11]

The interpretation developed above is the most natural interpretation of Romans 5 in light of the total Scripture, but can there

7. Romans 1:18-32; 3:9-19.

8. John 1:13; 14:6; Acts 4:12; Romans 3:20; Ephesians 2:1.

9. Romans 6:1-14; Philippians 2:12-13; Hebrews 8:10-12; 10:15-17.

10. II Corinthians 5:21; Galatians 3:13-14; Hebrews 9:27-28; I Peter 2:24.

11. See J. Murray, *The Imputation of Adam's Sin* (Grand Rapids: Wm. B. Eerdmans, 1959).

be some other tenable interpretation of the text that is consistent with the evolutionary view of the origin of man? If the view is held that Adam is only a symbolic representation of the evil or imperfection in all men, then Paul's analogy must be followed through to its logical conclusion. If the half of the analogy involving Adam is regarded as expressive of our proneness to do evil as depicted by the symbol of Adam's fall, then we are forced to an interpretation which states that the half of the analogy involving Christ expresses our proneness to do good or our inherent goodness. Or perhaps it is telling us to do good by imitating Jesus. The most consistent evolutionary interpretation would be that as Adam is a symbolic representation of the evil inherent in human nature, so Jesus is a symbolic representation of the good that is inherent in human nature. Needless to say, this interpretation does violent injustice both to the text of Romans and also to the whole thrust of the Biblical teaching regarding Christ and what He did for men.

An entirely different evolutionary approach to Romans 5 might maintain that Adam was a real individual who plunged his descendants into sin and misery. For example, a recent view of evolution sees man's culture and instincts as gradually developing from his animal ancestors. In animals, instincts oftentimes lead to hostility between neighbors or struggles for social status and power. In man such hostility and social struggles are regarded as sin, but in animals they are not. Suppose that man had evolved from the animals to such an extent that he developed complete control over all his instincts. As such he would be able to resist all temptations to trespass or retaliate or strive to overthrow his superior. We might call this individual, Adam. His loss of control over his instincts might be the fall into sin. Apart from the question of whether or not science would look favorably upon this possibility, the whole interpretation is fallacious because of the fact that any evolved creature is going to die whether or not he has complete control over his instincts. Death is a normal aspect of evolutionary theories. The evolutionary Adam would die even if he didn't sin. And at this point there is an irreconcilable contradiction with Romans 5. Death entered the human race through the sin of one man, not through his biology (verse 12). There simply is no Biblical way to find support for the evolution of man from animals in the passage from Romans 5.[12]

12. See also the analogy between Adam and Jesus Christ in I Corinthians 15:21-22.

Many genealogies of the human race are given to us in the Scriptures. These genealogies begin with Adam and proceed to individuals who are unquestionably historical individuals (Genesis 5:1-32; 11:10-26; I Chronicles 1—8), or they begin with obviously historical individuals and trace their lineage back to Adam (Luke 3:23-38). The way in which the various Biblical genealogies are constructed suggests that the writers of those genealogies had no belief whatsoever that Adam was anything other than a genuine historical individual who was the first member of the race.

Several texts of Scripture point to the idea that man was specially created by God. The idea of theistic evolution of man is an unbiblical idea and ought to be abandoned by those who profess to believe in a genuinely Biblical Christianity.

The Bible and Science at Odds

The Biblical idea of the origin of man and the evolutionary origin of man are mutually exclusive. At this particular point there must be conflict between Christianity and modern science as long as science maintains its current attitude with regard to the origin of man. Virtually any other areas of significant conflict between the Bible and earth history can be removed once it is seen that the Bible by no means unequivocally teaches a 144-hour, purely miraculous creation which took place only a few thousand years ago. Other conflicts are really pseudo-conflicts, but the conflict over the origin of man is real. It cannot be removed by reinterpreting the Bible, for the total Biblical data do not permit the latitude in interpretation that is afforded in Genesis 1. There is no point in Christians' retreating on this question simply to gain favor with the scientific community. Biblical Christianity must challenge science at this point.

The only way to soften this conflict is for all parties concerned to understand the nature of scientific inquiry. Laymen and scientists, Christian and non-Christian alike, must realize that science is incapable of explaining phenomena in other than natural, *mechanistic* terms. This is the essence of the method. The scientific approach to the world is incapable in itself of postulating and testing a supernatural activity of God or the devil. Hence it must be recognized that *scientific inquiry has its limits.* Science cannot exhaustively interpret everything. For example, science cannot determine whether or not a certain mountain-top vista is "beautiful." Truth may not always be explicable scientifically. The terms "true" and "scientific," although so often naively assumed to be interchangeable, are by no means identical. Science can "discover" and "explain" only in terms of the natural, but it is foolish to reason from this that something other than the natural is impossible.

In the matter of the origin of man on the earth, essentially four possibilities are available. Man could have been miraculously, directly created by God or some other supernatural agent. Man could have evolved gradually from pre-existent forms of life. Man could have developed by spontaneous generation from the earth. Man could have arrived on the earth from some other part of the universe. This last possibility, of course, simply pushes back the matter of ultimate origin and is therefore not a legitimate alternative. Of the three remaining choices, special creation cannot be verified *scientifically*. Science is thus left with two possibilities. Quite obviously the spontaneous generation of men from inanimate material is an absurdity, and so science really has available to it only one viable option, namely, the evolution of man from pre-existent animals. Now the fact that there are considerable variation in man and some apparent change in time is evidence that this choice may be correct. But, in effect, science has available to it only one hypothesis, evolution, and must do the best it can to fit the facts into that hypothesis.

There is, of course, great danger when science has only one hypothesis open to it and the available data at least crudely support that hypothesis. The result of such a situation is often scientific dogmatism. Science is guilty of dogmatism on this particular question. Evolution is the only hypothesis regarding the origin of man available to science, the evidence seems to support the hypothesis, therefore evolution is true. The faulty logic in this syllogism is revealed in the false identification of scientific verification with the truth. People will not accuse the Bible of error on the matter of the origin of man if once they realize that no other alternative is really possible for science. Science, by its very inability to verify a special creation, must therefore logically conflict with a theory of special creation. In such a situation science must recognize its limitations and must not be so insistent that its theory is true. This is especially vital in an emotional matter like the origin of man, a question on which scientific thinking has changed frequently as new discoveries are made. Knowledge of the prehistory of man is far too fragmentary for scientific dogma on this critical question. Science simply is not in a position to charge the Bible with error in this matter. Its tools are inadequate.

The Fossil Evidence

To appreciate more fully the debate over the origin of man, it would be helpful to have at least a rudimentary knowledge of the fossil material.[13] Fossil remains of men are found in rocks and deposits that are thought to be Pleistocene in age. The Pleistocene epoch has a complex history as evidenced by complicated stratigraphy. Much of Pleistocene stratigraphy is based on deposits that were formed during or between four major advances of the margins of great continental ice sheets in the northern hemisphere. Times during widespread advance of the sheet margin are termed *glacials;* times when the glacier margins receded very significantly are termed *interglacials.* Technical names for the glacials and interglacials are listed in Table 3. Human fossil remains are commonly dated in reference to the glacials and interglacials.

TABLE 3

Glacial and Interglacial Stages

	North American	European
4.	Wisconsinan (Middle and Late)	Würm
		Riss-Würm (Third Interglacial)
3.	Wisconsinan (Early)	Riss
	Sangamonian	Mindel-Riss (Second Interglacial)
2.	Illinoian	Mindel
	Yarmouthian	Günz-Mindel (First Interglacial)
1.	Kansan	Günz

Skeletal materials that have been found at archaeological sites from historical times are essentially the same as those of modern man, *Homo sapiens.* Progressively older hominid remains, however,

---

13. A helpful reference work on human fossil material is M. Day, *Guide to Fossil Man* (Cleveland: World, 1965).

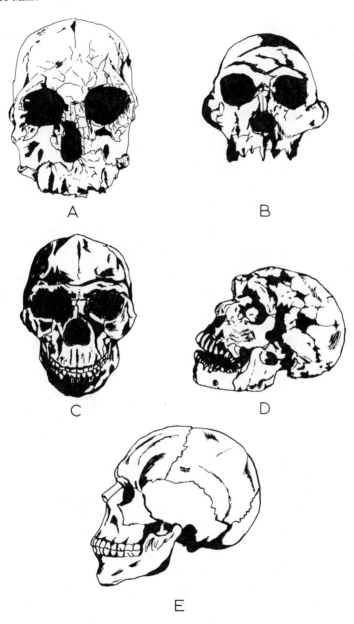

Figure 8. Skulls of fossil hominids and modern man. A. Skull 1470, the recent find of Richard Leakey in Kenya. This skull is older but more modern in appearance than most other ancient hominid remains. B. *Australopithecus* skull from Sterkfontein, South Africa. C. Peking skull (*Homo erectus*) from Choukoutien, China. D. Neanderthal skull (*Homo sapiens neanderthalensis*) from France. E. Modern man.

show increasing differences in skeletal structure from present-day
man (Figure 8). Numerous remains have been discovered in deposits
that date from the fourth (Würm) glaciation. Among these remains
are those of so-called Cro-Magnon man. Skeletal remains with the
general features of this race of men have been found throughout
western Europe. The general skeletal characteristics indicate that this
creature was very similar in appearance to modern man. The layman
finds the skulls of Cro-Magnon man to be virtually indistinguishable
from those of modern man. Associated with Cro-Magnon man are
advanced cultural remains. Stone and bone items were evidently used
as tools and ornaments. Cave paintings also were produced by these
extinct men. Remains of various animal species in caves with Cro-
Magnon man have helped to date these human remains from the time
of the fourth glaciation.

Numerous skulls and skeletons of Neanderthal man have also been
found in caves throughout much of Europe, in particular France and
Germany. Finding tool cultures and faunal remains associated with
many of the Neanderthal remains has helped to date Neanderthal
man from the fourth (Würm) glaciation. Neanderthal skulls differ
noticeably from those of modern man, yet they do appear to be
obviously human. The skulls are as large as those of modern man, but
the forehead recedes and the vault is low. The bone above the eye-
brows is quite pronounced and the jaw is slightly more pronounced
than in modern man. The rest of the skeletal material indicates that
there were other features characteristic of the Neanderthal. These
characteristic features do, however, fall within the wide range of the
skeletal variation of modern man. It is currently believed, contrary to
earlier opinion, that Neanderthal man stood and walked in an upright
position as does modern man. Evidence from the manner of the
burial of the skeletons suggests a belief in an afterlife on the part of
the Neanderthal. Neanderthal man is generally regarded today as a
subspecies of *Homo sapiens.*

Human remains from other parts of the world bear similarities to
both Neanderthal and modern man. Fossils from caves on Mount
Carmel in Israel (Tabun and Skuhl remains) are somewhat similar to
Neanderthal man and date from about the time of the Würm glaciation. Another skull, missing the lower jaw, was found in an excavated
cave in Zambia. The evidence suggests that the skull, referred to as
Rhodesian man, dates from the Upper Pleistocene epoch. Despite
many similarities to Neanderthal man, such as low forehead, some

investigators have pointed out that in many respects the Rhodesian man resembles *Homo sapiens*. Several skulls of so-called Solo man were discovered in Upper Pleistocene river terrace gravels in Indonesia. Some have considered Solo man as a primitive Neanderthal type, but one recent taxonomic classification has proposed the inclusion of Solo man as a subspecies of *Homo sapiens* (*Homo sapiens soloensis*) distinct from Neanderthal man (*Homo neanderthalensis*), Rhodesian man (*Homo rhodesiensis*), and modern man (*Homo sapiens*). Evidence from all these Upper Pleistocene remains suggests a rather wide range in variations of human skeletal structure. Probably these remains simply represent various races of ancient men.

Fossils that are similar to modern man have also been discovered in deposits that are older than the fourth glaciation. In Fontechevade, France, deposits dating from the third (Riss-Würm) interglacial yielded the top part of a human skull as well as another smaller skull fragment. Several anthropologists have suggested that these fragments are from individuals that more closely resembled modern man than Neanderthal man. On this account it has been suggested that Fontechevade man may be an ancestor of modern *Homo sapiens*, but this is by no means universally accepted.

A fairly complete skull was unearthed from a gravel deposit in Steinheim, Germany, that dates from the second (Mindel-Riss) interglacial age. No cultural artifacts were discovered with the skull. The skull shows a number of features that are similar to those of Neanderthal man and *Homo sapiens*, and it has been suggested that Steinheim man is ancestral to *Homo sapiens*.

A third very old find that greatly resembles modern man is a group of skull bones from Swanscombe, England. Three skull fragments fit together perfectly to form a nearly complete top part of a skull. The bones were discovered in river gravels that have been dated to the second (Mindel-Riss) interglacial time. The skull measurements indicate close similarity to modern man. Anthropologists J. S. Weiner and B. G. Campbell have emphasized the interrelatedness of such forms as Solo, Rhodesian, Neanderthal, and modern man. They regard these forms as a spectrum of varieties within one species, *Homo sapiens*, and have suggested that Swanscombe man was a Neanderthaloid type similar to the Steinheim and Skuhl specimens. A wide spectrum of essentially "modern" types of men has thus been discovered from deposits believed to be as old as 250,000 years.

A number of finds have been made in materials of Middle Pleistocene age which appear to be more primitive than the remains mentioned above. Included here are fossils from China and Indonesia, known colloquially as Peking man and Java man. In the past these forms have been given a variety of technical names such as *Pithecanthropus pekinensis,* but the designation *Homo erectus* has been increasingly applied to both types of remains. The deposits containing these fossil remains have been estimated to be from about 350,000 to 550,000 years old—about the time of the first (Günz) glaciation and first interglacial.

Remains of *Homo erectus* are represented by a number of complete skulls, skull fragments, and other skeletal parts. Available evidence indicates that on the average these men had a smaller braincase that modern man and the extinct races of *Homo sapiens.* In addition the jaw is slightly more pronounced than in Neanderthal man, as are the eyebrow ridges. The forehead also is quite flattened in comparison with modern man. Other skeletal evidence indicates that these extinct men walked upright. Crude-tools have been found with some of the remains as well as ash heaps and pieces of charcoal that indicate that *Homo erectus* used fire.

The finds thus far discussed suggest that as we go back in time men were more "primitive" in their appearance. There has been progressive change in skull morphology through time. Despite these changes, the layman, upon looking at photographs of these various fossil skulls, would likely not hesitate in referring to any of them as genuine men.

A more perplexing group of extinct creatures are the australopithecines. Remains of several forms of *Australopithecus* have been discovered in parts of eastern and southern Africa in cave deposits and stratified sedimentary layers ranging from about one to three million years in age. Many of these remains, including skull fragments and other parts of the skeleton, have been uncovered in the now famous Olduvai Gorge of Tanzania by the Leakey family. In a general way forms of *Australopithecus* have been grouped into two species. One species, *Australopithecus africanus,* was a smaller, light-framed variety whereas *Australopithecus robustus* was a heavier variety. Both types were much shorter (about four feet tall) and had a much smaller brain (about one-third the cranial capacity) than modern man. Skeletal evidence indicates that these creatures walked essentially erect.

The skulls are considerably different from the forms previously noted. The forehead and top of the cranium are very much flattened. In many specimens there is a bony ridge (sagittal crest) running along the top of the cranium. The cheekbones are very wide and the jaws are quite pronounced (prognathous) so that the creature had a slightly muzzled appearance that is lacking in modern man. The general impression one has of the skulls is that they represent extinct apelike rather than manlike forms. This impression of apelikeness must, however, be tempered by two further observations. The first observation is that the teeth of specimens of *Australopithecus* bear far more resemblance to those of man than to those of extinct or modern apes. Evolutionists have suggested that this feature indicates a significant tendency or transition toward humanization. The second observation is that very primitive kinds of stone and bone tools have been discovered at the australopithecine sites, suggesting that these creatures used tools and perhaps even made them.

The Bible and the Antiquity of the Human Race

What is the Bible-believing scientist to do with these fossils? Can he tell where in time among this group of fossils the creation of Adam took place? Can he tell which of these ancient manlike fossils represent genuine men? It might be objected by many Christians that none of the fossils we have discussed, with the possible exception of Cro-Magnon, could be true men inasmuch as the Bible teaches that the human race is only a few thousand years old at the most. Hence, Neanderthal "man" could not have been a real man if he lived forty thousand years ago. But in the area of the antiquity of man considerable caution must be exercised. In the first place it cannot be proved from Scripture that man is only a few thousand years old. A literal reading of the genealogies of Genesis 5 and 11 does indeed suggest that the human race has been in existence only a few thousand years, but various scholars, especially Warfield,[14] have shown that Hebrew genealogies differ from western ones. When, for example, the Hebrew in Genesis 11:12 says that Arphaxad lived 35 years and begat Salah, it is not necessary to believe that Salah was the son of Arphaxad in the strict sense of the term. Salah could just as well have been the

---

14. B. B. Warfield, "On the Antiquity and the Unity of the Human Race," in *Biblical and Theological Studies* (Philadelphia: Presbyterian and Reformed, 1952), pp. 238-61.

grandson or great-grandson of Arphaxad. The point is that Hebrew genealogies may very well be omitting one or more generations when they say that x begat y. That this is the case is evident from the example we have chosen, for the New Testament account in Luke 3:35-36 indicates that Cainan was an ancestor of Salah and a descendant of Arphaxad. Cainan's name is omitted in the Genesis genealogy. It is therefore entirely possible that one, or a few, or a great many generations may have been omitted from the two Genesis genealogies. A similar kind of omission was previously seen to occur in the Matthew 1 genealogy. Sufficient Biblical data are simply not available for the rendering of a firm decision one way or another. Thus we do not really know how long a time span is covered by Genesis 5 and 11. It may be only a few thousand years. It may be tens or hundreds of thousands of years. We simply do not know. The Bible does not tell us the age of the human race.

It might also be objected that the so-called fossil men could not have been true men because their life spans, according to scientific investigation, were about the same as ours whereas the Bible teaches that early man had an extremely long life span. The first descendants of Adam lived to be 900 years old! Paleoanthropology has found no evidence of men who lived anywhere near that long. Again caution is in order. A careful look at the text of Genesis discloses that lives of great duration are ascribed only to the descendants of Seth, that is, to a particular branch of the human race that ultimately led to the appearance of Jesus Christ. This branch is the so-called godly line that included such saintly men as Enoch, Noah, and Abraham. The Bible says nothing about the life spans of the descendants of Cain, one of Adam's other sons. Why then should it be a necessity to believe that these individuals lived such long lives? There is good reason for believing that many individuals in Cain's line (and possibly those descendants of Seth who were not in direct line from Seth to Abraham) were relatively short-lived because there is good reason to believe that sin abounded among his descendants in a way that it did not among the members of the godly line. In the fourth chapter of Genesis are records of two murders. The first of the murders is of righteous Abel by his brother Cain. Later Cain's descendant Lamech boasts to his wives about a murder that he has committed. In Genesis 6 is a report of extremely great wickedness of the human race outside of Noah's immediate family. If murder was a common practice and men were given over to debauchery and debasement, there seems no pressing reason to doubt that where sin abounded, there also life spans were shortened. So it should not be a great surprise that fossils of ancient men give no evidence of great longevity, for the number of individuals who actually did live long lives may have been small.

The Christian and Paleoanthropological Investigation

Another consideration in the matter of the antiquity of man is that the ages assigned to fossil men may not be entirely correct. As science progresses, dating techniques may be refined and new facts may be discovered that will alter our present ideas about dating earth materials. If so, it may turn out that fossil men did not live as long ago as science presently believes. On the other hand new data may suggest that these remains are actually older than is currently believed. The whole area of the antiquity of the human race demands considerable caution.

Furthermore no one knows what Adam looked like. Much as we might desire it, no photographs of Adam and Eve have been provided on the page opposite the text of Genesis 2. What might Adam have looked like? Did he necessarily have the skeletal and facial structure of modern man? Could he have looked like a Neanderthal man? Even more daring, could Adam have been a creature like *Australopithecus*? In order to answer these questions properly, we must first answer the question, "What is man?" Is man simply to be identified by a particular skeletal structure or range of structures? Is man identifiable and distinguishable from other animals on the basis of ability to make and use stone and bone tools? Is he identifiable on the basis of artistic ability or use of fire? Is he identifiable on the basis of some sort of religious expression?

The only way that the question, "What is man?" can be properly answered is by appeal to Scripture. Scripture indicates that the characteristic which distinguishes man from all other creatures is his image-bearing nature. Man bears the image of God. No other creature does. What this must mean above all is that man is a religious creature. The one feature which will prove the identity of a fossil as being truly man is solid evidence of religious belief. Recall the case of the Neanderthal burials. On the other hand, no evidence of religion has been found with the remains of *Australopithecus*, but this does not necessarily mean that he was not a religious being.

But can other criteria be relied on to help determine whether or not a certain fossil creature was genuinely man? For example, does not the use of tools indicate the presence of genuine man? Keep in mind, however, that some animals of the present do use simple kinds of tools and some in a sense manufacture them. Bowerbirds use tools. So do chimpanzees. Perhaps the possibility should be kept open that there have been highly intelligent apes, now extinct, which were capable of making simple stone and bone tools, perhaps in imitation of real men who were in the vicinity. Although various fossil creatures do have simple tool cultures associated with them, this does not mean that these creatures were necessarily true men. Further research may shed some light on this problem.

The Christian anthropologist who believes the Biblical doctrine of the special creation of man is thus confronted with a real dilemma. His problem is that he cannot identify from the fossil remains the time when true man first appeared on the earth. He cannot do this because he is unable to say with certainty whether or not such primitive, "transitional" forms as *Australopithecus* and *Homo erectus* were genuinely human.

Suppose, for example, that the Christian paleoanthropologist believes that *Australopithecus* is an extinct ape and that *Homo erectus* and those fossil manlike forms dating after *Homo erectus* are genuine men. Suppose that this belief is based on the appearance of the skulls. After all *Homo erectus* looks more or less human whereas *Australopithecus* doesn't look human. On this basis further suppose that our Christian paleoanthropologist dates the special creation of man at about 500,000 years ago. There is real danger in postulating this kind of an idea, especially in a scientific journal, for postulating that man was specially created at a certain time runs the risk that someday much older forms of *Homo erectus* might be found. In this case the date for special creation would have to be moved back to, say, one million years before the present. An idea of the date of special creation could also be overthrown by further discoveries of manlike forms that might be transitional between *Homo erectus* and *Australopithecus africanus*.[15] If such a discovery were ever made (it is, of course, also possible that no such transitional form ever did

---

15. Fascinating new discoveries have been made since the writing of the text of this book. For one popular account, see R. E. Leakey, "Skull 1470," in *National Geographic* 143 (1973), pp. 819-29.

exist), then man would have to be redefined. Could one consider the new form genuine man or not? Again the Christian, who rejects the idea of the transition from ape to man in history, would be faced with the problem of identifying true man! On the basis of these considerations it is probably virtually impossible for the Christian to identify, from the fossil record, the time when special creation occurred. Nor does Scripture help him to identify this time. Perhaps the most useful task for the Christian paleoanthropologist would be to evaluate the available fossil material carefully and cautiously and to show that the evidence for an evolution from ape to man is much more tenuous than we are sometimes led to believe. It might be learned that man has simply undergone a small degree of physical change through time and that physically he is much more variable than was hitherto thought.

Evolution and Its Theological Consequences

A further aspect of the origin of man now confronts us. If science is so strongly in favor of the idea that man has evolved from animals and if the Christian can never prove special creation from the fossil record, then is there any reason to hold so vehemently to special creation? Is anything lost to the Christian religion if the evolution of man from animals is accepted? Even if convinced that Scripture teaches the falsity of an evolutionary origin of man, do we really lose anything if it is simply admitted that Scripture is in error at this point?

The admission of error in Scripture is extremely serious, and the theological consequences of a fallible Bible are profound. This point will not be pursued, however, in spite of its great importance. What cannot be overlooked is the fact that the evolutionary origin of man has radical implications for the whole Christian story. If man evolved, the whole of Christian, genuinely Biblical theology and ethics falls to the ground.

Suppose, for the sake of argument, that mankind really has evolved from some sort of prehuman animal life over a period of millions of years. Also assume, as theistic evolutionists insist, that God has directed providentially the entire process of man's evolution. Then consider the nature of such a being with particular reference to the presence of evil within him.

In order to discuss the nature of an evolved man, one must rely to a large extent upon current scientific opinion about the nature of evolving animals. It is increasingly believed that animals have various behavioral and social patterns or instincts which characterize particular species.[16] For example, many animals have very strong territorial instincts and will seek to defend their territory against intruders. Most dogs will become antagonistic when another dog or even a person strays across a certain boundary. A battle between the intruder and the defender may ensue. The same can be said about fish, birds, and other animals. The point is that the trespassing of property boundaries by intruder animals is a natural thing. There is nothing unusual about this sort of action. It is not a sin against the law of God. It is only a way of life among the animals. Moreover, the "hostility" or "hatred" and the violence on the part of the defender are also instinctive. This responsive action is expected. It is the way of life and cannot be construed as a sin, for it is the natural manner for the animal to react. Hostility and infringement of territorial rights are part of the very fabric and structure of animal life. The animal cannot be condemned for behaving in such a manner. He is behaving only in accordance with his instincts.

Moreover, many animal species demonstrate a certain social hierarchy, pecking order, or stratification. Each member of a certain group has its place within the group and in all probability the group has its recognized leader. At times lower members of the group may attempt to move up the social scale or attempt to become the group leader. Such attempts to take over leadership will be answered with repressive or hostile measures. The pretender to leadership is firmly dealt with and put back in his place. Such actions in the animal realm can only be regarded as instinctive. They are natural and therefore cannot be regarded as some kind of sin. It is difficult to conceive of God as one who would punish a bird that sought to take over by force the position of leadership from the top bird in the flock. The power struggle, like the defense of territory, is but one aspect of the way of life for the bird.

If man is regarded as having evolved from the animal kingdom, there should be no real difficulty in seeing the strong sense of property ownership and defense and the development of social strati-

---

16. For a fascinating popular presentation of these ideas see R. Ardrey, *African Genesis* (New York: Dell, 1961), and *The Territorial Imperative* (New York: Dell, 1966). The ideas popularized by Ardrey have, of course, not been universally accepted by anthropologists.

fication or authority structure as having been brought along via evolution from man's animal heritage. If human evolution is true, there is little reason to doubt that these social structures were derived from animals. The existence of these patterns in the animal and in man, however, is not the point of concern. Rather the question must be raised as to the meaning of the actions of individual animals or men in the context of these structures or patterns.

It has been noted that among animals there are individuals which for some reason or other trespass the boundaries of a neighbor's territory or challenge the authority of the leader of the group. Those whose boundaries are crossed or whose authority is challenged retaliate. It has been noted that these actions are simply part of the way of life for animals. No sin against the law of God is involved. Now it is difficult to see why an evolved human race would not also have individuals that trespass boundaries or seek to challenge established authorities. And it is difficult to see why an evolved human race should not have individuals whose normal response to trespassing or to challenge against authority will be some sort of hostile retaliation. Furthermore if these actions are to be expected in an evolved human race, then it is clear that these actions are simply a part of human nature. It is human nature to try to overthrow governmental authority occasionally. It is human nature to liquidate the political opponent who seeks to remove the reins of government from your hands. It is human nature to curse angrily at someone who steps on your flower garden. These are normal, expected actions that have been derived from our animal ancestry. If this is human nature, that nature has been given to us by God. He has, according to the theistic evolutionist, controlled the evolutionary process which culminated in man. If this is indeed so, then the hostile actions of human beings cannot be regarded as sins. They cannot fairly be punished with eternal destruction if God has made man this way. The exceeding sinfulness of sin, however, really consists in the fact that man originally, by nature, was capable of keeping perfectly God's law. He was utterly free of hatred and hostility. The evolutionary process, however, renders him incapable of keeping that law perfectly.

Acceptance of an evolutionary view of the origin of man thus introduces a distortion into the gospel. Sin is not a transgression of the law of God, nor a violation of the original nature of man. Sin is now really nothing more than an unpleasant characteristic or action that it would be nice to eliminate from society. The sinner, when confronted with the fact of his sinfulness, can with a considerable degree of legitimacy make excuses for his sin. He can to a large degree blame his behavior on his biological heritage. He can even to some extent lay the blame, according to the theistic evolutionist construction, on God. After all, has not God directed the process which has given him a certain biochemical structure together with all of its instinctual behavior patterns? How then can the sinner truly be guilty before God when sin is built into his very structure?

There also remains the further problem, in the theistic evolutionist interpretation, of the meaning of Christ's death. What is meant by the statement that Christ died for our sin? Careful reading of the Bible, and particularly the New Testament, ought to make very plain that Christ's death on the cross did not change our biochemical structure so that we no longer follow certain instinctive behavioral patterns. In fact it ought to be clear Christ died so that His people might have their sins forgiven by God, and that through His Spirit He might renew the innermost being of His people by giving to them a new heart of flesh and spirit. Adopting a theistic evolutionist approach to the origin of man places the entire structure of Christian theology and ethics in a most precarious position.

8

The Fall,
the Curse, and Science

If the Biblical view of the beginnings of man is adopted, that is, man as a special creation of God originally characterized by genuine holiness and righteousness, then the Biblical view of the origin of sin in the human race must also be adopted. The Christian who believes in the special creation of man must also trace sin to the fall of Adam and Eve in the Garden of Eden as recorded in Genesis 3. As a result of the fall, a curse was pronounced by God. It is particularly important to discover, if possible, the nature and extent of that curse. In Genesis 3, as a result of the disobedience of Adam and Eve and the subtle treachery of the serpent, a threefold curse was pronounced on the serpent, the woman, and the ground. Are the consequences of this curse limited essentially to mankind and to the realm of spiritual beings, or has the curse also wrought drastic consequences on the entire cosmos that can be detected geologically or that will affect the practice of geology?

Neo-Catastrophism and the Curse

The problem of the cosmic relevance of the curse is especially important because the curse has played a very significant role in the geological theory of the Biblical neo-catastrophists. Prior to Adam's fall, it is said, the universe operated in accordance with creative,

159

order-building laws of thermodynamics. Since the fall the universe
has been subject to the familiar laws of thermodynamics of the present time. The first law of thermodynamics states that matter and
energy cannot be produced or destroyed in any natural process. The
second law states that during every natural process some of the
energy involved in the energy exchange is converted into forms that
are no longer available for performance of useful work. That is, the
amount of energy that is available for work is continuously de-
creasing. Another way of viewing this law is to note that the universe
is gradually becoming more disordered. Scientists observe that the
entropy of the universe is always increasing, so that in effect the
universe is running down. Neo-catastrophists see the entropy principle as a principle of *decay* which cannot have been built into the
structure of the "very good" world as originally formed by God
(Genesis 1:31). This principle of decay must have become enmeshed
in the cosmic fabric as an aspect of the curse pronounced after the
sin of Adam. The universe is thus said to share in the punishment of
the sin of Adam.

Another aspect of the neo-catastrophist interpretation of the curse
is that prior to the fall there is said to have been no death, disease, or
pain in the world. Genesis 1:29-30 is said to teach that both Adam
and all the animals were strictly vegetarians. Because of the lack of
death in the prelapsarian world no fossils, in particular no animal
fossils, could have been formed until after Adam first sinned. Death,
disease, and pain were all introduced into the world as punishments
for the sin of Adam.

The Biblical Data on the Curse

Only a very careful look at Scripture will reveal the actual implications of the curse. The account of the curse is presented in Genesis
3:14-19. The curse is pronounced on three recipients: the serpent,
the woman, and the ground. In the case of the ground, however, it is
not the ground itself but the man Adam who is addressed by God.
The curse is pronounced on the ground for Adam's sake. Nowhere in
this narrative is it said that the entire cosmos underwent any kind of
drastic transformation, and nowhere is it said that the animal world
experienced sudden structural changes (that lions, for example,
suddenly developed large canine teeth for freshly arisen carnivorous
tendencies).

The curse on the serpent cannot be extrapolated to the total animal kingdom. It is true that the Authorized Version says that the serpent is cursed above all cattle, and above every beast of the field, suggesting that the cattle and beasts of the field were also cursed but to a lesser degree than the serpent. E. J. Young, however, maintains that this is not at all the case. He says that

> the thought is not that of comparison, as though the Lord had said that all the beasts would be cursed, but that the serpent would be cursed more than any. Rather, in the curse the serpent is separated from the other beasts. Whereas they are free, he is now in a peculiar bondage. Upon him alone of all the beasts does God pronounce the curse, for he alone had tempted the woman.[1]

With this point Keil is in agreement: "the curse . . . was not pronounced upon all the beasts, but upon the serpent alone."[2]

Young also notes that some people have suggested that with the curse structural changes occurred in the snake. His comments on this point are most instructive.

> But did the serpent always go upon his belly? Did he always crawl along in the tortuous manner that we now see? There are those who think that before the fall, he was upright, and that he walked upright. It was the fall, so they hold, which brought about an actual change in his mode of locomotion. Before the fall, we are told, the entire animal world was different from what it is now, and so the serpent must have undergone a great change. It also must have been bright and attractive so that it would have drawn Eve's attention. This may be but we must remember that the Bible is written for men who live after the fall took place and after man was driven from Eden. When, therefore, the Bible speaks of a serpent, we bring to mind only the reptile which we know. We know no serpents but those which crawl about in what seems to us a tortuous fashion. If before the fall the serpent possessed some other mode of locomotion, we do not know that fact, and there is really nothing in the Scripture to indicate it.
>
> In the eyes of man the repulsive manner in which the serpent crawls is his punishment.[3]

Scripture makes no mention of the sudden introduction of death or violence into the animal world *or even into the realm of the*

---

1. E. J. Young, *Genesis 3* (London: Banner of Truth, 1966), p. 97.

2. C. F. Keil and F. Delitzsch, *Biblical Commentary on the Old Testament, I, The Pentateuch* (Grand Rapids: Wm. B. Eerdmans, 1949), p. 98.

3. Young, *Genesis 3*, pp. 97-98.

serpent itself. Although Keil views the vanity of the irrational creation as related to the sin of man, he agrees that this vanity "is not to
be regarded as the effect of the curse, which was pronounced upon
the serpent, having fallen upon the whole animal world. . . ."[4] The
curse on the serpent is that he is doomed to be regarded as a dis-
gusting, degraded, repulsive creature. There are, to be sure,
extensions of the curse on the serpent to Satan and the demonic
realm, but we tread on very thin ice if we extend this curse to other
animals or even to the rest of the physical world. The curse on the
serpent does not involve death for other animals nor does it involve
structural changes in the animal world.

The curse on the woman seems to be relatively straightforward. It
is difficult to see any cosmic implications here. If the curse does have
cosmic implications they must be derived from the curse on the
ground for Adam's sake. To find such implications, however, seems
to be a dangerous practice bordering on speculation. E. J. Young
writes:

> Ground is something inanimate and not responsible. How is it possi-
> ble for a curse to be placed upon it? What is meant of course is that
> the curse upon the ground is with respect to man, so that the one
> who will feel the effects of the curse is not the ground inasmuch as
> the ground is insensible and without life but man himself.[5]

Young also observes that whereas the curse on the woman strikes in
the heart of her being, the curse on the ground "strikes the man in
that it affects the basis or foundation from which he must derive his
substance."[6] Adam will now find that "no longer will the earth
produce with the ease that was characteristic of Eden."[7] In light of
these observations it seems difficult to believe that all matter in the
cosmos is cursed and suddenly begins to operate under an entirely
new set of laws.

The fact that thorns and thistles will come forth for man does not
mean that thorns and thistles did not exist before the fall. It may
simply mean that they did not exist in the garden where work was a
pleasure and that man is now being driven into a more hostile en-

4. Keil and Delitzsch, *The Pentateuch*, p. 98.

5. Young, *Genesis 3*, p. 131.

6. Ibid., p. 132.

7. Ibid.

vironment characterized by such plants.[8] Or it may simply mean that thorns and thistles will become much more abundant than they once were. In either case man's labor is to become far more difficult than it was in Eden. Genesis 3, however, tells us nothing about any drastic cosmic renovations or devastations that accompanied the fall.

Appeal is made by Whitcomb and Morris and the neo-catastrophist school to Romans 8:18-23 as evidence for a cosmic curse. The creation groans and travails in pain. The creature is subject to the bondage of corruption. There seems to be little doubt that Paul is here envisioning the effects of sin in the universe, but is he here thinking of the universe as operating under a whole new set of thermodynamic laws because of the curse? Young has briefly reflected on this point:

> It is true that the whole creation is under bondage and groaneth and travaileth together, as the apostle says in Romans 8; but this is not the curse mentioned here (the curse on the serpent). The creation is in bondage because of man's sin; it was man himself who plunged the whole creation into bondage, not the serpent. In this curse the serpent stands above and unique, and in this curse he is separated from the animals. He of all the animals receives the curse, whether they be the tame animals or the wild beasts which roam the fields.[9]

Is Romans 8:18-23, in reflecting on the bondage in the world, referring back to the curse on the ground in Genesis 3:17-19? Numerous exegetes, such as Hodge, Murray, and Vos,[10] do refer this text to the fall of Adam. One must, however, exercise considerable caution in interpretation of the text. The thought is developed that the creature, viewed by most commentators as the irrational creation, both animate and inanimate, was made subject to vanity. The text, however, does not tell when this occurred. Nor is it possible to speak with exactness about the meaning of the subjection to vanity, the corruption, and the bondage. Does this text refer to the death of animals? That is a possibility, but the text itself does not directly speak of death, nor does it speak of death in relation to man's sin. If

---

8. A. H. Lewis, "The Localization of the Garden of Eden," in *Bulletin of the Evangelical Theological Society* 11 (1968), pp. 169-75.

9. Young, *Genesis 3*, p. 97.

10. Cf. C. Hodge, *Commentary on the Epistle to the Romans* (Grand Rapids: Wm. B. Eerdmans, 1886), pp. 269-75; J. Murray, *The Epistle to the Romans*, Vol. I (Grand Rapids: Wm. B. Eerdmans, 1959), pp. 300-05; and G. Vos, *The Pauline Eschatology* (Grand Rapids: Wm. B. Eerdmans, 1961), pp. 84-85.

Romans 8:18-23 is reflecting on Genesis 3:17-19 and the curse on the ground for man's sake, neither text says anything specific either of death or of the animals. It is particularly important in dealing with the passage in Romans 8 to recognize that the contrast presented by the material is not between *what once was* and *what now is.* Rather the emphasis is on the contrast between the present and the eschatological. Paul does not refer to *past* ideal conditions; he does refer to *future* ideal conditions. He refers to the glory that *shall be* revealed in us, to the glorious liberty of the children of God, and to the redemption of the body. Romans 8 looks forward, not backward. Hence although the curse may form the background for the deficient present situation described in the text, there is no express statement to that effect and it is unwarranted to infer too much about the nature and extent of the curse from this text.

Scripture does not say anywhere whether or not animals died before the fall. The only mention of death in the Genesis account is with reference to *man.* If man eats the forbidden fruit, then in the day he eats thereof *he* will surely die (Genesis 2:17). To extend this death penalty to the irrational animals is a speculation. In fact the argument has been used that if Adam were to have some idea of what is meant by death, he would need to have some example of death around him. If Adam were to understand the threat of death spoken by God, he would likely have observed this phenomenon in the animals around him. Moreover, there is no reason to see death in the animal realm as being unnatural or unusual before the fall. For man, however, death would be a great horror, for man and man alone was made in the image of God. These arguments in support of the idea that death occurred in the animal kingdom before the fall must be regarded only as educated speculations. Scripture is silent on the question of the death of animals prior to the fall.

It is possible that the vanity and bondage of the creature mentioned in Romans 8 are not merely death, but rather the needlessly cruel and unnatural exploitation and abuse of the creation by man. When man was created he received the cultural mandate (Genesis 1:28). Man was not only commanded to be fruitful and multiply and fill the earth, but he was also told to subdue the earth and to exercise dominion over the fish, the fowl, and every living thing that moved on the earth. Man, as God's representative, was to utilize the creation that God had provided for him and to develop it for the glory of God and the service of man. Now almost certainly the idea of man's dominion would necessitate the death of some of the animate creatures. Does not the cultural mandate give to Adam the right to eat a fish or a clam? Could not Adam have used the skins of animals for clothing in the event it should be needed? If the objection is made that God permitted Adam to eat only plant material (Genesis 1:29), it must be observed that no prohibition of meat-eating is anywhere to be found. This observation is especially striking in the light of Genesis 2:17, where God did circumscribe man's activity. There man was not prohibited from eating meat but from eating the fruit of a specific tree. It is thus entirely possible that the cultural mandate involves man's careful, selective use of the entire spectrum of created things for his own good and God's glory. There is no pressing reason to argue that this excludes death. How else was Adam to have dominion over the fish?

When man fell into sin, however, he no longer observed the cultural mandate. He no longer acted as God's steward over the creation. Instead he regarded the earth as his own property rather than God's. Since the fall man has ruthlessly exploited creation. Mankind now needlessly tortures and slaughters the animal. Are not animals subject to vanity and corruption now because men act as tyrants rather than benevolent rulers? Men recklessly slash the backs of Florida's manatees with rakes and the propellers of their high-speed motorboats. Young boys corner ground hogs and senselessly stab them with knives. Men, just for sport, fill the bellies of ducks and pheasants with buckshot. The seabirds have become soaked with oil because of our carelessness. Is it any wonder that the fear and dread of man is upon the beast when we are so often the purveyors of meaningless and cruel death and torture? And has man been a good steward of the earth itself? Or has he selfishly exploited the earth for his own ends? Are we not guilty of subjecting creation to vanity and corruption when we continually pour filth into our rivers and lakes, when we throw trash out our automobile windows, when we scar the earth in digging for its treasures and then fail to heal the wounds? There is no question that the universe is in anguish because of man's sin. Even the moon has now begun to be a refuse heap of the solar system. The plain fact is that man as sinner automatically carries with him the curse. He will succeed in marring creation wherever he goes. There is no question that creation groans and travails in pain because of man, but the Scriptural data are not sufficiently specific to state that death first occurred in the animal realm at the fall of

Adam. Above all it would seem to be an utterly unwarranted speculation to say that the first and second laws of thermodynamics took
effect at the fall of Adam. What is clear from Romans 8 is that
creation will be delivered from the present state of affairs at the
return of Christ and in this fact the Christian is to rejoice.

Psalm 104 lends some credence to the idea that death occurred
before the fall and that the animals could eat meat. This psalm
reflects on the six days of creation and praises God for His ordering
of the universe in such a way that His creatures are blessed and
enriched. Psalm 104:21 reflects on the activity of the lions in the
light of God's regulation of night and day by means of the sun. The
predatory activity of the lions is viewed as a perfectly natural
phenomenon in the context of the activity of the sun with respect to
the earth. In other words God created the sun in such a way that the
lions, among other creatures, might be able to carry out the func-
tions which God had ordained for them. Similar thoughts are expressed in verses 25-30, where the food-gathering activities of man
and beast in the sea are viewed in the light of creation. Verse 29 even
reflects on the death of the creature. All the thoughts of this psalm
are seen in the light of God's good creation. There is no indication in
the psalm of a drastic disruption of nature because of the fall.

Further insight into the nature of the curse is afforded by a glance
at a few additional texts of Scripture. There are several instances in
which effects in the realm of nature are related to the wickedness of
the people. Isaiah 24:4-7 speaks of the earth-devouring curse in relation to the transgression of the earth's inhabitants. In Psalm
107:33-34 we read of God's turning rivers into a wilderness, water-
springs into dry ground, and fruitful lands into barrenness because of
the wickedness of those who dwell in the land. Jeremiah 50:38 says
that a drought is upon the waters of Babylon because it is a land of
graven images. Haggai 1 speaks of the leanness of the land—heaven
withholds the dew and earth its fruit. A drought is pronounced on
the land, the mountains, the corn, the new wine, the oil, the
products of the ground, the men, the cattle, and all the labor of the
hands. This curse is the result of the fact that the house of God is
still in ruins while the people dwell comfortably in their ceiled
houses.

The curses pronounced in these texts do not involve new regimes
in the government of the universe. They do not involve structural
changes in the cow, the grape, or water. They do not involve the

introduction of new laws into the universe. These curses come about through God's providentially ordering the existing laws and structures and processes of nature so that they result in punishment rather than blessing for man.

It would seem that if this idea is applied to the initial curse at the fall of Adam, some of the more fantastic theories that arise in connection with the curse can be avoided. The curse on the ground does not involve the creation of new kinds of plants known as thistles. It does not involve a whole new set of laws in the government of the universe. The curse means rather that God will now so order the existing structures of the cosmos through the laws He has already created that man's life will be a struggle instead of a blessing. God now orders the weather patterns in such a way that Adam will have to sweat out an existence from the ground. It will be much easier for the hardy thistles to survive in the thirsty ground than for the life-giving crops which Adam will have to grow. A curse in Scripture always involves that which was meant originally to be a blessing for man. Because of sin the elements of nature are turned against man by God, who controls whatever comes to pass.

Prophecy, to some extent, bears on conditions in the world prior to the entrance of sin. Many passages in Scripture promise an eschatological restitution and renovation of the heavens and the earth. When Christ returns to set up His everlasting kingdom, all sorts of wonderful transformations will occur. Isaiah 11:6, for example, sees that in the days of Messiah "the wolf also shall dwell with the lamb, and the leopard shall lie down with the kid; and the calf and the young lion and the fatling together; and a little child shall lead them." Other texts speak of similar conditions in the great Messianic future. Many commentators view these passages as implying a return to prelapsarian conditions and therewith postulate that prior to Adam's fall there was no violence or antagonism whatsoever among the animals. It is, however, unwarranted to insist on the basis of the prophetic texts that so-called ideal conditions existed at first. Moreover, the eschatological projections do not simply depict a return to the conditions of Eden; instead they depict a decided advance or progress over those conditions. According to Genesis, in the primitive earth there was a sun, a moon, day and night, and a sea. Revelation, however, in speaking of the Messiah's eternal kingdom, namely the new heavens and new earth, reports in symbolic terms that the city of God has no need of the sun or the moon (Revelation 21:23).

There is no night in the city of God (Revelation 22:5). There is no more sea in the new order of things (Revelation 21:1). Man himself is not to be restored to the state of Eden but will advance beyond it. Man will no longer marry but will be as the angels in heaven (Mark 12:24-25). His resurrection body will be like that of Christ (I Corinthians 15:50-53; Philippians 3:21; I John 3:2). I Corinthians 15 in particular presents a sharp contrast between the original Adam and Christ, between created man and resurrected man. The first Adam was created a living soul; the second Adam was a life-giving spirit. The first Adam had a physical body; the resurrected Christian will have a spiritual body. Men now bear the image of the first Adam in their possession of *physical* bodies, bodies that are fitted to existence on this earth, bodies that are susceptible to corruption because of the very possibility of falling into sin. Christians will at the resurrection bear the image of the second Adam from heaven in their possession of *spiritual* bodies, bodies that will be infused with life, bodies that will be utterly insusceptible to death and corruption because there will be *no* possibility in heaven of another fall into sin. In light of these Scriptural statements it can clearly be seen that not all the glorious conditions of the eternal kingdom were present on earth prior to the fall.

In summary, the most that can be said with certainty about the effect of the fall on geological phenomena is that it introduced death and suffering into the human race for the first time. Genesis 2:17 and Romans 5:12 make this crystal clear. It cannot be proved from the Scripture that the curse resulted in anything other than pain, sorrow, agonizing labor, and death for man and degradation for the serpent. Ideas about structural changes in the animals, death among animals, and drastic transformations in the laws of nature such as the laws of thermodynamics must from a Scriptural perspective forever remain pure speculations. The Christian geologist is under no Biblical obligation to tie himself to some curse-controlled theory of paleontology or cosmology. This conclusion further supports the idea that the Christian geologist may study the rocks of the creation period in terms of the laws and processes that now are operative in the world.

Part of the curse on Adam and Eve is that they were driven out of the garden, out of the presence of God, and into a world where man would be subject to the hostilities of disease and violence, heat and cold, and all other kinds of annoyances. Revelation 22 tells us that in the new heavens and the new earth the curse will be lifted (verse 3) and that the people of God will again have access to the tree of life and to the perfect conditions of the kingdom in which they shall reign for ever and ever with the Lord God who gives them light.

9

The Flood

No study of the relationship between Scripture and earth history would be complete without a consideration of the role of Noah's flood in geological history. The story of this flood is recorded in Genesis 6:1–9:17. Despite the attempt of critics to regard the story as we have it as a compilation from different sources, the story is here regarded as a unity. The account of the flood says that all the fountains of the great deep were broken up and the windows of heaven were opened. The rains fell for forty days and nights, and eventually the mountains were covered. All flesh, inclusive of the birds, the beasts, the creeping things, and man, was destroyed from the face of the ground. At the end of about one year the flood waters receded, and Noah and his family disembarked from their ark onto dry ground. The story is not only very impressive as an account of God's judgment upon the sin of a wicked world but also as a description of an apparently significant geological phenomenon.

The report of Noah's flood has, perhaps more than any other story in the Bible, exercised men's imaginations. The flood story has, of course, been regarded as pure myth but generally is seen as having roots in some historical event. In the Bible-believing world the flood story has always been accepted as a true account of a real, historical phenomenon. Some have regarded the flood as a very large-scale inundation of the Mesopotamian region, but other scholars have insisted on the global nature of the flood. Indeed some have maintained that the flood rearranged the entire face of the earth. Moreover, scholars of varying shades of opinion have thought they have discovered fairly convincing physical evidence for the flood. Sir Leonard Woolley, the great archaeologist, found thick layers of flood silt in his diggings at Ur and related them to the activity of Noah's flood.[1] A host of Christian writers have attempted to explain fossiliferous strata as the result of a global flood. A sizeable literature has been built up to support the idea of a global flood and to interpret the geological phenomena of the earth in terms of it.[2]

The Role of the Flood in Geological History

The Biblical data tend to support the idea that the flood was essentially global in nature, although it is worthy of consideration that the story was written from the point of view of an individual experiencing the flood. The arguments for a local flood seem to be rendered rather weak in the light of God's promise never again to cut off all flesh or destroy the earth with a flood (Genesis 9:11), a promise that seems to have universal implications.

If the Bible is indeed speaking of a global flood, it is not necessary to be committed to some specific flood theory. There are alternative ways of reconstructing a global flood. On the one hand the flood might have consisted of great rains and tidal waves which resulted in the widespread deposition of unconsolidated surface materials such as gravels and silts. On the other hand the flood might have been the overwhelming catastrophe postulated by Whitcomb and Morris. Belief in a global flood does not by any means force one to an acceptance of the Whitcomb-Morris theory of a geological catastrophe.

The fact that the Bible lays such stress on an obviously great geological phenomenon like the flood does not thereby imply that that particular phenomenon was the most important event in all of geological history since the beginning of creation. After all the prime

1. L. Woolley, *Excavations at Ur* (New York: Thomas Crowell, 1965), pp. 27-36.

2. In particular, J. C. Whitcomb and H. M. Morris, *The Genesis Flood* (Philadelphia: Presbyterian and Reformed, 1961), and D. W. Patten, *The Biblical Flood and the Ice Epoch* (Seattle: Pacific Meridian, 1966); see also A. M. Rehwinkel, *The Flood* (St. Louis: Concordia, 1951).

significance of the Biblical flood lies in the fact that it was a tremendous *ordeal*. The flood was a cataclysmic *judgment* upon a wicked human race whose every imagination of the thoughts of the heart was only evil continually; moreover, the flood was a *means of gracious deliverance and salvation* for Noah and his family, who found grace in God's eyes. Now while much geological activity may have been performed by the flood and while much of the judgment may have been meted out by a geological agent effecting geological processes, the stress of Scripture is really on the combined judgmental and preservative character of the flood rather than on its geological effects.

It is perfectly legitimate to assume that in the past there may have been other geological cataclysms which performed as much activity as the Genesis flood. Scripture, however, knows nothing of any other such events. The reason for this is not to be sought in the possibility that no other major geological events could have taken place but rather in the fact that such events, if they did occur, did not play an immediately revelatory role in the plan of God in the sense in which the flood did. No other geological event *revealed* as pointedly and clearly as did the flood the wrathful and gracious character of the holy God. Even if no other major cataclysmic event ever occurred, there is absolutely no reason to believe that a sequence of numerous short-term geological events could not produce more geological work than a single great flood. But again Scripture is not interested in such events because they play no immediate, direct role in redemptive history. After all, the main concern of Scripture is with sin and grace, judgment and salvation, rather than with geology. If Scripture does speak of a great geological event Christian geologists should indeed search for the evidence of that event in nature and integrate that evidence into all the other available evidence in building up a model of geological history. But the false assumption must be avoided that simply because the Bible mentions a great geological event it must automatically be the most important event in geological history.

An analogy from archaeological history may be helpful at this point. In terms of history the Bible is concerned with the nation of Israel. The events of the world are viewed from the perspective of Israel. The other nations appear in incidental fashion. From an Old Testament point of view Israel appears as the most important of the nations. Hence one could easily make the false assumption that somehow ancient history was dominated by Israel. But archaeology informs us that the ancient world was dominated by other peoples, by Sumerians and Assyrians and Egyptians and Hittites. Israel played a lesser role in the overall historical panorama. This is by no means to say that the Bible has overestimated Israel or that archaeology has underestimated Israel. It is rather to say that in Scripture Israel is important because it is God's people, it is the recipient of God's revelation, it is the vehicle through which God works out His redemptive plan. This by no means implies that Israel dominated the ancient world culturally, economically, or politically. So it is with the flood.

There is also the very strong possibility that a great flood could have produced rather ephemeral kinds of geological deposits. One might expect the development of widespread silt and gravel deposits and piles of debris that could well be eroded away quickly. It is entirely possible that the Genesis flood may have in some fashion covered much of the globe's surface and produced a great re-distribution of materials. Since that time much of the physical evidence for such a flood could easily have been destroyed or rendered difficult to decipher. Remnants of flood deposits scattered around the world would be extremely difficult to correlate stratigraphically or geochronologically.

The Neo-Catastrophist Idea of the Flood

The preceding observations must be kept in mind when reflecting on the meaning and nature of the flood, lest the Christian commit himself too hastily to some catastrophic scheme such as the Whitcomb-Morris theory. The Bible does not specifically teach the Whitcomb-Morris theory. Though it is an interpretation that can be built around *selected* Biblical facts, the very data of geology render this theory virtually untenable. At this point a critique of the Whitcomb-Morris theory is in order. This critique is not to be taken as an attack on the idea of a global flood but rather on one inter-pretation of a global flood. The arguments against the Whitcomb-Morris theory are chiefly of a geological nature, although certain Scriptural considerations also militate against it.

The charge could be leveled that the geological arguments against the hypothesis developed in *The Genesis Flood* are constructed on the basis of and in the context of a false, unbiblical uniformitarian scientific philosophy that is alien to the thinking of Whitcomb and

Morris. In order to avoid that charge and to render the geological arguments more cogent, we will present them in the context of the scientific philosophy that Whitcomb and Morris have themselves constructed. Thus a review of the salient features of the catastrophic flood hypothesis as developed in *The Genesis Flood* is in order before the critique is presented.

On the basis of the genealogies of Genesis 5 and 11 Whitcomb and Morris believe that the fall of Adam and the consequent curse occurred only a few thousand years ago. Therefore the flood itself may have occurred only five to seven thousand years ago.[3]

According to the Whitcomb-Morris theory death did not occur until the pronouncement of the curse on Adam. Therefore all the fossils in various sedimentary rock strata must have become fossilized *after* the curse. The obvious implication is that the strata in which the fossils are entombed were themselves deposited and lithified *after* the curse. Most of these sedimentary layers, it is believed, were laid down during the great flood when everything on the face of the earth that had the breath of life died. Thus the vast majority of all fossiliferous rocks were formed during the flood year. For apart from some catastrophic sedimentation the amount of time after the curse would be insufficient to account for the great volume of fossiliferous sedimentary rock actually observable in the earth's crust. Great tectonic and magmatic events, so it is maintained, accompanied the deposition of these strata during the flood. This is said to be implied by the breaking up of the fountains of the great deep.

Another main feature of the catastrophic flood scheme is that the present laws of nature were put into effect by the Creator at the time of the curse as an integral aspect of that curse. This shift in the laws of thermodynamics became operative at the time of the curse. Therefore those events that have transpired since the imposition of the curse, and their end products, with the exception of pure miracles, may be investigated by scientific procedures, that is, by projecting or extrapolating backward to those times the *laws* that are operative in nature today (*without necessarily projecting the present rates of those processes backward in time*). This means that the flood and its effects may be examined scientifically in the context of existing laws of nature. That Whitcomb and Morris do precisely this themselves

---

3. Whitcomb and Morris, *The Genesis Flood*, pp. 474-89.

may be seen in their application of the principles of hydrodynamics to the processes of diluvian sedimentation.[4]

Finally, the flood is viewed as a truly *catastrophic* event. An enormous amount of geological work was accomplished during the span of essentially *one year* in contrast to the thousands and millions of years of slow process in uniformitarian geology. It is important to realize that according to the Whitcomb-Morris theory the rates at which geologic processes transpire were vastly speeded up during the flood year as compared with the present. As a result flood deposits ought to demonstrate evidence of such catastrophic development; thus the great interest of Whitcomb and Morris and other catastrophists in those sedimentary deposits that obviously were developed at unusually rapid or catastrophic rates.[5] Not only do Whitcomb and Morris believe that the rates of such processes as erosion and sedimentation were greatly increased during the flood year because of the abundant precipitation, they also suggest that volcanic activity was greatly intensified and that even the rates of decay of radioactive isotopes were increased.[6] The effect of a speeding up of radioactive decay processes would be to increase greatly the apparent ages of those rocks and minerals containing the radioactive atoms. Hence the apparent or radiometric ages of those rocks would be far greater than their true ages.

A Geological Critique of the Neo-Catastrophist Flood Geology

Four major objections from the field of geology should suffice to demonstrate the untenability of the catastrophic flood hypothesis, although numerous other objections could also be utilized. The objections presented here are not the typical objections that commonly derive from the fields of paleontology, sedimentation, stratigraphy, and structural geology. A number of objections from those fields were presented in a critical paper by Van de Fliert.[7] Whitcomb

---

4. Ibid., pp. 265-66.

5. Ibid., pp. 136-69; see also N. A. Rupke, "Prolegomena to a Study of Cataclysmal Sedimentation," in *Why Not Creation?* (Philadelphia: Presbyterian and Reformed, 1970), pp. 141-79.

6. Whitcomb and Morris, *The Genesis Flood*, pp. 346-55.

7. J. R. Van de Fliert, "Fundamentalism and Fundamentals of Geology," in *International Reformed Bulletin* 32-33 (1968), pp. 5-27.

and Morris anticipated and attempted to answer many of those kinds of objections in *The Genesis Flood.* For the most part, however, *The Genesis Flood* did not deal with the kind of objections and criticisms here presented largely from the fields of petrology, geochemistry, and geophysics.

1. Heat Flow from Crystallizing Magmas

The first argument is derived from the field of igneous petrology, that is, the branch of geology which is concerned with the development, emplacement, and crystallization of masses of molten rock material, termed *magma,* within or on the surface of the earth. We will consider only igneous rocks that must have been formed during or after the flood year according to the Whitcomb-Morris theory. Such rocks are those that can be demonstrated to have crystallized from a mass of magma that was intruded into sedimentary rocks presumably consolidated from sediments laid down either by the flood or at least during the flood year by a process in some way related to the flood. It will be demonstrated that many such igneous magmas could not possibly have lost their heat rapidly enough to crystallize during the flood year or soon after the termination of the flood year.

An example of an igneous body "intruded during the flood year" is the Palisades sill in northern New Jersey. A sill is a tabular body of igneous rock whose boundaries are parallel to the layers of rock above and below it. The Palisades sill crops out as a very prominent cliff (the Palisades) on the western side of the Hudson River opposite the city of New York. This sill, composed of a rock type known as diabase, is one of the most thoroughly studied igneous bodies in the world so that its geometrical relationships to the surrounding rocks are very well established.[8] Figures 9 and 10 diagrammatically portray in map and cross section the relationships of the sill to the surrounding rocks. The Palisades sill itself is overall a flat, sheetlike, tabular body of rock that is approximately a thousand feet thick. It is sandwiched in between a stack of layered red sandstones and shales that is several thousand feet thick. This thick stack of sedimentary rocks

---

8. A recent comprehensive report of the Palisades sill has been published by K. Walker, *The Palisades Sill, New Jersey: a Reinvestigation* (Geological Society of America Special Paper 111, 1969).

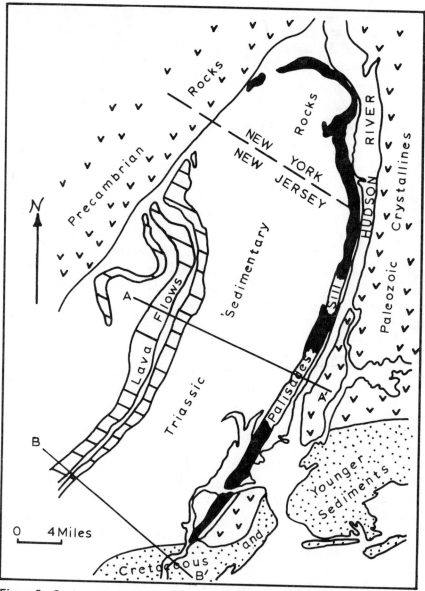

Figure 9. Geological map of the New York City-upper New Jersey region showing the relationship of the Palisades sill to surrounding rock types. Rocks of the sill are exposed at the surface in the blackened area.

is known as the Newark group and is believed by uniformitarian geologists to be Triassic in age. The entire sequence of layers is tilted gently towards the west at an angle of about eleven degrees.

Although the boundaries of the sill are generally parallel to the sandstone and shale layers immediately above and below, there are a number of locations where the boundary or contact of this igneous body can be seen to cut directly across the sedimentary layering. This feature, although proof of the once mobile nature of the material of the sill, does not conclusively prove the magmatic nature of that material. It does, however, strongly suggest that the sill material was once a magma. There are also several locations where slabs of various sizes of the surrounding sedimentary rock are enclosed by the sill rock. Many of these slabs have been rotated, and many occur several feet from the nearest undisturbed sedimentary layers. These slabs of sedimentary rock are again proof of the mobile nature of the

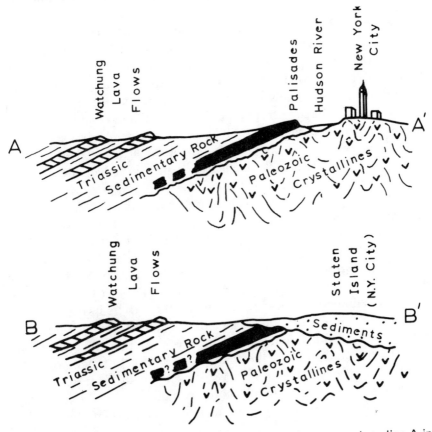

Figure 10. Two schematic cross sections (section A-A' corresponds to line A in Figure 9, section B-B' to line B) showing relationship of the Palisades sill (black) to surrounding rocks.

sill material. As the mobile material squeezed in between the sedimentary rocks, chunks of the latter were ripped apart and rafted or floated into the mobile material. The presence of the included slabs, though by no means conclusive proof, strongly suggests the existence of a magma at one time. It is after all possible to conceive of some kind of very fluid mass of material that is not necessarily as hot as a magma would be. For example, under certain conditions cold sand can be fluidized and then intruded into cracks and solidified. In these rare cases the cross-cutting sandstone bodies have an igneous appearance.

The magmatic origin, and therefore the extremely hot nature of the original liquid, is confirmed by chemical, mineralogical, and textural evidence. The chemistry and mineralogy are not similar to any known sedimentary rock that might fortuitously become mobilized, but they are virtually identical to the chemistry and mineralogy of rocks known as basalts, rocks that are obviously magmatic inasmuch as they are repeatedly erupted as lavas from volcanoes around the world. The internal texture of the sill, that is, the relationship of the various mineral grains to one another, indicates that the minerals crystallized in sequence from a liquid as that liquid cooled through a falling temperature range. The sill also shows mineralogical variations throughout which indicate that the mineral crystals settled through liquid. The igneous, that is, magmatic origin of the Palisade sill rock is thus unequivocally established.

The stack of layered sandstones and shales of the Newark group that was intruded by the Palisades magma contains at various localities fossil dinosaur tracks and numerous fossil fish.[9] Therefore, if we accept the Whitcomb-Morris flood theory, it is virtually certain that the Newark group was deposited during the flood year. It follows that the Palisades magma was intruded during or after the flood year when the sedimentary rocks were actually there to be intruded.

If it is concluded that the magma of the Palisades sill was intruded during or after the flood year, then it is clear that the sill did not begin to crystallize before the time of the flood. In other words the sill must have been able to lose a sufficient quantity of heat in the few thousand years since the flood to crystallize from an initially hot magmatic liquid. As a matter of fact, on the basis of the existing

9. W. F. Rapp, "Check List of the Fossil Reptiles of New Jersey," in *Journal of Paleontology* 18 (1944), pp. 285-88.

geological relationships the Whitcomb-Morris theory would indicate that the sill must have both intruded and crystallized *during* a small part of the flood year. The evidence for this conclusion derives from the fact that Newark group rocks, and the Palisades sill, particularly in central New Jersey, are themselves overlain by thick sequences of *fossiliferous,* completely unconsolidated formations of sand, clay, marl, and gravel that are presently exposed all along the coastal plain of New Jersey. Whitcomb and Morris quite likely would regard these thick, unconsolidated deposits as having been laid down during the waning stages of the flood. Now both the consolidated Newark group sedimentary rocks *and the Palisades sill* are overlain by these unconsolidated formations, so that the sill must have intruded after the deposition of the Newark group but before the deposition of the unconsolidated coastal sediments. There is *absolutely no evidence* of any intrusive relationship of the Palisades sill to the unconsolidated formations. Rather the Palisades sill has clearly been eroded and overlain by these formations. Erosion of the Palisades sill is indicative that crystallization had taken place before deposition of the unconsolidated coastal sediments. The geological time sequence of these regions of New Jersey could then be summarized as follows: (1) deposition and consolidation of sedimentary rocks of the Newark group, (2) intrusion and crystallization of the Palisades sill, (3) gentle westward tilting of this sequence of rocks, (4) erosion of Newark group rocks and the Palisades sill, (5) deposition of the unconsolidated coastal plain sediments (refer to Figure 10). The geological time sequence just developed is based solely on the geometrical field relationships of the various formations involved and says nothing of the amount of time involved—yet. The relative time sequence above is independent of either uniformitarian or catastrophist prejudices. Whitcomb and Morris would no doubt arrive at the same conclusion regarding the relative sequence of geologic events in this area.

An acceptance of this time sequence and of the idea that virtually all these sedimentary materials were deposited during the flood year compels us to accept the intrusion *and* crystallization of the magma of the Palisades sill during the flood year. The question which must now be faced is whether or not it is possible, in accordance with the laws of nature that are currently operative, to crystallize a thick sheet of magma the size of the Palisades sill in *less than one year.*

How rapidly a body of liquid can crystallize depends on many variables such as the initial temperature of the magma, its composition and therefore its heat capacity, the latent heats of crystallization of the various minerals crystallizing from the magma, the heat-conducting properties of the magma and the surrounding rocks, the initial temperature of the surrounding rocks, and the depth of burial of the magma at the time of its intrusion.[10] Most of these variables can be determined with a reasonable degree of accuracy. For example, the chemical composition of the original magma is very well known as a result of numerous chemical and mineralogical studies of the sill. From knowledge of the composition, reasonable estimates of such variables as heat capacities and latent heats of crystallization can be determined through laboratory experiments.[11] Temperatures of crystallization of the magma can also be estimated rather accurately. The type of rock found in the sill is generally known as *diabase*. Diabase is composed chiefly of the very common minerals pyroxene and plagioclase feldspar. Minor amounts of olivine, magnetite, potassium feldspar, and quartz also are present. It is a relatively simple matter to determine the temperature of a liquid magma that will form pyroxene and plagioclase upon crystallization, for laboratory experiments can be performed in which mixtures of pyroxene and plagioclase are intensely heated. It has for many years been possible to heat these mixtures to temperatures above which they will be completely melted. In other words a synthetic magma essentially identical to a natural magma can be generated in the laboratory and its temperature measured. Magmas that crystallize pyroxene and plagioclase in approximately the same proportions as exist in the Palisades sill require temperatures on the order of $1100°C$ or greater to be completely molten. Variations in pressure and chemi-

---

10. The cooling properties of magmas are related to such variables as the thermal conductivity, that is, how rapidly heat is conducted through a given volume of a specific material; the density, that is, mass per unit volume of material; specific heat, that is, the amount of heat that must be absorbed or lost by the magma per unit volume in order for that unit volume to have its temperature raised or lowered by one degree Centigrade; the latent heat of crystallization, that is, how much heat is released per unit mass of material upon crystallization of minerals from the magma; and temperature. Other variables may also be involved. An extended discussion of the cooling of magmas is given by J. C. Jaeger, "Cooling and Solidification of Igneous Rocks," in *Basalts: The Poldervaart Treatise on Rocks of Basaltic Composition*, Vol. 2 (New York: Interscience, 1968), pp. 503-36.

11. R. A. Robie and D. R. Waldbaum, *Thermodynamic Properties of Minerals and Related Substances* (U. S. Geological Survey Bulletin 1259, 1968).

cal composition, especially in the concentration of H_2O in the magma, will influence to some degree the temperatures at which crystallization will first take place. The point is, however, that prior to the initiation of crystallization the temperature of a magma whose composition is like that of the Palisades sill is extremely high and easily exceeds $1000°C$.[12]

The data gathered from numerous painstaking laboratory investigations have been corroborated by several measurements in the field on lavas that have just been erupted.[13] Such field data are particularly abundant from Hawaii, where the erupted magmas (lavas) are chemically and, upon crystallization, mineralogically very similar to the Palisades diabase. Temperatures of Hawaiian lavas have in general varied between 1050 and $1200°C$.

The problem now confronting the Whitcomb-Morris theory is how to cool a sheet of liquid which is a thousand feet thick and whose temperature is about 1100 to $1200°C$ down to essentially room temperature in the span of one year or less! The mathematical theory of heat conduction from cooling igneous magmas is too complex for discussion here, but on the basis of this mathematical theory reasonable estimates have been made for the time it would take to cool igneous bodies such as the Palisades sill. On the basis of the data from the Palisades sill, it can be estimated that approximately *a few hundred years* were required for the complete solidification of the Palisades sill. This result alone casts severe doubt on the validity of the Whitcomb-Morris theory. But the Palisades sill is a relatively small igneous body in comparison with some of the world's great igneous complexes and therefore could be expected to crystallize far

---

12. The temperatures of crystallization of basaltic igneous rocks may be readily inferred on the basis of experimental investigations such as those of H. S. Yoder and C. E. Tilley, "Origin of Basalt Magmas: An Experimental Study of Natural and Synthetic Rock Systems," in *Journal of Petrology* 3 (1962), pp. 342-532; and D. H. Green and A. E. Ringwood, "The Genesis of Basaltic Magmas," in *Contributions to Mineralogy and Petrology* 15 (1967), pp. 103-90.

13. See W. U. Ault, J. P. Eaton, and D. H. Richter, "Lava Temperatures in the 1959 Kilauea Eruption and Cooling Lake," in *Geological Society of America Bulletin* 72 (1961), pp. 791-94; G. A. Macdonald, "Physical Properties of Erupting Hawaiian Magmas," in *Geological Society of America Bulletin* 74 (1963), pp. 1071-78; and D. L. Peck, J. G. Moore, and G. Kozima, "Temperatures in the Crust and Melt of Alae Lava Lake, Hawaii After the August, 1963 Eruption of Kilauea Volcano—A Preliminary Report," in *U. S. Geological Survey Professional Paper* 501-D (1964), pp. D1-D7.

more rapidly than those larger bodies. For example, it has been estimated that the large Muskox intrusion in the Northwest Territories of Canada required about 7000 years to crystallize. Hess estimated that about 50,000 years were needed for the crystallization of 60 percent of Montana's Stillwater igneous complex. Irvine calculated that the Bushveld complex of South Africa, the largest known layered igneous body in the world, took nearly 200,000 years to cool. According to Larsen the immense granitic batholith of southern California, that, like the Palisades, can easily be demonstrated to have intruded "during the flood year," required a period of about one million years in order to crystallize completely.[14]

The numbers make the point. Although it is perfectly true that the values determined by these geologists are estimates, they are nonetheless important and instructive because of the order of magnitude suggested. Some of the smaller major igneous bodies, even those intruded at relatively shallow depths (like the Palisades sill) and therefore likely to cool relatively quickly, take on the order of hundreds of years to crystallize. Enormous bodies of igneous rock, like the massive granitic batholiths of California, Idaho, and British Columbia, intruded at great depths in the crust into metamorphosed fossiliferous sedimentary rocks, would have required tens or hundreds of thousands or even a million years to cool. These figures are not figments of some scientist's imagination. They have not been conjured up to fit into some preconceived theory of the earth. They are estimates arrived at by applying to measurable or reasonably inferred properties of rock and mineral materials a mathematical theory of heat conduction in solids and liquids that holds true for materials today. Inasmuch as the theory of heat flow is based on laws

---

14. See T. N. Irvine, "Heat Transfer During Solidification of Layered Intrusions. I. Sheets and Sills," in *Canadian Journal of Earth Sciences* 7 (1970), pp. 1031-61. Several of the igneous intrusions noted in the text, such as Canada's Muskox intrusion, Montana's Stillwater complex, and South Africa's Bushveld complex are Precambrian in age. Quite probably Whitcomb and Morris would view these rocks as having been created in place and would reject the validity of the estimated times of cooling. The point, however, is that the principles employed by uniformitarian geologists in investigating the heat conducting properties of these intrusions are exactly the same as are employed in investigating later intrusions that occurred "during the flood." For large intrusions injected "during the flood" we are talking about times of cooling measured in hundreds to many thousands of years. A prime example is the southern California batholith, which took approximately one million years to cool.

in operation today, Whitcomb and Morris ought to be willing to accept the applicability of that theory to the flood period. Presumably they do not desire to rely upon pure miracle. They have so indicated nowhere in their writings. The burden now lies upon flood geologists to explain, in terms of sound theoretical principles of heat conduction in liquids and solids, just how igneous bodies of various sizes, intruded during the flood year, could succeed in completely solidifying during the flood year or shortly thereafter.

2. Radiometric Dating and the Flood

The problems are compounded for flood catastrophists if consideration is given to the results of radioactive age dating of those igneous bodies that have been intruded into fossiliferous sedimentary formations. Several catastrophists have made valiant attempts[15] to discredit the radiometric methods. Whitcomb and Morris, for example, have argued for the validity of the concept of creation of apparent age as described in chapter three. For the sake of argument, it could be assumed that the concept of apparent age is true. Radiometric methods would then be invalid for any of the so-called Precambrian rocks because these rocks presumably were created during creation week. In spite of such a concession, the flood theory still encounters extreme difficulty when confronted with the radiometric methods. One that is particularly devastating to the Whitcomb-Morris theory is the rubidium-strontium isochron method, based on the radioactive decay of rubidium 87 (Rb^{87}) into strontium 87 (Sr^{87}). It is interesting that flood catastrophists have had very little to say about the Rb^{87}-Sr^{87} method. This method is very useful in determining, among other things, the time of crystallization of a body of igneous rock.

One of the criticisms leveled against the radiometric methods by flood catastrophists is that the amount of a radiogenic daughter

---

15. Whitcomb and Morris, *The Genesis Flood*, pp. 331-68; D. O. Acrey, "Problems in Absolute Age Determination," in *Scientific Studies in Special Creation* (Philadelphia: Presbyterian and Reformed, 1971), pp. 72-78; M. A. Cook, "Radiological Dating and Some Pertinent Applications of Historical Interest: Do Radiological 'Clocks' Need Repair?" in *Scientific Studies in Special Creation* (Philadelphia: Presbyterian and Reformed, 1971), pp. 79-97; R. L. Whitelaw, "Radiocarbon Confirms Biblical Creation (And So Does Potassium-Argon)," in *Why Not Creation?* (Philadelphia: Presbyterian and Reformed, 1970), pp. 90-100, and "Radiocarbon and Potassium-Argon Dating in the Light of New Discoveries in Cosmic Rays," in *Why Not Creation?*, pp. 101-05.

element[16] present in a rock or mineral at the time of its formation is not known; hence the age determined for the rock or mineral is a function of the estimate one makes of the amount of that element initially present. On this basis catastrophists accuse uniformitarians of pure guesswork when it comes to radiometric age determination. For example, atoms of argon 40 (Ar^{40}) form by radioactive decay of atoms of potassium 40 (K^{40}) at known, measurable rates. If the amounts of Ar^{40} and K^{40} in a rock are measured, it ought to be possible to calculate the age of the rock on the basis of the rate of decay of K^{40} into Ar^{40}. If, however, a significant amount of Ar^{40} was initially present in the rock at the time of its formation, the calculated or measured age will be considerably greater than the true age of the rock. The geologist must therefore devise some means for determining the amount of Ar^{40} initially present. In all radiometric methods the amount of radiogenic daughter element initially present must be known or estimated if we wish to be able to determine the true ages of rocks.[17]

Now the Rb^{87}-Sr^{87} isochron method is very useful in that it eliminates the need for guessing how much Sr^{87} was initially present in a rock when it was formed. The Rb^{87}-Sr^{87} isochron method actually tells us how much Sr^{87}, in terms of the ratio of Sr^{87} to Sr^{86}, was initially present. Intelligent guesswork is thus eliminated.

Let us assume that a mass of granitic magma devoid of any suspended crystals is intruded into some other set of rocks in the earth's crust. As a granitic magma, the liquid is rich in atoms and ions[18] of the elements oxygen (O), silicon (Si), aluminum (Al), potassium (K), and sodium (Na). Minor but significant amounts of calcium (Ca),

---

16. In the study of radioactive processes, an atom that undergoes radioactive decay, such as rubidium 87, is termed the *parent*. The atom into which the parent is transformed, such as strontium 87, is termed the *daughter*.

17. There is a great wealth of material available that discusses the details of the common radiometric dating methods, e.g., P. Pasteels, "A Comparison of Methods in Geochronology," in *Earth-Science Reviews* 4 (1968), pp. 5-38; and E. I. Hamilton, *Applied Geochronology* (New York: Academic Press, 1965).

18. Individual ions (simply atoms with an electrical charge) of the various elements may be thought of as approximately spherical in shape. As such they may be said to have ionic radii. Various ionic radii have been measured by means of several sophisticated instrumental techniques such as molecular refraction and X-ray diffraction and are on the order of 1 Å (Ångstrom unit), which equals 0.00000001 centimeter.

iron (Fe), titanium (Ti), and magnesium (Mg) also are present. When the magma ultimately crystallizes, the resulting rock, granite, will consist chiefly of the minerals quartz (SiO_2), microcline or ortho-clase feldspar ($KAlSi_3O_8$), and plagioclase feldspar ($NaAlSi_3O_8$ with some Ca atoms substituting for the Na atoms). Minor amounts of such iron- and calcium-bearing minerals as hornblende and pyroxene, or of such potassium-bearing minerals as biotite and muscovite may also be present. The granitic magma will also contain traces of rubidium and strontium, but concentrations of these elements will not be sufficient to permit the crystallization of any rubidium- or strontium-rich minerals. Therefore these two elements are, upon crystallization of the magma, incorporated in trace amounts in the common minerals like the feldspars. These trace elements will tend to occupy particular positions in the mineral structures that are suit-able for them on the basis of their size and charge. For example, a rubidium ion has the same electrical charge (+1) as and in terms of its radius[19] is but slightly larger than an ion of potassium. Because of these similarities between ions of potassium and rubidium, the latter tends to occupy the same position in a crystal structure as the former. In other words some rubidium ions act as proxies or substi-tutes for what, in a crystal structure, would ordinarily be ions of potassium. Thus we find trace amounts of rubidium in potassium-rich minerals like microcline, biotite, and muscovite. On the other hand, rubidium is much rarer in potassium-poor minerals. Similarly, ions of the element strontium are the same charge (+2) as and very similar in size to ions of the element calcium. Therefore strontium ions commonly replace calcium ions in crystal structures and are found in trace quantities in such calcium-bearing minerals as plagio-clase feldspar, hornblende, and pyroxene.

Most strontium is composed of the nonradiogenic isotopes[20] Sr^{86} and Sr^{88}, but a substantial percentage of strontium is composed of the radiogenic isotope Sr^{87}. Ions of Sr^{87} and Sr^{86} have the same size

19. The radius of the potassium ion (K^{+1}) is about 1.33 Å, and the radius of the rubidium ion (Rb^{+1}) is about 1.45 Å.

20. An isotope is a particular atomic form of a chemical element determined solely by the number of neutrons in the nucleus of the atoms of that element. For example, all atoms of strontium have 38 protons in their nuclei, but some strontium atoms have only 47 neutrons (Sr^{85}), some have 48 neutrons (Sr^{86}), and some have 49 neutrons (Sr^{87}). The various forms of strontium atoms with their variable numbers of neutrons are said to be isotopes of strontium.

and charge, and both isotopes enter into calcium-rich minerals. The ratio of Sr^{87} to Sr^{86} in a mass of magma should be essentially the same throughout. This may be designated $(Sr^{87}/Sr^{86})_0$. Upon crystallization of the various calcium-bearing minerals the ratio Sr^{87}/Sr^{86} ought to be the same as before inasmuch as there is no evidence to suggest that any mineral structure preferentially incorporates either Sr^{87} or Sr^{86}. But after a significant period of time has passed since completion of crystallization, the ratio Sr^{87}/Sr^{86} will vary in different minerals because of the addition of Sr^{87} generated by the decay of varying amounts of radioactive Rb^{87}.

In essence then the granitic rock immediately upon crystallization has a homogeneous distribution of strontium isotopes throughout, which we term $(Sr^{87}/Sr^{86})_0$. After the magma crystallizes and time proceeds, more and more of the Rb^{87} initially present in the granite decays radioactively to Sr^{87}. The ratio Sr^{87}/Sr^{86} in the granite as a whole increases since the amount of the nonradiogenic Sr^{86} remains constant while Sr^{87} is continually being produced. Different parts of the granite body will have, at the time of crystallization, different amounts of Rb^{87}. A piece of granite that is rich in microcline and poor in plagioclase will have a high initial amount of Rb^{87}. A piece of granite rich in plagioclase and poor in microcline will have a low initial content of Rb^{87} inasmuch as the rubidium occurs chiefly in the microcline. At some time later, the rock with a high initial amount of Rb^{87} will have produced more radiogenic Sr^{87} than will the rock with a low initial amount of Rb^{87}. Hence the former will develop a higher Sr^{87}/Sr^{86} ratio than the latter even though they started with the same ratio. It follows that if several different samples of the granite are examined to measure the present ratios of Rb^{87}/Sr^{86} and Sr^{87}/Sr^{86}, it is possible graphically to determine the original Sr^{87}/Sr^{86} ratio of the granite magma. The mathematical demonstration of this graphical method is presented in the Appendix.

The time of crystallization of the granite (or another igneous rock) may be determined from the slope of a straight line plotted on a graph depicting the ratios of Sr^{87}/Sr^{86} and Rb^{87}/Sr^{86}. The straight line is determined in the following manner. We select about five or six large chunks of the granite with variable rubidium contents and after elaborate preparation analyze these chunks by means of a mass spectrometer in order to determine the present-day ratios of Sr^{87}/Sr^{86} and Rb^{87}/Sr^{86} in each chunk. These values are then

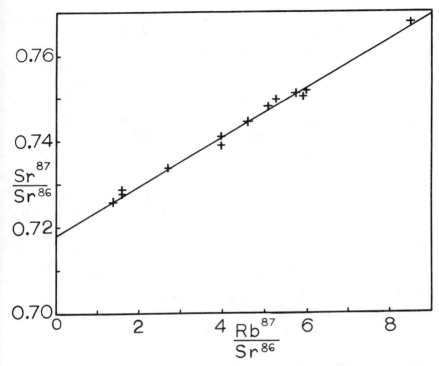

Figure 11. Rubidium-strontium whole rock isochron plot. The data points (crosses) represent actually measured values of the present isotope ratios of Sr^{87}/Sr^{86} and Rb^{87}/Sr^{86} in several large chunks of granite from a single granite body which presumably crystallized during a short time interval. The slope of the line (isochron) through the data points is a function of the age of the granite and the intersection of the line with the Sr^{87}/Sr^{86} axis yields the ratio of Sr^{87}/Sr^{86} possessed by the granitic magma when it initially crystallized.

plotted on the graph (Figure 11). If the assumption with respect to the initial homogeneity of the ratio Sr^{87}/Sr^{86} throughout the original mass of granitic magma is valid and if there has been no significant loss or gain of rubidium or strontium since the time of crystallization, then the analytical data, assuming also that the analysis was performed properly, ought to be defined as a straight line on the graph. In the great majority of actual experimental determinations a straight line plot has been obtained. This straight line is known as the *isochron*. The slope of the isochron is a function of the time of crystallization[21] of the igneous body. From the slope of the isochron

---

21. The slope of an isochron on a plot of the ratios of Sr^{87}/Sr^{86} and Rb^{87}/Sr^{86} is equivalent to $e^{\lambda t} - 1$ where λ is the decay constant of Rb^{87} and t is the

we therefore obtain the age of the granite under discussion without any prior knowledge of or guessing at the actual amount of Sr^{87} that was present in the granite at the time of crystallization. Instead this rubidium-strontium isochron method has actually told us what the initial Sr^{87} content was in terms of the ratio of Sr^{87}/Sr^{86} inasmuch as the y-intercept[22] of the isochron has the value $(Sr^{87}/Sr^{86})_0$. This method therefore eliminates the guesswork about which many of the flood catastrophists have complained. The results of hundreds of analyses have yielded ages on the order of hundreds of millions of years.

Not only can guesswork, even highly educated guesswork, regarding the initial Sr^{87} content of a sample be eliminated by the isochron method, but the results of this method have demonstrated just how well educated have been the guesses where guesswork is required by other radiometric methods. Values of $(Sr^{87}/Sr^{86})_0$ generally vary between 0.699 and 0.725 but the great majority of values are between 0.702 and 0.708. If the age of a mineral is being determined by only one rubidium-strontium measurement, it is necessary to make some estimate of the initial Sr^{87} content or an initial $(Sr^{87}/Sr^{86})_0$. It is important to note that in such cases geochronologists have made "intelligent estimates" of the initial $(Sr^{87}/Sr^{86})_0$ on the order of 0.70 to 0.71. From this it is rather obvious that geochronologists know what they are doing and have not been making wild guesses at the initial Sr^{87} contents of minerals simply to force prejudicially the age results into some preconceived uniformitarian scheme.

The overall usefulness and consistency of radiometric age results may further be illustrated by comparing them with the geological time scale. In a majority of thousands of analyses, the ages obtained from rocks by radiometric means agree quite consistently (within the limits of analytical error) with the *relative* ages of materials that have been determined by strictly geological or paleontological criteria. As an example, consider a group of small igneous bodies that occurs

---

amount of time elapsed since the rock material in question crystallized. For relatively young rocks the slope is approximately equal to λt. Hence the slope is a function of the time of crystallization.

22. The y-intercept is the point on the y-axis (the vertical axis or ordinate) which is intercepted by the isochron line. Its value is equal to the original Sr^{87}/Sr^{86} ratio of the magma at the time of crystallization.

near Beemerville, New Jersey. These bodies are composed chiefly of a relatively uncommon rock type known as nepheline syenite. The field relationships clearly indicate that the nepheline syenite has intruded the Martinsburg Formation, a unit composed chiefly of shale that, on paleontological and stratigraphic grounds, is believed by uniformitarian geologists to be of Middle to Late Ordovician age. Moreover, it is fairly evident that the nepheline syenite has not intruded but is overlain by the Tuscarora Formation, a quartzite that is believed to be Early Silurian in age. Figure 12 schematically portrays the field relationships. The following time sequence would no doubt be agreed on by uniformitarian and catastrophist alike: the Martinsburg was deposited, consolidated, and intruded by the nepheline syenite; this group of rocks was then eroded in part and overlain by a blanket of quartz sand which ultimately lithified into the Shawangunk Formation.

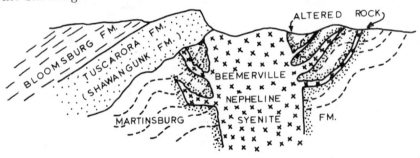

Figure 12. Field relationships of the Beemerville nepheline syenite. This body of igneous rock in northern New Jersey intrudes the Ordovician Martinsburg Formation. It does not intrude but is overlain by the Lower Silurian Tuscarora Formation. On the basis of these field relationships an age of about 425 to 450 million years would be predicted for the nepheline syenite. Radiometric dating has yielded a date of 437 million years!

Now from radiometric data around the world it has been possible for uniformitarian geologists to estimate when events of the Ordovician, Silurian, and other periods prevailed on the earth. Thus a prediction could be made as to the approximate age of the nepheline syenite on the basis of its field relationships. The latter part of the Ordovician period is believed to have occurred about 450 million years ago, and the earlier part of the Silurian period is believed to have occurred about 425 million years ago. Geologists would therefore predict that the Beemerville nepheline syenite was intruded about 425 to 450 million years ago. The uniformitarian geologist is

rightly impressed by the reliability and consistency of the radiometric methods when he learns that the results of a geochronological
study of the Beemerville material yield ages of 424 ± 20 million years
and 436 ± 41 million years for two mineral specimens by the
rubidium-strontium method and 437 ± 22 million years for two different analyses by the potassium-argon method.[23] The success of
radiometric methods is evident.

A similar appeal can be made to a radiometric study of the
Palisades diabase sill[24] which on stratigraphic grounds is thought to
be of Late Triassic age. Available data suggest that the Triassic period
extended from about 230 million years ago to about 180 million
years ago. The fact that potassium-argon dating of minerals in the
diabase yields ages of 190 ± 5 million years again points to the
reliability and consistency of the radiometric methods.

Both the Palisades sill and the Beemerville nepheline syenite
would, according to catastrophist principles, have been intruded
during the flood year. The flood geologists must somehow be able to
explain the tremendous ages yielded by the radiometric methods
when "in reality" these igneous rocks were formed only a few
thousand years ago. They might object, and indeed have objected, to
arguments similar to the preceding on the basis of the fact that it is
only an unproven assumption that the decay constant for a particular
radioactive element is indeed a constant through all time under all
conditions. Whitcomb and Morris are aware of the fact that decay
constants generally are not subject to any more than insignificant
variation because of external thermal, mechanical, or compositional
factors. They have, however, argued that a significant increase in the
cosmic ray flux on the earth's surface would succeed in greatly
speeding up the rate of decay of radioactive elements. Thus in order
to explain the great apparent ages of rock presumably formed during
the flood, the flood geologists are led to suggest that at the time of
the flood a very great increase in cosmic ray influx in turn caused
greatly increased radioactive decay.

---

23. R. E. Zartman et al., "K-Ar and Rb-Sr Ages of Some Alkalic Intrusive Rocks
from Central and Eastern United States," in *American Journal of Science* 265
(1967), pp. 848-70.

24. G. P. Erickson and J. L. Kulp, "Potassium-Argon Measurements on the
Palisades Sill, New Jersey," in *Geological Society of America Bulletin* 72 (1961),
pp. 649-52.

This argument, however, does not salvage the flood theory. Although the earth's atmosphere succeeds in shielding us from the greater proportion of cosmic rays coming in from space, it is possible to learn the effects of high cosmic ray flux on radioactive materials by studying objects from space such as the moon and meteorites. Studies of meteorites by the cosmic ray exposure method have, for example, indicated that most cosmic radiation is successful in penetrating only the outermost few feet of an unshielded solid body.[25] In light of this observation, if the cosmic ray influx at the earth's surface somehow increased drastically, the effect on the radiometric age indicators of rocks that must have formed thousands of feet or several miles below the surface would be negligible. Moreover, the studies of meteorites have indicated that the cosmic ray flux in the solar system as a whole has probably been essentially constant for the last few million years.

Finally it ought to be observed that no mechanism has been suggested whereby the earth's shielding from high-energy cosmic radiation could be suddenly eliminated. Moreover, the surface of the moon, which has obviously had far more exposure to cosmic rays than the surface of the earth, has yielded radiometric ages that are perfectly consistent with other data on the age of the solar system. The available evidence indicates that cosmic ray fluxes that are greater than those at the earth's surface would not have any significant effect in increasing the apparent radiometric ages of materials forming at depth. Despite all the objections of flood geologists to radiometric dating we may confidently maintain that the *available* facts from the field of radiometric geochronology argue very eloquently against the Whitcomb-Morris theory.

3. Metamorphism

The Whitcomb-Morris theory is also ill-equipped to deal with a major argument from the fields of metamorphic and tectonic geology. The evidence derived from studies of the stability of metamorphic rocks in terms of ranges of temperature and pressure argues persuasively against the catastrophist view.

Much of the earth's surface is immediately underlain by vast tracts of crystalline metamorphic rock. Much of the exposed rock of the

---

25. Hamilton, *Applied Geochronology*.

eastern two-thirds of Canada consists of metamorphic rocks. The Blue Ridge Mountains of the southern Appalachians, the southern Piedmont, virtually all of New England, New York's Manhattan Island, and nearly the entire area between Philadelphia and Washington, D.C., consist of metamorphic rock. So do large areas of the mountainous western parts of the United States and Canada. Metamorphic rocks also are widely exposed in other parts of the world such as Australia, Scandinavia, Siberia, and India. A great many of these crystalline metamorphic rocks, as, for example, most of those in Canada, are believed to be Precambrian in age. Hence Whitcomb and Morris might be tempted to relegate such rocks to the activity of the creation week. It is evident, however, on the basis of Whitcomb-Morris criteria, that many metamorphic rocks would have had to form during the flood year.

Let us first consider the metamorphic terrain of New England. Despite the fact that many of these rocks have been very severely heated and deformed it is evident that they were chiefly of sedimentary and volcanic character prior to their metamorphism. This assertion is strongly backed by inferences from various compositional, textural, and structural characteristics; the original sedimentary character of many of the rocks is clinched by the fact that, in places, several fossils, albeit somewhat deformed, have been discovered within them.[26] It is true that fossils are very rare in metamorphic rocks, but the New England occurrences obviously are an exception. The Whitcomb-Morris theory virtually leads us, on the basis of contained fossils, to believe that the sedimentary material from which these metamorphic rocks developed was deposited during the flood year. In southern New England the metamorphic rocks are unconformably overlain by unmetamorphosed fossiliferous sedimentary rocks. Therefore flood geologists are faced with the necessity of concluding that the metamorphic rocks of New England metamorphosed during the time span of less than one year.

In order to see what is involved in this assertion consider the degree to which the New England rocks were metamorphosed. This means that we must discover what kinds of pressures and tempera-

---

26. E.g., A. J. Boucot et al., "Metamorphosed Middle Paleozoic Fossils from Central Massachusetts, Eastern Vermont, and Western New Hampshire," in *Geological Society of America Bulletin* 69 (1958), pp. 855-70; and A. J. Boucot and J. B. Thompson, "Metamorphosed Silurian Brachiopods from New Hampshire," in *Geological Society of America Bulletin* 74 (1963), pp. 1313-34.

tures were superimposed on the rocks during metamorphism.[27]
These variables can be determined from knowledge of the mineralogy
of the rocks. At equilibrium each mineral and each set of minerals
can form only under certain temperature-pressure conditions. For
example, it has long been known that at atmospheric pressure and
814°C a piece of quartz under equilibrium conditions is converted
into a different mineral, tridymite. In order for the conversion of one
mineral to another mineral to take place at equilibrium it is very
often necessary for the conversion or reaction to take place *very
slowly.*

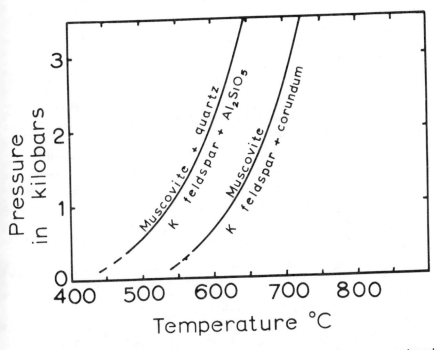

Figure 13. Diagram showing experimentally-determined stability of the mineral
muscovite in terms of pressure and temperature. For example, pure muscovite
can exist stably at temperatures lower than those of the right-hand curve, but at
higher temperatures the atomic structure of muscovite breaks down and re-
assembles as the structures of the two minerals corundum and potassium (K)
feldspar.

---

27. Several texts treat of the problem of determining the physical conditions of
metamorphism, e.g., F. J. Turner, *Metamorphic Petrology* (New York: McGraw-
Hill, 1968).

Now it has been possible to determine the range of stability of almost all important metamorphic minerals in terms of pressure and temperature. It has also been possible to determine the pressure and temperature at which many important metamorphic mineral reactions may occur. Figure 13, for example, shows the experimentally-determined upper temperature limit of the common mica mineral, muscovite, as well as the upper temperature limit of the reaction of muscovite and quartz.[28] These stabilities have in many cases been determined by several investigators with highly sophisticated equipment. Hence geologists may with a considerable degree of reliability apply experimental knowledge of mineral stabilities to actual rocks. The data available for the mineral assemblages of New England rocks[29] indicate that many of these rocks must have been subjected to temperatures on the order of 600°C and pressures on the order of five kilobars.[30] In order to be subjected to such a pressure a rock must be buried under a load of rock that approaches ten to twelve miles in thickness.[31] To produce the observed mineral assemblages the rock had to originate at the earth's surface as layers of sediment, for example, mud or silt, be gradually buried under successively accumulating layers of sediment and converted into rock, be buried still more deeply in order to be metamorphosed progressively, ultimately be buried to a depth of several miles, then finally uplifted and eroded until the original material was again exposed at the surface as a metamorphic rock. Hence the flood geologist is under

28. B. Velde, "Upper Limits of Stability of Muscovite," in *American Mineralogist* 51 (1966), pp. 924-29; and B. W. Evans, "Application of a Reaction-Rate Method to the Breakdown Equilibria of Muscovite and Muscovite Plus Quartz," in *American Journal of Science* 263 (1965), pp. 647-67.

29. See the summary article on New England metamorphism by J. B. Thompson and S. A. Norton, "Paleozoic Regional Metamorphism in New England and Adjacent Areas," in *Studies of Appalachian Geology: Northern and Maritime* (New York: Interscience, 1968), pp. 319-27.

30. One kilobar pressure is equal to approximately 15,000 pounds per square inch.

31. Lateral compressive stresses on rocks at depth, known as tectonic overpressures, may contribute an important component of pressure on buried rocks. It is possible that a rock subjected to a pressure of five kilobars was not buried at depths approaching ten to twelve miles *if* the tectonic overpressure was sufficiently great. Most geologists, however, do not believe that lateral pressures are as important as what is known as burial, overburden, or lithostatic pressure, that is, the pressure due to simple burial under an overlying load of rock.

the obligation of explaining in terms of his theory how it would have been possible *in less than one year* for the New England rocks to be heated to around 600°C and cooled back down to surface temperature, as well as buried to a depth of around twelve miles and brought all the way back to the surface!

The New England situation presents quite a predicament for catastrophism, but it is mild compared with evidence obtained from rocks of California's Franciscan Formation and similar rocks in Japan.[32] The Franciscan Formation is a chaotic complex of mildly metamorphosed sedimentary and volcanic rocks, chiefly graywackes and cherts. In many places the metamorphism has not been sufficiently severe to destroy the original sedimentary texture of these rocks. Fossils are very rare in the Franciscan Formation, but those present, together with other lines of evidence, indicate that it is Jurassic in age. While the temperature of Franciscan metamorphism was relatively low (between 150 and 300°C), the mineralogical evidence overwhelmingly indicates there were *extremely* high pressures on the rocks during metamorphism. The minerals yielding this evidence are utterly out of character for sedimentary deposits and must be attributed to the metamorphism. Among these minerals are lawsonite, jadeite, and aragonite. The combination of jadeite and quartz in particular indicates formation under extremely high pressure. Figure 14 shows some of the experimental data that are relevant to Franciscan metamorphism. The available data indicate that in order to form the combination of the minerals jadeite and quartz from the common mineral albite, the pressure during Franciscan metamorphism in places must have exceeded eight kilobars. In other words these rocks most likely must have been buried on the order of at least eighteen miles.[33] The flood catastrophists must therefore explain how it was possible *in the span of one year* for the originally sedimentary rocks of California's coastal ranges to be buried at least eighteen miles and uplifted all the way back to the earth's surface.

---

32. W. G. Ernst and Y. Seki, "Petrologic Comparison of the Franciscan and Sanbagawa Metamorphic Terranes," in *Tectonophysics* 4 (1967), pp. 463-78.

33. W. G. Ernst, "Do Mineral Parageneses Reflect Unusually High Pressure Conditions of Franciscan Metamorphism?" in *American Journal of Science* 270 (1971), pp. 81-108.

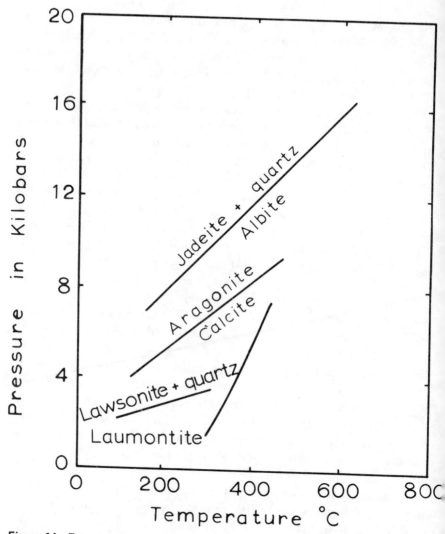

Figure 14. Experimentally-determined curves showing the stability of certain minerals found in rocks of California's Franciscan Formation. The presence in these rocks of minerals such as lawsonite, aragonite instead of calcite, and jadeite and quartz instead of albite is an indication of the very high pressures that were operative during metamorphism.

4. Plate Tectonics

The geological critique of the Whitcomb-Morris theory concludes with an appeal to plate tectonics (also known as the new global tectonics). The dynamic nature of the earth's crust and mantle is stressed in the new global tectonics, which is essentially a composite of two major theories, continental drift and sea-floor spreading. The theory of continental drift views the continental masses as having been shifted continuously in their relative positions on the earth's surface. Particularly well-known is the idea that South America and Africa together with India, Australia, and Antarctica were at one time joined together in a single land mass known as Gondwanaland. The theory of sea-floor spreading suggests possible means by which the continents have drifted in time.

The theory of continental drift was proposed long ago. In the 1920s and 1930s the idea was somewhat widely held by geologists who studied rocks within the southern hemisphere. Germany's Alfred Wegener,[34] a meteorologist, was also an ardent proponent of the idea. As a rule, however, European and American geologists were very cool to the continental-drift hypothesis chiefly because it was thought to be dynamically impossible. Since the early 1960s, however, the drift idea has gained new impetus. In fact acceptance of the theory was just beginning to gather momentum at the time when *The Genesis Flood* was first published. Owing to the recent proliferation of knowledge concerning the large-scale structure of the oceans and continents, the idea of continental drift is now all but universally accepted by geologists.

It is clear that Whitcomb and Morris did not recognize that continental drift is a formidable foe to their theory. *The Genesis Flood* mentions continental drift only twice. One reference is in relation to mountain building.

> In general, there are currently two main hypotheses of mountain-building. One depends on thermal contraction of the crust, the other on subcrustal convection currents. Another, the theory of continental drift, is presently running a poor third. None of them is based on present measurable processes, but solely on hypothetical speculations which may or may not be meaningful.[35]

A second reference to continental drift is in the context of climate and glaciation. Whitcomb and Morris are concerned to show that, on account of the global water vapor canopy, worldwide climates were warm and equable before the flood. This notion seems to be contra-

---

34. A. Wegener, *The Origin of Continents and Oceans* (New York: Dover, 1966).

35. Whitcomb and Morris, *The Genesis Flood*, pp. 140-41.

dicted by the evidence for glaciation—an indication of harsh climate—in rocks of supposed Permian age. Whitcomb and Morris must somehow explain away *this* glaciation (not to be confused with the relatively recent ice age). They say:

> This remarkably extensive glaciation is anomalous and difficult to explain, occurring as it did so near the equator and also largely near sea level. Gignoux believes the only possible explanation is the theory of continental drift, previously advocated strenuously by Wegener, du Toit and others, according to which the southern continents, and possibly others as well, were once parts of one great continental mass, since broken and drifted apart.
>
> This theory of course bears quite hard on the uniformist concept, and so is rejected by most geologists.[36]

In effect Whitcomb and Morris saw no danger to their theory from the quarter of continental drift. Now, however, the evidence in favor of drift is overwhelming; hence we must pay due heed to this evidence and its consequences for the Whitcomb-Morris theory.

Quite simply the theory of continental drift states that the present continental land masses have not always been in a fixed position relative to one another on the earth's surface. Rather, all the continents, at least in Late Paleozoic time, were joined together into one or two supercontinents that began to split up around Triassic or Jurassic time and subsequently moved away from one another to their present position. The rate of movement is very slow, on the order of a couple of centimeters per year, but is believed to be still going on. It will soon be possible to test the present rate of continental drift by means of a system of lasers and laser-beam reflectors on the various continents and on the moon. The drift theory has also been extended back in time beyond the Late Paleozoic age: it is believed that smaller isolated continental masses drifted together, collided, and were welded together to form the supercontinents of that age. Evidence for such earlier drifting is still a bit nebulous, but extrapolation of the drift idea to earlier times is a reasonable extension of the theory. The evidence for the latest (post-Paleozoic) phase of drifting is very convincing.

The most obvious line of evidence is the remarkable similarity in the shapes of the coast lines of eastern South America and western Africa. If the outlines of the two continents are juxtaposed and

---

36. Ibid., p. 246.

slightly rotated, one obtains an almost perfect jigsaw-puzzle fit. Also remarkable is the good fit between the eastern coast of North America and the northwestern coast of Africa. Other large land masses also fit together quite well. The evidence is even more remarkable if instead of the coast lines we compare the true edges of the continents, namely the borders of the continental shelves. The closeness of the fit of several of the continents is seen in Figure 15.

Some of the geologic evidence in support of the drift theory is presented in a series of maps which speak for themselves. Figure 16-A shows the distribution of Precambrian shield areas in South America and Africa. Whitcomb and Morris would likely consider these as rocks of the creation period. The map suggests the one-time continuity of these shield areas. Figure 16-A also shows the spatial trends of various geological structures such as folds and faults on the southern continents, and Figure 16-B illustrates the distribution of radiometric ages on those continents. The maps clearly point out the continuity of structural trends and radiometric age provinces from one continent to the other.

Figure 17-A shows the present distribution of Paleozoic mountain chains, like the Appalachians, around the Atlantic Ocean. These mountain belts appear to be unrelated until the continents are fitted together as in Figure 17-B, which clearly shows the continuity of the Appalachians, the Scottish Highlands, and the Norwegian mountains.

The occurrence of certain rare rock types has also lent strong credence to the theory of drift. For example, the rock type anorthosite, composed chiefly of plagioclase feldspar, is a rather unusual type of rock that appears to be restricted to Precambrian areas. Anorthosite occurs as large batholiths with outcrop areas measured in hundreds of square miles. The individual anorthosite batholiths occur in long chains like beads on a string in what appear to be the eroded remnants of the deepest roots of ancient mountain belts. The best examples of this linear distribution of anorthosite bodies are to be found in the Grenville province, a belt of Precambrian rock extending from New York's Adirondack Mountains through southern Quebec and into Labrador, and in the Ghats region of eastern India. The linear distribution of anorthosite bodies along ancient folded mountain chains appears to be a characteristic of the occurrence of anorthosite. Isolated bodies of anorthosite occur on virtually all the continents, but if the continents are fitted together, the result is a remarkable linear distribution (see Figure 18).

Figure 15. Reconstruction of the continents bordering the Atlantic Ocean. The dark boundaries represent the present shore lines of these continents. The light boundaries represent the edges of the continental shelves, the true edges of the continental masses. The excellence of the fit between the edges of the continental shelves of adjoining continents can be readily observed, providing strong support for the theory of the breakup of an original large continent and subsequent continental drift to present locations. Blackened areas between continents represent regions where adjoining continental shelves would overlap.

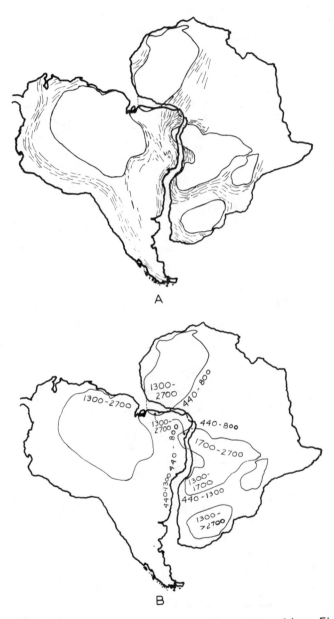

A

B

Figure 16. South America and Africa adjoined in predrift positions. Figure 16-A shows ancient Precambrian shields (enclosed areas), and trends of folds and faults (dashed lines). Figure 16-B shows general distribution of radiometric ages. The continuity of shield areas, trends of folds and faults, and radiometric ages from South America into Africa is strong support for the theory of continental drift.

204

Creation and the Flood

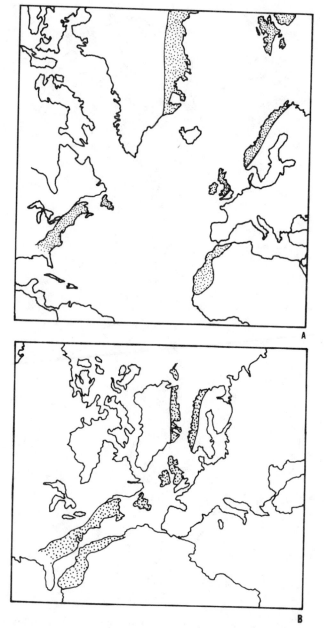

Figure 17. A. Present arrangement of continents around the Atlantic Ocean showing the location of several mountainous belts of Paleozoic age (stippled). B. Predrift arrangement of Atlantic continents showing location of the same Paleozoic mountains. The suggestion of one long continuous belt of mountain-building activity supports the idea of drift.

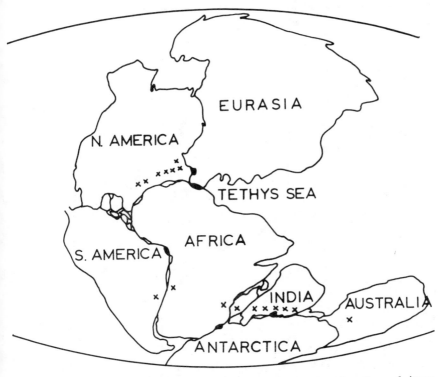

Figure 18. Predrift reconstruction of continents showing location of large bodies of the rock type anorthosite (crosses). The strongly linear arrangement of these bodies from South America into Australia in this reconstruction supports the theory of continental drift inasmuch as anorthosite bodies today are arranged in linear chains, as in eastern North America and eastern India.

Evidence from several continents suggests that considerable glacial activity occurred during Permian time. This evidence is summarized in Figure 19, which shows that a large continental glacial ice cap once covered a now broken-up supercontinent. Evidence for drift also comes from the sea floors. On various geological grounds it has been postulated that the ancient supercontinent, generally referred to as Pangaea and composed of two subcontinents termed Laurasia[37] and Gondwanaland,[38] began to break up during Early Mesozoic time.

---

37. Laurasia was the northern protocontinent. It included present-day North America, Greenland, Europe, and Asia.

38. Gondwanaland was the southern protocontinent. It included present-day South America, Africa, India, Australia, and Antarctica.

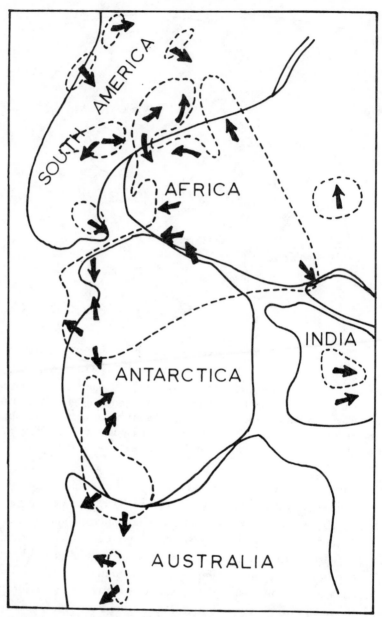

Figure 19. Permian glacial activity. Southern hemisphere continents are here shown in predrift reconstruction with heavy lines representing continental boundaries. The enclosed dashed areas show location of Permian glacial ice caps with inferred directions of ice movement (arrows). The closeness of these ice caps of essentially the same age in this reconstruction supports the theory of the former closeness of these continents and therefore continental drift.

It is believed that as the continents separated from one another new basaltic oceanic crust was gradually being developed at the original site of the continental rupture. This site is presently marked by the great submarine mountain range known as the Mid-Atlantic Ridge. If the Atlantic Ocean basin crust has been forming only since Early Mesozoic time when the continents first separated, we would not expect to find any sedimentary deposits on the Atlantic Ocean floor that are older than Early Mesozoic. As a matter of fact, the oldest known sediments on the Atlantic Ocean floor are Jurassic in age. If the Atlantic Ocean floor is itself older than Jurassic, then where are the older sediments? Several other lines of evidence also strongly support the theory of continental drift, and the reader can discover much of that evidence in some very readable, fascinating recent publications.[39]

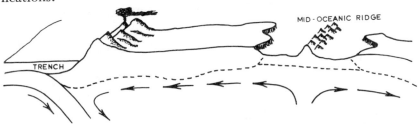

Figure 20. Convection cell hypothesis. According to this idea, warm mantle moves upward towards the earth's surface beneath mid-oceanic ridges where it adds new material to the crust. The warm mantle then spreads out laterally beneath the overlying continental masses, carrying them along in piggyback fashion. Upper mantle and oceanic crust then plunge slowly back down into the deeper mantle underneath oceanic trench areas.

How can the westward drift of the Americas relative to Africa since Early Mesozoic times be envisioned mechanically? Our present knowledge of continental and oceanic structure and composition suggests rather strongly that the continental plates and the newly developed oceanic crust and uppermost mantle, being *relatively* low density materials, "float" somewhat buoyantly and passively on top of higher density material somewhat lower in the mantle. Some theoreticians have suggested that these crustal plates float on top of convection cells in the upper mantle (see Figure 20). These

39. See H. Takeuchi, S. Uyeda, and H. Kanamori, *Debate About the Earth* (San Francisco: Freeman-Cooper, 1970); and J. T. Wilson, *Continents Adrift* (San Francisco: W. H. Freeman, 1972).

"conveyor-belt" convection cells are believed to be moving upward beneath the submarine ridges like the Mid-Atlantic Ridge. Here hot magma is brought to the surface and contributes to newly developing oceanic crust. The crustal plates move away from the oceanic ridges and towards great submarine trenches such as the Puerto Rico trench or the Marianas trench off the Philippines. At the trench sites the convection cells move downward and tend to drag crustal material with them. Some geophysicists are sceptical of the convection cell idea and have proposed that "plumes" of very hot material come up from the deep mantle to form new oceanic crust. Because of a slight bulging or doming effect at the submarine ridge sites, continental-oceanic plates are said to float or drift away from these sites chiefly under the influence of gravitational forces. This idea is illustrated in Figure 21. Despite disagreement about the exact mechanism, it seems clear to most geologists that new crust is continuously generated at

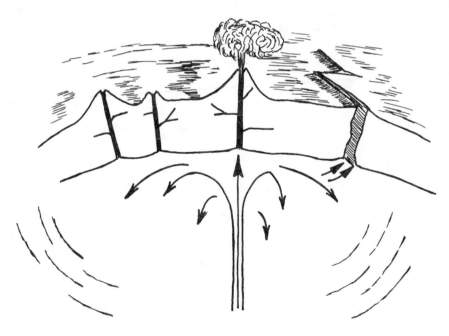

Figure 21. Plume hypothesis. According to this idea, a narrow pipe of hot mantle material moves upward as a "plume" doming up the overlying crust. Because of the doming effect, the overlying crust tends to glide away from the dome under the influence of gravitational forces, thus providing a mechanism for continental drift. Neither the plume nor convection cell hypothesis has been proved as the mechanism of drift.

submarine ridge sites and gradually drifts away from those sites until it ultimately reaches a submarine trench site where the crustal material tends to be consumed.

If we now envision the Americas as moving westward through time we would suspect the likelihood of some kind of disturbance developing along the leading edge of the continent, particularly if that leading edge runs into a submarine trench where material tends to get dragged back down into the mantle or if it runs into a land mass drifting in the opposite direction! Plowing and buckling of material as the leading edge of a continent collides with oceanic crust can easily be envisaged. Thus it would appear to be no accident that the entire western coast of the Americas is a great mountain range that is still characterized by such profound disturbances as earthquakes and volcanoes. Not only this, but geologic mapping has demonstrated that the mountain-building events of the Rockies, Sierra Nevadas, and Andes occurred in Late Mesozoic to Tertiary time (indeed, they are still continuing), that is, after continental drifting began. A similar situation can be observed in the eastern hemisphere where the Indian subcontinent is believed to have drifted away from Africa in a northerly direction until it ultimately collided with the Asian land mass. The result of this collision between two great land masses is the Himalayan mountain belt! Moreover the geologic relationships in the Himalayas indicate that the mountain-building events were Tertiary and Quaternary, that is, *after* the beginning of continental drift.

The ramifications of the theories of continental drift and sea-floor spreading are indeed fascinating but space does not permit discussion of all of them. Instead consider briefly how the idea of drift is devastating to the theory of *The Genesis Flood.* We have just reviewed some of the great mass of evidence which indicates that the continents were at one time joined together. In particular, the evidence from glaciated Permian rocks indicates that the continents were together in Late Paleozoic time. If we follow through on the Whitcomb-Morris theory, it seems the continents must have been joined together before the flood took place and, as a matter of fact, even early in the flood year, because the Permian rocks are fossil-bearing. Thus the flood catastrophists must find some way of explaining how the continents could drift from their originally united position to their present positions in a few thousand years. But in that case drift must have occurred at an extremely rapid rate and in historical times there does not appear to be evidence to support an extremely rapid rate of drift. In any case geological evidence from mountain belts indicates that fossiliferous sediments were still being deposited and deformed during the pronounced uplifts when continents ran into oceanic crust or other continents. In reality then Whitcomb and Morris must achieve the drifting of continents during the latter part of the flood period, that is, in less than one year. It is unlikely that Whitcomb and Morris can find a way to explain how continents could drift distances of hundreds or even thousands of miles in only a few months unless they wish at this point to resort to pure miracle. Their only remaining options are either to deny the overwhelming evidence for continental drift or to find some other satisfactory explanation for it.

Scriptural Arguments Against the Whitcomb-Morris Theory

The Whitcomb-Morris theory regarding the flood may to some extent sound plausible as long as one speaks in vague generalities. As soon as one considers specific details in actual geologic contexts, it is seen that the theory simply doeś not stand up and therefore must be rejected. Geology refutes the whole theory and Scripture certainly does not require it. In fact there are also some Scriptural data which tend to negate the Whitcomb-Morris theory. For one thing it was already pointed out in chapter six that the vapor canopy idea, which posits a now-defunct, prediluvian vapor canopy that served as a source for the abundant flood rains, is not really in accord with the actual facts of Scripture.

A second Scriptural consideration concerns the nature of prediluvian topography and geography. It is an important implication of the Whitcomb-Morris theory that the earth's surface was completely renovated during the flood year. Prediluvian topography would have been exceedingly different from postdiluvian topography. That this is so can be inferred from the fact that virtually the entire sedimentary cover of the earth is said to have been produced during the flood epoch. These sediments must have been derived from pre-existing uplands and have filled in large pre-existing basinlike areas. With the amount of geological activity attributed to the flood by Whitcomb and Morris there is no reason to expect anything other than a wholesale redistribution of the earth's surface features.

The Bible, however, strongly suggests that prediluvian geography did basically *resemble* postdiluvian geography. This is especially seen in the description of the location of the Garden of Eden (Genesis 2:8-14). The garden is located in terms of four rivers, two of which are still familiar to us, the Tigris (Hiddekel) and Euphrates. Whether or not the Pison and the Gihon were known to the ancient Israelites we do not know. Perhaps these rivers disappeared through course of time or were captured by other streams. The rapidly shifting nature of river courses in the Mesopotamian flood plain is well known. While the Authorized Version of the Bible says that the Gihon is in Ethiopia, it has been suggested by some[40] that the word translated "Ethiopia" (the land of Cush) could as well have been translated as the "land of the Kassites," a group of people who were located to the east of the Tigris-Euphrates basin, so that the Gihon most likely was a tributary of those two great rivers. Whatever may be said about the exact location of the Pison and Gihon rivers, the Tigris and Euphrates were and are the major rivers of the Middle East, the Nile excepted, and would obviously be well known to the inhabitants of that general part of the world, just as every citizen of the United States has a general idea of the location of the Mississippi River. When Moses located the Garden of Eden for his readers in terms of great rivers and a country (Havilah) famous for certain gemstones, it seems fairly clear that he was talking about rivers and places that were generally familiar to his readers. Else why the detail involved in the attempt to locate the garden? When Moses spoke of the rivers and of Havilah, presumably part of Arabia, his readers' attention would immediately be focused on the region of Mesopotamia. If prediluvian geography had been radically different from that familiar to the Israelites, there would have been little point to Moses' reference to the Tigris and Euphrates. If Noah's flood had been as catastrophic and devastating as Whitcomb and Morris' flood, it is rather unlikely that the Tigris and Euphrates, the gold and onyx of Havilah, and even Havilah itself, existed prior to the flood.

The fact that Noah used pitch in building the ark in obedience to the Lord's command (Genesis 6:14) is yet a further Scriptural evidence against the Whitcomb-Morris theory. The use of pitch is perfectly consistent with geographical and geological conditions that are like those in the modern day Mesopotamian region. The presence of pitch implies that there has been no radical renovation of the face

---

40. E. A. Speiser, *Genesis*, The Anchor Bible (New York: Doubleday, 1964), p. 20.

of the earth. Indeed if we accept the catastrophic theory it seems unlikely that any pitch would ever exist until the time of the flood. Pitch is an organic material that is generally regarded as forming from decayed plant and animal material as does petroleum. Thus we would expect no pitch to have been formed during creation week, when presumably there was no death. Furthermore the extent of death in the few thousand years between the fall of Adam and the flood would not likely produce much in the way of petroleum products. It was during the flood, according to the neo-catastrophists, that a vast quantity of petroleum and related organic materials were generated, owing to the staggering amount of plants and animals killed by the flood and buried in sediment. Thus it is extremely unlikely that Noah would have been able to find pitch in the prediluvian world. He would have been able to find it if he lived in a Mesopotamian world that was geologically and geographically similar to what it is now.

We have seen that the Scriptural account of the flood by no means demands adherence to the Whitcomb-Morris catastrophic construction of the flood. Much Scriptural evidence argues against the catastrophic view. The geological evidence is strongly opposed to the catastrophic view. The Christian, whether scientifically oriented or not, must not make the mistake of assuming that the Whitcomb-Morris version of the flood is what Scripture teaches.

Unfortunately it is a much easier matter to say what the flood did not do than what it did do. Arguments can be adduced to suggest that the flood was a gigantic local deluge; other arguments suggest the universality of the flood. Whatever view is ultimately adopted, it must be kept in mind that the flood was a genuine historical event. The flood story is not a myth or legend. It is history. The flood was fundamentally a judgment of God and not a major geological event, certainly not an event which reshaped the globe. The Christian may believe the full historicity of the flood without committing himself to a theory of the flood which runs counter to parts of Scriptural revelation and to the general tenor of natural revelation.

Conclusion

A great many problems in the debate between theology and geology can be resolved if we reject theistic evolutionism and Biblical neo-catastrophism and adopt the third way developed in this book. By rejecting theistic evolutionism we reject faulty theological principles. By rejecting neo-catastrophism we reject faulty science. By adopting the approach we have outlined we can preserve both good theology and good science. The alternative we have developed allows the Bible to speak for itself. Ideas were not superimposed on the Bible as in theistic evolutionism. Our alternative involves thorough exegesis of all of Scripture, and does not build a scientific theory on a few selected texts as does neo-catastrophism. We recognize science for what it is and allow it to develop in a natural way without forcing discovery into a preconceived mold. To be sure problems still remain, but our approach is faithful to both Scripture, God's special revelation, and nature, His general revelation. Only an approach that is faithful to all of God's works has any real hope of resolving any problems in the fascinating area of the relationship between geology and the Bible.

Appendix

The rubidium-strontium isochron method may be derived mathematically as follows. The fundamental equation for the radioactive decay of atoms is

$$\frac{dN}{dt} = -\lambda N \tag{1}$$

where N is the absolute number of atoms of a particular radioactive element in a mineral or rock, dN/dt is the rate of decay per unit time of the radioactive element into its daughter product at the moment when N atoms of the radioactive element are present in the sample, and λ is an experimentally determined decay constant whose value is different for each of the radioactive isotopes.

By transposition of variables we obtain

$$\frac{dN}{N} = -\lambda\, dt \tag{2}$$

and, by integration between definite limits, we further obtain

$$\int_{N_o}^{N} \frac{dN}{N} = -\lambda \int_{t=0}^{t} dt \quad \text{or} \quad \ln\frac{N}{N_o} = -\lambda t \tag{3}$$

where N_o is the number of atoms of the radioactive element in the sample at time t=0 or the time when the sample was first formed.

Equation (3) may also be written as

$$N = N_o e^{-\lambda t} \tag{4}$$

Now let us confine our mathematical analysis to the decay of rubidium into strontium. We may then write an equation of the form of equation (4) for Rb^{87} which states

$$Rb^{87} = Rb_0^{87} e^{-\lambda t} \tag{5}$$

Equation (5) says that the number of rubidium 87 atoms in a sample, say, of a large chunk of granite is equal to the number of rubidium 87 atoms initially present in the rock at the time of its original crystallization (assuming no loss or gain of rubidium 87 with respect to the chunk of rock) times an exponential expression that depends on the decay constant and the amount of time that has elapsed since the original crystallization of the rock.

But the number of Rb^{87} atoms that was initially present (Rb_0^{87}) in the chunk of granite is equal to the number of Rb^{87} atoms now present in the chunk plus the number of Sr^{87} atoms that have been derived radiogenically from the original Rb_0^{87}. If, however, some Sr^{87} was also originally present in the chunk the total number of Sr^{87} atoms in the rock at present will exceed the number of Sr^{87} atoms derived radiogenically from the initial Rb_0^{87}. We assume that no Sr^{87} has been gained or lost from the chunk. We will return to the problem of gain or loss shortly. Let us now designate the initial Sr^{87} content of the chunk of granite as Sr_0^{87} so that

$$Sr^{87}_{radiogenic} = Sr^{87}_{present\ now} - Sr_0^{87} \tag{6}$$

Hence we may conclude that, apart from gain or loss,

$$Rb_0^{87} = Rb^{87} + Sr^{87} - Sr_0^{87} \tag{7}$$

By substituting equation (5) into equation (7) we obtain

$$Rb^{87} = (Rb^{87} + Sr^{87} - Sr_0^{87})\ e^{-\lambda t} \tag{8}$$

Since with mass spectrometers it is easier to measure the ratios of isotopes to one another than to measure absolute amounts of isotopes in a sample, we introduce ratios into the mathematical treatment by dividing equation (8) by the quantity Sr^{86}, that is, the number of strontium 86 atoms in the sample at the present time. It is also important to note that inasmuch as Sr^{86} is not radiogenic, it remains constant in amount through time so that $Sr^{86} = Sr_0^{86}$. Hence we may now write

$$\frac{Rb^{87}}{Sr^{86}} = \left(\frac{Rb^{87}}{Sr^{86}} + \frac{Sr^{87}}{Sr^{86}} - \left[\frac{Sr^{87}}{Sr^{86}}\right]_0\right)\ e^{-\lambda t} \tag{9}$$

If we rearrange the variables we may write

$$\frac{Rb^{87}}{Sr^{86}} + \frac{Sr^{87}}{Sr^{86}} - \left(\frac{Sr^{87}}{Sr^{86}}\right)_0 = \frac{Rb^{87}}{Sr^{86}}\ e^{\lambda t} \tag{10}$$

Further

$$\frac{Sr^{87}}{Sr^{86}} = \frac{Rb^{87}}{Sr^{86}}\ e^{\lambda t} - \frac{Rb^{87}}{Sr^{86}} + \left(\frac{Sr^{87}}{Sr^{86}}\right)_0 \tag{11}$$

And finally we obtain

$$\frac{Sr^{87}}{Sr^{86}} = \left(\frac{Rb^{87}}{Sr^{86}}\right)\left(e^{\lambda t} - 1\right) + \left(\frac{Sr^{87}}{Sr^{86}}\right)_0 \tag{12}$$

We have just derived an equation which has the exact mathematical form of the equation for a straight line, $y = mx + b$ (the y-axis is plotted against the x-axis, m is the slope of the straight line and b is the intercept of the line on the y-axis). Hence if equation (12) is of a straight line, the ratio Sr^{87}/Sr^{86} is plotted along the y-axis, the ratio Rb^{87}/Sr^{86} is plotted along the x-axis, $e^{\lambda t} - 1$ is the slope of the straight line, and $(Sr^{87}/Sr^{86})_o$ is the y-intercept.

If there has been significant loss or gain of strontium or rubidium in the chunk of granite since its time of crystallization, the data on isotope abundances in the rock will not yield a well-defined straight line on the isochron plot.